RICH

$\mathcal{R}$ICH

THE RISE *and* FALL *of* AMERICAN WEALTH CULTURE

LARRY SAMUEL

AMERICAN MANAGEMENT ASSOCIATION
New York • Atlanta • Brussels • Chicago • Mexico City • San Francisco
Shanghai • Tokyo • Toronto • Washington, D.C.

This publication is designed to provide accurate and authoritative information in regard to the subject matter covered. It is sold with the understanding that the publisher is not engaged in rendering legal, accounting, or other professional service. If legal advice or other expert assistance is required, the services of a competent professional person should be sought.

Library of Congress Cataloging-in-Publication Data

Samuel, Larry.
    Rich : the rise and fall of American wealth culture / Larry Samuel.
        p.   cm.
    Includes bibliographical references and index.
    ISBN-13: 978-0-8144-1362-3
    ISBN-10: 0-8144-1362-5
    1. Rich people—United States.   2. Wealth—United States.   I. Title.
HC110.W4S26   2009
305.5'2340973—dc22
                                                        2008055731

Printing number

10   9   8   7   6   5   4   3   2   1

"As one digs deeper into the national character of the Americans, one sees that they have sought the value of everything in this world only in the answer to this single question: how much money will it bring in?"
—ALEXIS DE TOCQUEVILLE,
DEMOCRACY IN AMERICA, 1835

CONTENTS

ACKNOWLEDGMENTS

M ANY THANKS TO BOB SHUMAN FOR RECOGNIZING THIS WAS a story worth telling and to all the other fine folks at AMACOM for bringing it to life. Much gratitude to the staffs at the New York Public Library, Miami-Dade Public Library, and University of Miami Richter Library for steering me in the right direction. Finally, special appreciation to Paul Groncki and Susan Hirshman at JP Morgan for sparking my interest in the American rich and for allowing me to add my own two bits to the story.

RICH

INTRODUCTION

"WITHIN THE LAST TEN YEARS NO END OF PEOPLE HAVE become rich," a *Los Angeles Times* reporter once wrote, telling readers that "a man with a million dollars cannot, in these days, be counted as really rich." This reporter wasn't writing a few years ago, alarmed at how hedge fund managers were pulling further and further away from the mere rich, or even in the late 1980s as investment bankers made unprecedented gobs of money. No, this reporter was writing shortly before the market crash in 1929, another time in which it seemed that a million dollars just wasn't what it used to be.[1]

Rich reveals many such stories, which tell us a lot about how the cultural dynamics surrounding the wealthy elite have both changed dramatically and remained remarkably the same over the past century or so. The first full examination of the American rich since 1920, this book traces the cultural trajectory of the wealthy elite and completes a surprisingly overlooked and important chapter of the nation's history. As well, *Rich* puts today's obsession with all things monetary into much needed perspective and context, exposing the backstory that has shaped today's fascination with the rich. Who were the Gateses, Bransons, and Trumps of the past? How did the rich show off their status? What did they splurge on, and how did they scrimp when times got tough? Who were the VIPs of yesterday and, some are sure to wonder, the Paris Hiltons? We're reminded, for example, that bling is hardly a new phenomenon and that today's McMansions are shacks compared to some estates of the past. The book may surprise some readers with the news that recent lifestyles of the rich and famous—building world-class art collections, collecting vintage cars, throwing $1 million parties, heading off to remote locales to escape the hoi polloi—have their roots in similar passions of the wealthy decades ago. Today's inclination for the super-rich to give away hundreds of millions of dollars to ensure their legacy also echoes the past, the current batch of gazillionaires merely following a long tradition of attempts by the wealthy to achieve a kind of immortality.

Importantly, rather than try to establish its own definition of "rich" or "wealthy" as a certain level of net worth, income, or percentage of the population owning or earning an arbitrary dollar level, *Rich* relies on how its sources used these terms. Not only has what constitutes being "rich" and "wealthy" constantly shifted over the last century, but a single definition of either of these terms would have to address inflation and a host of other economic factors, much too complicated an exercise for the reader (and, even more so, for a cultural historian).

If there is any single grand narrative of the rich, it is that American wealth culture—the beliefs and behavior of the upper class—became increasingly democratized over the past century. In this country there are now more people with more money than any other civilization in history, suggesting that the story of wealth culture is perhaps the biggest story of our time and place. (Recent media attention about the "rich versus the super-rich " is entirely a result of the hedge fund phenomenon of the last few years. By

virtually any measure—asset and income level, house and car ownership, pairs of Jimmy Choos in one's closet—America and Americans have undoubtedly gotten richer since 1920.) Over the last
decade, despite the economic downturn, we've reached a new plateau in individual and collective prosperity, making the examination of the American rich that much more significant. If the West's
greatest achievement over the last two centuries was to create a
mass middle class, as Dinesh D'Souza argued in a 1999 article
called "The Billionaire Next Door," the United States was, at the
end of the millennium, about to outdo even that milestone. The
emergence of what Russ Alan Prince and Lewis Schiff called in
their 2008 book *The Middle-Class Millionaire* will thus be the
major focus of this book.[2]

Although they've splintered into a million little pieces—
actually about 10 million; according to Transaction Network Services (TNS) there were 9.9 million millionaire households in June
2007—and although the economy has headed south, the wealthy
elite have never been more influential than now.[3] "Being rich has
never exactly been a downer but today it is all the more sweet,"
wrote Harvard economics professor N. Gregory Mankiw for the *New
York Times* in 2008, after reviewing data that showed that the
super-haves were pulling further away from the pack of haves.[4] Recent TV shows like ABC's *Dirty Sexy Money*, CBS's *Cane*, and
HBO's *12 Miles of Bad Road* reveal our current celebration of and
fascination with the super-rich (and recall the 1980s televisual
troika of *Dallas*, *Dynasty*, and *Falcon Crest*). Despite a shaky-at-
best economy, some of today's plutocrats are still spending $1,000
a month on their hair and $36,000 a year on skin maintenance;
others travel in style in submarines and Hermes-outfitted helicopters. Hiring baby nurses who've worked for celebrities has become
a status symbol within some circles, and house detailing—where a
dozen maids wielding extra large Q-tips go over every inch of a
10,000-square-foot home—is all the rage among a certain segment
of the upper crust. A wide range of other service providers—art
conservators, family CFOs, nutritionists, and medical concierges,

to name just a few—are also popular among the very rich, sure signs that the American wealthy elite is alive and well.[5]

The global wealthy elite, especially the uppermost end, is also very much alive and well in 2008, despite the economic "meltdown." The international ultra-rich, who David Rothkopf calls the "superclass," are largely resilient to downturns such as the current one, maintaining or even escalating their spending on luxury goods and services. Record prices were set at a Christie's art auction in May 2008, for example, with Europeans, Russians, and a few Americans springing for Monets and Rodins like they were blue light specials. (Between 2007 and 2008, the number of billionaires grew by 20 percent to 1,125, with more now in Moscow—74—than New York—71—quite tellingly.) Luxury brands like Prada and Hermes are doing gangbuster business, and top-shelf real estate in New York is as strong as ever. "Bespoke" lifestyles have also taken off, as the ultra-rich forgo off-the-shelf luxury in exchange for customized, one-of-a-kind jewelry, vehicles, clothing, handbags, and even doghouses. Last but not least, today's super-yachts—especially Larry Ellison's *Rising Sun*, Paul Allen's *Octopus*, and Roman Abramovich's in-the-works *Eclipse*—are making Aristotle Onassis's *Christina* look like a rowboat, another sign that, for at least a privileged few, it's not the economy, stupid.[6]

In fact, one of the most interesting stories in *Rich* is the natural ebb and flow of the upper class and their enormous fortunes. The death of Big Money has been a running theme over the past century, with social critics of the 1930s, 1970s, late 1980s, and even today predicting the end of prosperity and the demise of the American rich. What such critics have failed to understand is that even if the super-rich lose a fair chunk of their investments in a financial "tsunami," to use Alan Greenspan's term, many or most of them will remain wealthy by any measure. (Even when a third of a $25-million nest egg evaporates, for example, a ridiculous amount of money remains, in a historical or comparative sense.) Critics also tend to forget that what Americans do best is make (and spend) money, making a recession or even a depression more of a temporary setback or inevitable correction than a fatal blow. In fact, there has always been a bigger and faster way to make money waiting around the corner, as this book vividly shows, suggesting that the best days for the American rich lie ahead.

Tracking the virtual demise of Old Money as we knew (and mythologized) it is equally as important as mapping the consistent rise of a mass-affluent class. How are today's rich different from the rest of us, we should ask, besides having (a lot) more money? Much has changed, of course, since Fitzgerald famously observed in 1925 that the rich were different (and since Hemingway apocryphally replied that yes, they had more money). Most notably, the democratization of wealth in America has diluted most of the social signifiers or markers of elitism—sense of privilege and entitlement, discreetness, understatedness, noblesse oblige, snobbery—that once were assigned to the rich. Less than 10 percent of today's rich inherited their fortunes, according to a recent Mendelsohn Affluent Survey; the deterioration of Old Money is a running theme over the last century. The American rich are now primarily "instapreneurs," as Robert Frank called them in his book *Richistan*; these folks bear a striking resemblance to the "blue-collar billionaires" described by Peter Bernstein and Annalyn Swan in *All the Money in the World*. Because today's rich look and act a lot like us, as Steven Winn wrote in 2008, the wealthy elite are no longer "remote, unattainable, or mysterious;" this supports the idea that their social downfall has come along with the demographic rise of the first mass-affluent class.[7] The unequivocal victory of New Money over Old has thus come at a significant cost—specifically the loss of an identifiable wealth culture. There are, of course, lots of rich Americans but very few "wealthy" ones, in the traditional sense of the word. Being rich just means having a lot of money, after all, while being wealthy means subscribing to a certain style of behavior and code of ethics that goes back centuries. Without Old and New Money, we are left with only Money, a more democratic but less interesting state of affairs.

This book shows, however, that Old Money was in fact an endangered species in Fitzgerald's prime, when our Aristocracy Lite imported from Europe had already begun to wear thin around the sleeves. As the nation ping-ponged between economic expansion and progressive reform over the next eighty-some years, a series of events and movements would largely dissolve the privileged few. Pick your culprit—modernity and youth culture in the 1920s, financial crisis in the 1930s, the rise of the middle and upper-middle classes in the postwar years, the countercultural, multicultural, and feminist movements of the 1960s and 1970s, and the emergence of a different kind of New Money in the 1980s, 1990s, and 2000s—but American wealth culture as we once knew it would no longer exist.

A BRIEF HISTORY OF
AMERICAN WEALTH CULTURE

Being rich in America was once a much simpler affair. Early Americans thoroughly endorsed the pursuit of wealth; their Protestant faith blessed the profits that came with hard work and from simply being good. "It is hard for an empty sack to stand upright!" was one of Ben Franklin's pithy lines in his *Poor Richard's Almanac*, not just a warning of the immorality of poverty but a tip of the three-cornered hat to those who (like Franklin) had fully filled their sacks. In her novels, Louisa May Alcott rewarded most of her good-but-poor heroines by marrying them off to the rich man next door, which also reflected the positive view of the wealthy in colonial and antebellum America. "Society" had been around in some form or another even before the nation's founding, with New England Puritans, Southern plantation owners, and New Yorkers of both Dutch and English descent all awarding the "best" families special social status.[8]

Alexis de Tocqueville weighed in on the American wealthy of the 1830s, of course, suggesting that it was better for a democracy like ours to have a few very rich than a lot of semi-rich. (The former could do great things with their money, he argued, while the latter were typically content indulging their consumer appetites.) Also not lost on de Tocqueville was Americans' passion for making and spending money, something that the Frenchman believed was unique to the new nation. He wrote, "I know of no country, indeed, where the love of money has taken stronger hold on the affections of men," an idea that seems even truer today than it did almost two centuries ago. "The love of wealth is . . . at the bottom of all that the Americans do," de Tocqueville concluded, our experiment in democracy custom-made for some, perhaps any, white male to get rich.[9]

Thoroughly woven into the tapestry of the American rich has been the mythology or cult of the millionaire, a term that originated in France with Disraeli in 1826 but was rarely used in the United States until the late nineteenth century.[10] The word was first used in America in a newspaper obituary for Pierre Lorillard I, founder of the tobacco empire. "Mr. Lorillard was a 'millionaire,'" the obit read, a result of selling something people could "chew that which they could not swallow."[11] There were only three millionaires in 1861, but that was about to change very quickly.[12] For centuries, even millennia, being rich depended on one thing: owning land. In the nineteenth century, however, industry emerged as a prime way to get rich; the turning of raw materials into products now became a path to fabulous wealth. By the end of the Civil War—an event that relied heavily on the fruits of industry—the first real leisure class in America had been born. These few hundred families took their cue from England's upper class, which exemplified extravagance during the Edwardian era. In New York, Boston, and the resorts of Saratoga, Newport, and Bar Harbor, "the best people," as they immodestly called themselves, turned turn-of-the-century America into their own personal playpen. Stories of unabashed excesses among these new millionaires—Pierre Lorillard V's creation of Tuxedo Park in 1886; E. Berry Wall's forty-time change of outfits in Saratoga Springs to become the indisputable "King of the Dudes" in 1888; San Francisco attorney Francis J. Carolan's stable party, in which some guests dressed (and raced) as horses; Mrs. Lowell Gardner's Fenway Court house-showing party in 1903 (with John Singer Sargent's daring portrait of the hostess on full display); and James Hazen Hyde's 1905 "$200,000 party," which turned Sherry's in New York into eighteenth-century Versailles—became legend, part of American folklore.[13]

Should there be any doubt that they were America's royalty, the richest of the rich did everything they could to prove it to themselves and to others. Failure to have all of one's servants imported from across the pond was a major faux pas; the cream of the crop stocked their palaces with English footmen complete with white wigs and maroon (Vanderbilt) or blue (Astor) livery.[14] With their wartime fortunes, the robber barons built European-style mansions in Newport and on Fifth Avenue, in the process raising the bar of what was considered ostentatious in America. In an early version of *Lifestyles of the Rich and Famous*, turn-of-the-century newspaper and magazine writers noted (or invented) the price of the latest purchase of one of the super-rich; knowing readers relished hearing about Jay Gould's "$500,000 yacht," J. P. Morgan's "$100,000 car," or Cornelius Vanderbilt's "$2 million home."[15]

Even these families who we now think of as being quintessential members of society were considered nouveau riche, as they tried to gate-crash their way into the ranks of the elite. The Astors, Whitneys, and Vanderbilts did just that around 1880, not impressing those wealthy families that had been around for a couple of centuries (Augustus Van Horne Stuyvesant always called them "the new ones").[16] Many of those who had made fortunes during the Civil War desperately wanted to be part of society, so much so they literally looked to Europe as a way to shortcut the process. Consuelo Vanderbilt's marriage to the Duke of Marlborough and Anna Gould's to Count Boni de Castellane were just a couple of quite a few swappings of fortunes for titles, as nothing said "society" to Americans like a real tiara. Seeing a truly golden opportunity, English lords and earls who had fallen on hard times made sure they were part of the social scene on the Continent, shopping around for a marriageable, American, and, above all, filthy rich young woman in what was popularly called "the Millionaire Market."[17]

Until relatively recently, the nearly desperate attempts by New Money to be perceived as Old served as a constant and reliable tension among the American rich, analogous perhaps to that which existed between the superpowers during the Cold War. In his 1960 book *Who Killed Society?*, for example, Cleveland Amory noted, "People have complained about Society not being what it was for some 350 years," a reminder of how integral this dynamic was to the American wealthy elite.[18] And in her 1920 novel *The Age of Innocence*, Edith Wharton wrote about the conviction among the New York upper crust of the 1870s that the New Money that had oozed out of the War Between the States and from the new oil fields out West was ruining society:

> It is undeniable that changes, and changes not for the better, have been taking place during the last few years in American social life in every quarter of the Union . . . Since the conditions of things during the war enabled men to amass fortunes in an incredibly short time, and the discovery of oil in almost worthless lands gave them suddenly immense value, the "shoddy" and "petroleum" element has been prominent in circles composed of wealthy persons inclined to scatter their money profusely for the purpose of display.[19]

More than just being seen as *arriviste*, liveried English footmen and all, the Vanderbilts, Astors, Rockefellers, Carnegies, and Morgans were universally despised, even among their own. In their day and for decades after, the robber barons of the Gilded Age were viewed as a much different kind of American rich than earlier generations, perceived as lacking the Calvinist principles of those in colonial and antebellum times. Not only were they not "the best people," but many thought they were quite possibly the worst. Only two voices of a loud chorus condemning the wily ways of the new rich, Edith Wharton denounced their "monstrous vulgarity," and Senator Robert LaFollette considered John D. Rockefeller nothing less than "the greatest criminal of the age." Even the rest of society didn't approve of how these men had made and were spending their money, with only nine of the ninety richest people in America in the 1890s invited to be part of Mrs. Astor's ballroom-sized list of "Four Hundred."[20]

The belief that they had upset the applecart of the nation's collective wealth was part and parcel of the turn-of-the-century loathing for the rich. As far back as 1869, and probably even earlier, social critics were disturbed by the growing inequality of wealth and rising number of millionaires. That year, an editor for a New Jersey newspaper, the *Washington Star*, included in his column this ironic diatribe against one of the richest men in America:

> William B. Astor rates his incomes at $4,330 per diem; sleeping or waking he finds a $3 bill dropping into his hat every minute of the twenty-four hours . . . At every turn cash stares at him in the most insolent manner. Banks fling their dividends at his head; ruthless financiers beat him with coupons; unpitying and soulless corporations dump their lucre at his doorstep, and contemptuous bill-stickers plaster his door with greenbacks. One might wonder what the fellow had done to merit such treatment. The only charge that can be brought is that he is a rich man's son and therefore must suffer.[21]

Despite what others were saying about them and their incredible wealth, robber barons like Astor believed their good fortune was divinely ordained and that they answered only to a much higher power. "God gave me my money," John D. Rockefeller once said, the perfect retort to those suggesting that no man, in America at least, should be that rich.[22]

No matter who had given him his money, the public was getting awfully tired of the excess displayed by Rockefeller and his partners in crime. The backlash climaxed in 1896 when a New York Society couple, Mr. and Mrs. Bradley Martin, threw a ball at the Waldorf-Astoria costing a reported $400,000. Many of those hearing about the party (again with a Versailles theme) judged it to be in bad taste and its expense absurd, forcing the host and hostess to flee to England, never to return. With the publication of Thorsten Veblen's popular *The Theory of the Leisure Class* three years later, public disfavor of the super-rich turned into pure outrage; the concept of "conspicuous consumption" was deemed unpalatable and contrary to the Puritan ethic of restrained and responsible wealth. "The attitude of the public towards great wealth, originally one of respect and admiration, changed to suspicion, antagonism, and hatred," wrote Arthur Train for *Forum & Century* in 1924.[23] Until the mid-nineteenth century, the (relatively few) American rich were looked up to (an "emblem of the nation's greatness—a living proof that it was the land of opportunity," according to Train), but this changed by 1900 as "he became anathema—a symbol of a people's bondage."[24] Up against the wall, as John Berendi explained in a 1990 article for *Esquire* called "The Quiet Rich," twentieth-century plutocrats adopted a new collective persona, what we now recognize as the dignified restraint of Old Money. Wearing clothing just slightly tattered, driving older cars, and contributing to deserving charities became the modus operandi of the wealthy elite, topped off by a repugnance of conversation that mentioned money. If only to preserve their dynasties, New Money morphed into Old Money, choosing to avoid the limelight and wear the camouflage of anonymity.[25]

Out with the Old, In with the New

Just as the Civil War had been a major turning point for the wealthy elite because of the creation of so many new fortunes, attitudes toward the rich changed dramatically after World War I, where Chapter 1 of *Rich* begins. American feeling toward the rich became "one of indifference," believed Train, as public sentiment regarding the very wealthy achieved a state of equilibrium.[26] "As far as the rich themselves are concerned," agreed Hoffman Nickerson of the *American Mercury* five years later, "the war and postwar periods have restored substantially the situation of 1865," the wealthy viewed as neither noble heroes nor heinous villains.[27] Any trend after the War to End All Wars was impossible to predict, however, and it was unclear to all which way the scales of the wealthy would tip. "How will the present prototypes of our only equivalent to royalty in America be recalled?" Train wondered, asking if they would be remembered as "amassers of tainted fortunes, or as trailing clouds of philanthropic glory?"[28]

The answer to that question could be found in the sheer volume of new rich being created when the postwar boom economy finally kicked in and as the stock market began to soar. "Millionaire-a-year men [are] increasing in number," the *New York Times* excitedly reported in 1924, when a whopping sixty-seven Americans claimed at least $1 million in income for the 1922 tax year. Many more, hundreds certainly, were also believed to have earned that much but had found ways to reduce their income to avoid paying more taxes. Because there were so many new rich, the very meaning of the term "millionaire" had in fact recently changed, from one whose total assets exceeded $1 million to one who made that much money in a single year (the term has since flipped back to its previous usage).[29] By the late 1920s, the number of millionaires and the size of some estates were becoming truly shocking, especially from a historical sense. (George Washington was one of the wealthiest men in the young nation when he died in 1799 but left an estate of just $530,000.)[30] A couple dozen women turned up on the Internal Revenue Bureau's 1927 tax rolls as earning a million dollars or more, among them, even more astonishing, a few unmarried ones.[31] Four months before Black Friday, it was believed that at least 30,000 Americans were millionaires in the older, asset-based sense of the word; the seeds of D'Souza's first mass-affluent class were planted, as a much more populist, democratic paradigm of the rich emerged.[32]

The rather sudden abundance of millionaires in the 1920s had such a redemptive effect on the wealthy elite that even politicians could now be rich and stand a good chance of getting into office.

The candidates for the presidential election of 1928 were nearly all rich, comprising a virtual millionaire's club. "The public no longer distrusts wealthy men in elective offices," thought an editor for the Danville (Illinois) *Commercial News* in 1927, suggesting it had to do with both "the diffusion of prosperity" and "an improvement in the morals of big business."[33] The winner of that election, Herbert Hoover, filled his administration with rich men, their dedication to public service perhaps more reason to forgive the wealthy for their past sins.[34]

The flourishing of the American rich in the 1920s also made it quite clear that any hopes of preserving a family dynasty in a democracy like ours would almost certainly be dashed. By 1927, the country's first few generations of the rich no longer had much influence, a trend that would accelerate over the course of the century. "Except in Philadelphia and the South," Montgomery Evans noted that year in *Forum & Century*, "few of the families whose names were household words before the Civil War are to-day more than faint shadows in social registers." It was inevitable that an aristocratic class like that in Europe be stopped in its tracks in this country, he and others believed. "The old Dutch families are gone, the early New England magnates are forgotten, and most of the fortunes of the railroad builders are already dissipated or the subject of bitter fights among heirs who will eventually relinquish most of them to lawyers," Evans noted, evidence supporting the well-known Yankee proverb "shirtsleeves to shirtsleeves in three generations."[35]

The market crash of 1929 further ensured that more grandchildren of the once-rich would be wearing shirtsleeves, Chapter 2 shows, and it served as a major blow to Old Money. "Few of our fortunes are more than a single generation old, fewer still can boast of two generations, and the three and four-generation money dynasties can be counted on the fingers of our hands," noted John T. Flynn in a 1930 article for *North American Review* titled "The Dwindling Dynasties." "The characters in that social group we call 'the rich' are constantly shifting," Flynn correctly observed, a con-

tinually revolving door of New Money.[36] It also became difficult to
say who was and wasn't rich as a new definition of "millionaire"
gained currency, so to speak, in the 1930s. Anyone with an annual
income of $50,000 was now considered to be a millionaire, an odd
but measurable way to determine who was rich. That number
plummeted from 43,000 in 1928 to 8,000 in 1932, and the number
of $50,000-a-year millionaires slowly increased up to 25,000 by
1942.[37]

Although it was a worse time to be poor, the Depression in
America was a bad time to be rich. The upper crust was blamed for
ruining the economy through their greed in the twenties. Proposals
to "soak the rich" ("share the wealth," more kindly) and make
them literally pay for their transgressions and redistribute what became increasingly considered "the nation's wealth" were taken very
seriously, a big part of our progressive, if not socialist, leanings.
"Idle" wealth just sitting in banks should be put to good use to
help America get back on its feet, lefties argued. One of them,
Senator Huey Long, even proposed that not just money but all
kinds of assets—cars, houses, stocks—be taken away from the rich
and shared among the people. A "wealth confiscation bill" actually
passed the Senate in 1935; this forgotten piece of history clearly
proved that wealth had become, rather suddenly, "un-American,"
a contradiction of our democratic ideals. A new inheritance (or,
more popularly, "death") tax also passed in the thirties, forcing the
rich to dispose of much of their holdings before heading to the big
country club in the sky, posing the serious question of whether the
rich would survive as a species if no longer allowed to pass on their
wealth to their heirs. In 1932, steel magnate Charles M. Schwab
famously declared that they were already extinct; his statement,
"There are no rich men in America today" sent shock waves
through society.

After sensibly laying low during the thirties, the surviving rich
came out of hiding during the war, the cause a fortunate opportunity to prove they loved their country as much as anyone, even if
they did have more money. The rich visibly displayed their patrio-

tism, enlisting as PFCs and cutting back on their opulent lifestyles. Every step of (or potato peeled by) "millionaire privates" seemed to make headlines (orchestrated by the media, no doubt), and society women's efforts in the cause also made good press. As in the thirties, politicians used the rich as a foil and to win votes. However, the declaration of war against the wealthy elite still remained very much in effect. Although plenty of new money was to be made from government contracts, Old Money, already seriously weakened by the Depression, took it on the chin during the war, their estates and private clubs considered wasteful white elephants during those years of sacrifice and restraint. Calls to shut the doors of private schools were made, one of many proposed measures to not just soak the rich but to "break" them because they violated the nation's creed of egalitarianism. Accusations that the rich were hogging private nurses and railroad cars during the shortage didn't help matters.

Perhaps the most virulent attack on the rich during the war was the federal government's (failed) attempt to prevent businessmen from "profiteering," something that occurred in spades during World War I. The war would have been in vain if the nation's wealth fell into the hands of a very few, said Vice President Henry Wallace in 1943, backed up by President Roosevelt himself (who was famously considered by his fellow rich as a true traitor to his class).[38] Roosevelt and other New Dealers batted around the idea of a "conscription of wealth," equivalent to the draft but enlisting financial versus human resources. Maybe worse for the rich, resort hotels were taken over, used for marching drills and as places for wounded soldiers to recuperate. Spending money was discouraged, especially in the thriving black market, making some believe that the days of extravagant and luxurious living were over forever.

Of course, that was not to be, as Chapter 3 illustrates; the postwar economy provided an ideal climate to both make and spend money. There was a surge in millionaires (now again defined as someone making $1 million or more a year) during the postwar years, their numbers finally returning to those of the late 1920s.

While sizable in number, these millionaires were significantly less flush than those of the past, another giant step in the democratization of wealth in America and the concomitant emergence of a mass-affluent class. Millionaires in the 1950s were increasingly made versus born, with wealth spread out more evenly than between the wars as very high tax rates (as much as 91 percent) flattened out the nation's socioeconomic curve. "The massive fortunes of the 'Pittsburgh millionaires' of the nineteenth century and the 'Detroit millionaires' of the Twenties are a phenomenon not likely to be repeated," thought Joseph Nolan of the *New York Times* in 1955. Many experts of the time concurred that the nature of being rich in America had substantially changed.[39] Most of the millionaires of the postwar years were what Alvin Shuster called in 1963 "a new breed," the very same folks who composed Vance Packard's "Semi-Upper Class" in his 1959 classic *The Status Seekers*. "It was easy in the old days to tell the millionaire from the rest of us," Shuster wrote in the *New York Times*, citing owning a private railroad car, canoodling with the likes of Lillian Russell, importing chefs from Paris to cook twenty-course meals served on gold plates, swimming in pools made of white Venetian tile or Carrara marble, and having a 110-room, 45-bath country house as the classic qualifications for being considered rich. The new rich of the postwar years were living well but not flamboyantly, embracing middle-class values and lifestyles, although their bank accounts had more zeroes than other Americans.[40]

In the mid-sixties, as Chapter 4 details, the American rich went through yet another sea change as "guiding East Coast social institutions—the *Social Register*, the Junior League, the Episcopal Church—started to lose importance as barometers of individual wealth and power," according to Katherine Betts.[41] Just a stroll around the lush campuses of Harvard, Yale, or Princeton suggested the wealthy elite was in a state of flux; Old Money was losing social status faster than you could say "Jeeves." The "Big Three" were increasingly choosing intellect over social status when it came to admitting new students, effectively destroying the prime launching pad of "the best families." Columbia University had long ago opened its gates to smart Jewish, Irish, and Italian students, but the other Ivies had held out, retaining their WASP-y identity. The change in admission policy among the best universities in the country was part of what Robert Trumbull described in 1964 as "the growth of a new kind of upper class in the United States, in which membership is obtained by accomplishment rather than inheritance." An "aristocracy of the able" indeed appeared to be emerging in America; the nation became more and more a "meritocracy," composed of those in the middle class and, shockingly, even some who were, economically at least, lower class.[42]

Charles McGrath, a writer for the *New York Times* who had attended Yale University in the late 1960s, witnessed this phenomenon firsthand, describing it as "the last wheezing gasp of the patrician ethos that held the ultimate status, the highest social perch." Already, McGrath remembered, there were "hints of a new elite"; there were students at Yale who cared so little about status that they didn't even own a pair of Weejuns, an essential part of the WASP uniform.[43] Again, the apparent demise of Old Money caused some to believe it was the end of truly big money. "The day of accumulating gargantuan new personal fortunes in the United States is just about ended," wrote Ferdinand Lundberg in his 1968 bestseller *The Rich and the Super-Rich*. No one was able to anticipate that another golden era lay ahead for the American rich.[44]

In *Old Money: The Mythology of America's Upper Class*, Nelson W. Aldrich Jr. proposed that it was during the 1980s, with President Ronald Reagan as the poster child for the self-made man and laissez-faire capitalism, when the tables of the American rich began to turn. Chapter 5 takes this idea and runs with it, showing how the values of Old Money, already considered anachronistic after the youth-oriented sixties and seventies, now became seen as almost prehistoric. Conversely, the values of the arriviste looked refreshingly hip and cool, even if they did engage in the kind of business practices that would have made the big daddies of New Money—Vanderbilt, Morgan, and Rockefeller—proud.[45] Achievement, something that Old Money placed little value on as a qualification for membership in its class, was in cultural ascent, an attribute New Money had in spades. A new kind of hero or antihero emerged in the 1980s, when real-life bond traders and corporate raiders—think Sherman McCoy in Tom Wolfe's novel *Bonfire of the Vanities* and Gordon Gekko in *Wall Street*—redefined what a rich person was supposed to look and act like. Our celebration of money arguably peaked with *Lifestyles of the Rich and Famous*, a television show that encouraged the purest imaginable form of lust and envy of the rich and represented a cultural zenith of sorts. The cult of celebrity in the eighties further chipped away at the social power of Old Money, making entertainers—traditionally *personae non gratae* within the circles of the upper crust—now the stars of the wealthy elite.

In just a few years, however, a new star would be born, a rather unlikely one after the likes of Cher and Lionel Richie. The tech boom of the late 1990s and early 2000s was truly different than other eras in the history of the American rich, Chapter 6 explains, a period that didn't really fit within its cultural trajectory. Each new wave of technological innovation had always produced a new crop of rich, but this one was unique, with stock options allowing employees of start-ups that went public to share in the wealth. A Ford assembly-line worker had never become rich overnight, at least from working at Ford. Most people, including those who were part of it, didn't quite know how to handle this phenomenon or make sense of it. A new malady was soon diagnosed—"sudden wealth syndrome"; its sufferers did not know how to deal with their overnight good fortune.

Not surprisingly, the tech boom further eroded Old Money, to the point where it hardly existed anymore, and swung wide open the doors of mass affluence. "Whatever happened to the leisure class?" asked Michael Lewis in 1995. The sheer volume of the money being made and the speed in which it was amassed made the reliable markers of Old Money—snobbery, filigree, understated-ness—seem increasingly irrelevant. Just as the European aristocracy—the very models of serious Old Money—had fallen on hard times, so had their American counterparts. Those with the biggest fortunes were anointed as our new royalty regardless of how long they had it.[46] "WASP, where is thy sting?" asked McGrath a few years later, noting that while the American rich of the Gilded Age went to Europe to instantly import class, "a prepackaged ancestral past" was now readily available at a premium department store or Ralph Lauren boutique.[47]

Others offered what were effectively eulogies for Old Money as the dot-com bubble ballooned in the late 1990s. "In the 1950s and early 1960s," wrote Joseph Nocera in a 1998 article for the *New York Times* called "The Arriviste Has Arrived," "the act of trying to get rich quick by, say, striking oil in Texas, was regarded with suspicion, if not outright hostility," while "today, it's Old Money that has become ever so slightly disreputable." Once willing to do pretty much anything to join the Old Money club, yearning for "the best families," respectability, status, and discreet good taste, New Money had completely obliterated Old Money. "Now the assumption is that the richer you are, the smarter you must be and the more status you have," Nocera concluded, the idea of merit finally and indisputably triumphing over what had long been the supporting foundations of wealth, privilege, and birthright. It had taken 200-plus years, but America had finally become the meritocracy the aristocratic founding fathers had dreamed of.[48]

OTHER THEMES

Although the emergence of the first mass-affluent class in history and the cultural erosion of the wealthy elite serve as principal themes in *Rich*, there are many other aspects of the story. The gap between the rich and poor seemed always to be widening over the past century or so; it was apparently okay for the rich to get richer but not for the poor to get poorer, especially at the same time.

Even if our entire economic system is dedicated to the idea of "to the winner go the spoils," critics consistently argued that the distancing of the haves and have-nots was somehow un-American, a disturbing, ugly reminder of the inequities of consumer capitalism. Confronted with shame and guilt about these tremendous inequities despite "the system" being at fault versus us, there were frequent calls for reform, a belief that we should do something about the gap. In a 2003 article in *Atlantic Monthly*, for example, Ray Boshara argued that the United States was "the most unequal society in the advanced democratic world." He then proposed "how to fix that" through what he called "the $6,000 solution."[49]

With the possible exception of the Draconian tax policies of the 1930s, remedies to "fix" the problem never took, however. Such remedies were themselves deemed "un-American" in our free-market economy. Similarly, calls to "redistribute" wealth (now expressed as proposals to raise the taxes on hedge fund managers and private equity partners) have often been made—the idea being to seize assets of the rich because they actually belonged to the nation rather than individuals. Underlying such proposals was the notion that inherited wealth is lazy, sinful, and antithetical to our Judeo-Christian work ethic, but taking action as through a "death tax" has generally been considered too European for our libertarian blood. Indeed, we've rhetorically penalized the rich through higher income taxes, while fully realizing the strategy is mostly a canard; the rich actually pay fewer taxes than the rest of us because they have access to exotic shelters, not to mention better CPAs and lawyers. Ways for the rich to avoid paying taxes (as well as paying alimony or giving money away to anyone not of one's own choosing) developed into a fine art over time, the preservation of wealth considered just as important as the making of it. Although it has usually been well-intended, charitable giving has also been considered merely a cost of doing business. (Americans' expectation for the rich to tithe and their anger at Scrooges when they don't is reason enough to occasionally write a check or attend a benefit.) The danger of leaving too much money to one's kids has also been a persistent thorn in the sides of the rich; the fear that they would catch a bad case of what would be called "affluenza" is always present in some form.

If it's not already clear from just these themes, we've had an intense love-hate relationship with the rich since 1920, our ambivalence rooted in the fuzzier side of Judeo-Christian theology. The love of money is the root of all evil, we've been told, but the devout often believed amassing fortunes to be divinely ordained, part of the Calvinist work ethic. The rich elicit an "oxymoronic barrage of responses," wrote Daphne Merkin in 2007, "our paradoxical romance with money rank[ing] among the oldest and the most enduring."[50] Some readers, especially younger ones, may be surprised to learn that the rich as a group have at times been disliked and even despised, considered enemies of the state. The government has often been aligned with the interests of the rich but sometimes not, another fact easily forgotten over the last decade or so. Periods in which the government and the rich have been kissin' cousins have, not surprisingly, been times when key members of the government *were* the rich, of course. "Young man wanna be rich, rich man wanna be king," Springsteen put it, the symbiotic relationship between wealth and politics one of history's more familiar tunes. Politics in the name of public service was nothing new in twentieth-century America, a perfect next career for men with big money and bigger egos. The desire for political power, including the opportunity to safeguard one's personal wealth and those of one's peers, accelerated rapidly through the century. "The millionaires-only club of American politics—once the small domain of men like Roosevelt, Rockefeller, and Kennedy—has expanded to include all sorts of Regular Rich Guys," wrote Romesh Ratnesai for *Time* magazine in 1997, the cost alone of getting elected to a major office now virtually requiring one to be a fat cat.[51]

Naturally, the lifestyles of the rich and famous have been an enduring theme within American culture (despite most people of wealth being the proverbial millionaire next door). What plutocrats are doing with their money has served as one of journalism's bread-and-butter stories, a sure way to attract readers, listeners, viewers, and Internet users. The size and cost of houses, yachts, jewelry, and parties have consistently been a source of endless fascination for Americans, the stuff of both envy and repugnance (typically at the same time). Family jewels became diamond-encrusted cellphone covers at some point, but the message was the same: Some people have all the luck, and some people just have no taste. The absurdly big house and world-class art collection have been the universals, but what one person's tremendous wealth could buy also frequently presented a good measure for how rich a rich person was. (For Bill Gates circa 1997, it was a pair of in-line skates for every man, woman, and child in the country, *Newsweek* magazine ridiculously reported.)[52] The designation of the richest of us all—canonized with the debut of the Forbes Four Hundred list in 1982—has informed us who's winning, important information in a highly competitive society like ours. Money is the easiest way to keep score, after all—the logical measure for constructing a social hierarchy in the absence of a monarchy.

Second only to the bling factor has been discovering how to get some for oneself. How-to-get-rich movements have generally come in generational waves (1920s, 1950s/1960s, and 1990s/2000s), each wave bigger and bigger, a reflection of escalating American "affection for money," as de Tocqueville put it. Throughout, the road to riches has been perceived and sometimes presented as secret and elusive; the cracking of some sort of code is required to strike gold. Despite the road being in fact pretty straightforward—make more money than you spend and eventually you'll be rich, if you're still alive—a billion-dollar cottage industry has sprung up to help people get to their destination faster. Interestingly, most millionaires have consistently made most of their money not through a magical formula or even by methodical, disciplined saving and scrimping but simply by allowing stock in a company they have an ownership stake in to rise in value or letting their real estate holdings appreciate over time.

Still, Americans have continually shifted gears to be where the money is. The process of getting rich is always in flux, but the issues surrounding wealth remain remarkably the same. The wealthy elite has been a revolving door, with people coming in and out, but the institution itself has been solid as a rock. The players are always changing, in other words, but the game has remained essentially the same. Because the pace of the game has accelerated, however, the rich have become decidedly younger, especially when it comes to how they look and act. Today's plutocrat is a far cry from your great-great-grandfather's millionaire (think Mark Cuban versus Henry Ford), a fair reflection of always-young-at-heart baby boomers. Young or old, the "self-made man" has been a constant presence within the wealthy elite. The idea that our rich weren't born that way is one of our core mythologies. Remarkably, the mythology is overwhelmingly true, the gradual demise of the family dynasty further strengthening this central trope within the American experience. The media, especially the business press, has loudly cheered on the self-made man (and woman), a validation of our allegedly equal playing field and undeniable entrepreneurial spirit.

Even the most successful members of the affluent class have at some point in their lives asked themselves, "What do I do now?" This is perhaps the most important theme running through the history of the American rich since 1920. The range of emotions that come with being rich are legion. The luxury to do what one wants without worrying about money is mostly a blessing but also potentially a curse. Adopting a cause, giving one's money and time to something one feels passionate about—usually with an equivalent amount of commitment—has typically been how A-types have channeled their energies, a fact that bodes well for us all in the future.

Finally, the question whether the rich are happier than the rest of us has been a staple, so much so that in 1997 *Forbes* considered this "one of mankind's most vexing questions."[53] The answer is complicated, but one thing seems sure: The journey to wealth has been a lot more fun than the arrival, according to most who've had the pleasure of experiencing the ride.

CHAPTER 1

THIS SIDE OF PARADISE:
1920–1929

"Let me tell you about the very rich. They are
different from you and me."
—F. SCOTT FITZGERALD,
"THE RICH BOY" (1926)

IN JANUARY 1927, CORNELIUS VANDERBILT IV, THE GREAT-GREAT-grandson of shipping and railroad tycoon Commodore Vanderbilt, mused over what possibly lay in store for America's richest families. Seeing vast changes in the nation's cultural landscape since the end of the Great War less than a decade before, Vanderbilt had good reason to wonder if these dynasties would continue to prosper or even survive. "What does the future hold for prominent American families, for those bearers of great names renowned in business, politics, and society whose ambition is to perpetuate and add luster to the dynasty?" he asked. He also wondered, "What are the chances in these days of killing competition in every line of endeavor, for reproducing the strain, courage, intelligence, and integrity which combined in the past to elevate the bearers of these names to positions of eminence?" Vanderbilt, himself to the manor born but straying from his family's legacy, provided his own, rather understated, answer: "Frankly the outlook could be brighter."[1]

Vanderbilt had good reason to believe that one era of the American rich had ended and another had begun. Industries like transportation and communication that the robber barons of the Gilded Age had dominated would be unrecognizable not only to the Commodore but to his children and his children's children. As well, a plethora of national, standardized brands and chain stores were fast transforming the American marketplace and, in the process, giving rise to the modern "consumer." Something unheard of a generation ago—mixing business with socializing—would have shocked the Old Guard too, with "flyers" (stock tips) now freely traded on the growing number of golf courses popping up across the country. Even more startling, young men and women were beginning to find each other not through social functions ruled by Mrs. John Jacob Astor or Mrs. Stuyvesant Fish but at college, a huge twist in the mating dance so integral to perpetuating the species of the wealthy elite.[2]

The future of the American rich, and the nation as a whole, was, in a word, unsure, a host of economic and political issues— inflation, labor problems, the growing threat of Bolshevism— having turned the prewar world upside down. With prohibition and women getting the vote, the social plates of America had also undeniably shifted, forcing the rich to think long and hard about how to move forward into what seemed like an entirely new age to many. Most troubling, perhaps, was the new casualness creeping into American society. The wealthy simply didn't command the kind of respect they used to, as modern times and the emergence of a more iconoclastic youth culture eroded all kinds of social divisions. After ordering some more bread at a fancy restaurant in 1920, for example, one plutocrat was horrified to hear the waiter respond not "Yes, sir" but "Sure thing," as clear a sign as any that it could indeed be the end of civilization.[3]

Indeed, for American wealth culture the 1920s would prove to be the most turbulent decade so far in the nation's history, as the world of Old Money crumbled and something new, different, and decidedly modern emerged. Driven by the changes in American life after World War I, the nineteenth-century model of wealth borrowed from the European aristocracy became seen as anachronistic and musty, as dated as a horse and carriage. With a less elitist "New Economy" in place, where anyone with a stockbroker could get in on the action "on margin," a new kind of rich American took a seat at the table. And unlike the Old Guard, the new rich were likely to be making their money fair and square and working for a living just like everyone else, thus inscribing wealth with wholesome Christian values. Most importantly, however, class would become seen as less an advantage (or disadvantage) when it came to accumulating wealth; one's surname was no longer the thing that would get one in the door (or thrown out on one's keester). This much more populist, democratic paradigm of the American rich in the twenties would play out in many ways, including the nation's first real how-to-get-rich movement, a spate of "mass luxury" goods for the swelling ranks of the wealthy, and a more activist form of philanthropy. As with many other things in the 1920s, it was out with the old and in with the new when it came to money in America.

WHAT IS THE USE IN BEING RICH?

Judging by how much it cost to keep up one's country house in 1920, Old Money had a perfect right to be concerned about their future. The tab for monthly wages in one Newport house was just over $1,500, for example, divided this way among some twenty servants:

> Chef $125
> Second cook 70
> Kitchen maids (2) ...... 50 each
> Butler 125
> Footmen (2) .... 75 each
> Useful man 60
> Parlor maid 50

```
Housemaids (3)  ........ 50 each
Laundresses (2) ............ 55/60
French maid  ...................55
Valet  ...........................80
Chauffeurs (2)  ......... 125/130
Gardeners (2)  .............100/80
```

In addition to this $1,515 a month, the Newportite paid almost as much to feed the staff—$2 a day, or $1,080 a month for the eighteen in the house (the gardeners fended for themselves). Add wardrobes for the chauffeurs, footmen, and all the maids, and we're talking real money in 1920, even for a rich man.[4] Other staff some houses employed included day and night nurses (typically with hospital experience), a hairdresser and barber, a masseuse, and, at the country house, a furnaceman, carpenter, and electrician.[5]

At least as annoying as the cost of being comfortable was, as it was known, "the servant problem." Domestics were not only demanding higher wages but insisting on many things they never would have before the war, taking full advantage of the fact that there were simply less of them than there used to be. Many men, of course, had not come back from the war, while many women had dropped out of service to work in munitions factories, become nurses, or get married. Tighter immigration laws were also reducing the flood of potential servants to a trickle, adding to the frustrations of many a wealthy homeowner in the early twenties. Compounding the problem was the increasing independence of servants, many of them no longer content to devote their working lives to the wishes of a rich man or woman. One butler in Manhattan, for example, left service to open up an automobile dealership, taking his $24,000 in savings (part of it resulting from a stock tip overheard at his employer's table) with him. The ex-Jeeves was, at last report, doing quite well, selling expensive cars to members of Mrs. Astor's "Four Hundred," whom he had previously and quite literally waited on hand and foot.[6]

The rich, taking this "disloyalty" personally, quite naturally felt betrayed by their longtime servants' newfound independence, a situation only made worse by the need to find replacements within a slimmer and slimmer pool of good candidates. Rather incredibly, money—even trainloads of it—was no longer a guarantee that one could have all the comforts one desired, a shocking revelation to those used to getting what they wanted whenever they wanted. "I do not give a hang whether my servants are Bolsheviks or Methodists," said one plutocrat, "but they must be trained servants." Finding good service, always a challenge in the United States but achievable if one could afford it, had now become nearly impossible as domestics' ranks thinned and the commitment level to their jobs got even thinner. (Many American rich actually traveled to Europe not to see its great capitals but to temporarily, at least, get great service.) Servants had begun acting like organized labor, demanding higher wages and benefits, and, because so sought after, they had far more success than your average union.[7] Kitchen maids, for example, universally considered the bottom of the servant barrel, were jumping on the fact that their position was, more than ever, the most difficult to fill. One applicant, told by her potential employer that the house in which she'd be working was in Newport, asked, "Well, how far is the house from the bathing beach?" Many other kitchen maids were refusing to make their own beds, effectively making another servant work for them. Besides the challenge of finding someone to chop vegetables, wash dishes, and help prepare the servants' food, there was the additional pressure of knowing that if one didn't have a kitchen maid—preferably two—one wouldn't be able to find or keep a cook. Because such a situation was simply unfathomable, kitchen maids in the early 1920s commanded as high a wage as parlor maids and even French maids (the personal maid for the lady of the house—yes, usually French) who'd worked in the same house for years, causing quite a lot of resentment among those women higher up the servant hierarchy.[8]

The American rich, startled to hear some of the requests being made by their staff, agreed to most nonetheless, afraid to create a hard-to-fill vacancy in their city or country houses. Some maids insisted they not be called by their first name, as was the custom, but rather their last, preceded by "Miss." (Upon hearing this request, one lady of a house agreed to call her maid "Countess" if she liked, as long as she stayed and did her job well.) Other servants insisted on having keys to the house to come and go as they liked (something not possible on larger estates, which typically employed watchmen). Maintaining a house in Newport during the season was the ultimate challenge, the law of supply and demand most drastically tipping the balance of power downstairs. Some Newport servants had taken to refusing to work at all in their employers' New York town houses in the summer, saying it was simply too hot. Servants in Newport increasingly were hired without references, not surprisingly resulting in a spike of thefts. "Today it is truly an exasperating thing to be rich and to live in Newport," said one lady without any sense of irony, capturing the degree to which the wealthy felt their world was changing.[9]

"The servant problem" had emerged despite the willingness among the wealthy to offer their servants not only more than decent wages but a very impressive set of perks, particularly for the early twentieth century. Often included in compensation packages were a month's paid vacation, an expense allowance, a big Christmas bonus (cash only, please), pensions for retirees, and funeral expenses. Medical expenses too were typically thrown in, with servants cared for by the same doctors who attended the family. Interestingly, high pay and wonderful benefits didn't always guarantee happy employees. More breakage and losses were reported in homes of the rich than in those of the upper-middle class, who also frequently retained a domestic or two in the 1920s. Compared to their counterparts in England, American domestics were generally downright miserable, this country having no real servant class like in Europe. Although employers here often told their staffs they were "part of the family," in England they really were, something clearly reflected by lengths of service and levels of contentment. The fundamental issue of "the servant problem" in the United States was that servants wanted to be more than servants, while in England they typically accepted and even embraced their positions, a function of course of the very different notions of class in each country. Many a fine English servant was "spoiled" after taking a position in an American home, where they, consciously or otherwise, soaked in the national creed of aspiration, much to the puzzlement of their new, much better-paying employers. Even if told they were cherished members of the family, the literal bottom line was that servants in the United States were ultimately hired help, a fact that would more often than not show up in sloppily made beds and dropped Wedgwood.[10]

If only to provide British-style service for a while before they went native, English butlers represented the top of the servant ladder for New York families insisting on the very best. Butlers coming from homes on Fifth Avenue, in Newport, or on Gatsbyesque Long Island estates were considered the next best thing; those from Riverside Drive (decidedly nouveau riche in the twenties) were to be avoided. Butlers with service for Midwest automobile tycoons on their resumes were deemed almost untouchable by the Manhattan elite, those men permanently tainted by their affiliation with simple "mechanics" who had hit it big. It was well known that all butlers were walking encyclopedias, having stored intimate details of their previous employers' personal lives that could only be acquired through their privileged position in the house. This information was naturally often shared with colleagues and passed down to successors, the stuff of a *Masterpiece Theater* miniseries a half century later.[11]

Discreet or otherwise, butlers earned every penny of their high monthly wages (up to $150 or more by 1927). Always called by their last names, butlers in the best houses changed their clothes no less than three times a day, each costume progressively more formal. Butlers hired the footmen (always called by their full first names) and watched over them like mother hens, as well as supervised all servants' travel between New York, Newport, and the country house, even buying their railroad tickets. Butlers were also in charge of two of the house's most precious assets: the silver (polished, counted, and locked up every night, being pure versus sterling) and the wine (the cellar key never out of reach or sight). Chefs, like French maids usually French, also worked hard for their money and were responsible for hiring the cook (a woman who prepared meals for the children and servants and did prep work for the chef) and managing the kitchen maids. Such elite servants were snobbish in their own way, fully prepared to leave their employers if they felt they were too common in order to protect their own reputations.[12]

The collegial atmosphere among servants combined with the ability for them to pick and choose where they wanted to work could and did result in one of the wealthy's worst fears—the dreaded "blacklist." Even some of the "best" families on Fifth Avenue and in Newport were blacklisted, meaning servants would simply not work for them under any circumstances (more than a dozen houses in Newport alone were blacklisted during the 1920 season, in fact). The reasons for this horrible fate were varied, ranging from employers' drinking (and forgetting what they had already requested), disagreeing with each other (creating a no-win situation for the servant), entertaining 'til the wee hours (keeping the staff up all night), and, perhaps worst of all, paying late. Although a butler or chef wasn't above leaving a note in the kitchen listing such sins as a warning to those following in their wake, the waiting rooms of employment agencies served as the central clearinghouses for information about wealthy heads of households, both favorable and unfavorable. Some agencies, fully aware of which families were blacklisted, would tell their client outright, saving them from disappointment when no servants, or even interviews, were produced. Employment agencies were hardly altruistic, however; a standard practice was to tip off servants when a better job opened up in order to quickly fill the spot and get their commission (10 percent of the monthly wage). This would, of course, leave another position open, meaning another quick commission, triggering a domino effect of additional open positions and commissions. With such an arrangement, it's not surprising that owners of employment agencies in the 1920s often arrived at work in limos, kept bankers' hours, and, a bit ironically, had servants of their own.[13]

Employment agencies' smart and lucrative decision to effectively partner with servants to create high turnover only added to the frustrations of the wealthy in managing their houses. Desperate for people to keep what was typically a large and complex operation running smoothly, the rich took waitresses into service, something that just would not have happened before the war. New employees, initially gung ho and motivated by their high wages and job perks, would inevitably soon adapt to the more lugubrious pace set by their co-workers. Heads of households grudgingly accepted the higher rate of "slippage" (especially when cooks over-ordered and took home that extra veal roast or game hen), looking at it as simply another cost of doing business. (Cooks got their just desserts, so to speak, when they went looking for a bottle of rum or sherry to make a cake or sauce and found that one of their colleagues had gotten to it first, a particularly disappointing bit of news in those days of prohibition.) Slowly but surely, the American rich were having to adjust to the idea that their fortunes would not necessarily buy good service anymore—a difficult and painful process. "What is the use of being rich?" asked one of its members in 1920, a question that would have been posed only recently, as modernity invaded American society with a vengeance.[14]

THE DOCTRINE OF STEWARDSHIP

One use of being rich was the ability to give away unimaginable amounts of money. If the late nineteenth century was a golden age of fortune building, the early twentieth century was a golden age of philanthropy, as rich industrialists, now elderly, knowing they couldn't come close to spending all their money, looked for ways to leave a legacy. The flow of money to worthy causes before the Great War began to gush after it ended, with the wealthiest men in the country taking the lead in the early 1920s in what to date were the largest acts of munificence ever attempted and achieved.

John D. Rockefeller, eighty-two years old in 1921, along with his only son, John D. Rockefeller Jr., age 47 that year, were devoting most of their lives to disposing of much of the greatest fortune ever acquired, perhaps as ambitious an enterprise as the father's making of it. For the past quarter-century, in fact, the two had been the world's most generous philanthropic tag team in history, following their carefully thought-out plan to attack not poverty itself but the causes of it. By damming up its streams ("disease, ignorance, and intemperance"), these men believed, there was a chance the big river of social ills could be stopped, or at least slowed. The Rockefellers' philanthropic focus on prevention versus cure was amazingly ahead of its time, serving as a model for how billionaires of the future could and would put their own fortunes to work.[15]

Much as was true of Bill Gates, Warren Buffett, or Richard Branson decades later, the senior Rockefeller had been the object of the American public's scrutiny for decades, as the man recast himself from ultimate businessman to ultimate benefactor. "If there is any subject regarding which every American citizen has an opinion, it is the fortune of John D. Rockefeller," wrote Albert W. Atwood in the *Saturday Evening Post* in 1921, arguing that the public's interest had evolved from a fascination with its sheer size to how it was made to, finally, how it was being given away. The Rockefellers had by then devoted a half-billion dollars to their particular causes, in the process bringing a number of key social issues to the forefront of the nation's consciousness. No single individual in the first half of the twentieth century made more people think about the tension between private rights versus public duty, selfishness versus service, than John D. Rockefeller or, more broadly, drew attention to both the privileges and responsibilities of the rich.[16]

His general mission to "promote healthy living conditions and educate the child to industry, thrift and self-sufficiency," Rockefeller's largesse was essentially a continuation of what he had been doing since his youth, now on a massive scale and full-time basis. As a child, Rockefeller gave pennies from his $4 a week salary to

FIGURE 1-1. John D. Rockefeller and John D. Rockefeller Jr. in 1925. The father and son team was now much more interested in giving money away than making more, the two applying their unsurpassed business skills to philanthropy. *(Hulton Archive/Getty Images)*

causes he believed in and, as a twelve-year-old bookkeeper, showed clear signs of the methodical generosity that lay in his future (as when he gave a quarter to a poor man in church and twelve cents to the Five Points Mission in New York, both dutifully recorded in his account book). Some seventy years later, it wasn't unusual for the Rockefellers' office to receive 2,000 letters a day, many of them petitions for money. The Rockefellers approached the giving of money much like the earning of it, applying the same kind of results-oriented decision making and efficiency for which they were famously known in their business dealings and investment philosophies. Being awarded Rockefeller money was important not only because of the gift's likely size (e.g., $35 million to the University of Chicago), but because it conveyed to other potential donors that the cause was deserving. The Rockefellers were very aware of this responsibility, making them even more careful to do their homework on each and every charity case.[17]

The Rockefellers' philanthropic empire was divided into four foundations or trusts in the early twenties; John Jr., who had never had an active career in business, was in charge of how to best conserve and utilize his dad's fortune. The biggest chunk was the Rockefeller Foundation, which at the time supported public health, sanitation, and medical education around the world. Many of its dollars were dedicated to eradicating diseases that took millions of lives each year, like hookworm, malaria, yellow fever, and tuberculosis. The Rockefeller Institute of Medical Research, the elder Rockefeller's favorite, was devoted to pure research in those days before for-profit pharmaceutical companies poured millions into R&D, hoping for a big payout. The General Education Board promoted education via gifts to college and university endowments, its dollars going toward increasing professors' salaries (as an incentive for them not to jump ship for higher paying jobs), underfunded areas like psychiatry, obstetrics, and dentistry, and, pretty forward-thinking for 1921, underrepresented practitioners such as blacks. The final piece, the Laura Spelman Rockefeller Memorial Fund, targeted pet causes of the octogenarian and, especially, those of his late wife, such as churches, missionaries, the YMCA and YWCA, and many local charities that put women and children first.[18]

Before giving a single dollar away, however, the Rockefellers were careful to do what today would be called due diligence, vetting the donee and its stated purpose to ensure legitimacy. Once donees received their checks, the Rockefellers' involvement was remarkably hands-off (unlike today's benefactors, who often want to play an active role in managing—and sometimes micromanaging—their "social ventures"). The Rockefellers were also determined to keep cause and ideology as separate as church and state, even when realizing they were likely supporting "radicalism" through their funding of university professors. For the same reason, the Rockefellers were sure not to offer money to newspapers and magazines, not wanting to mix politics or public opinion with philanthropy. Interestingly, the Rockefellers would sometimes deny a petition because it was clear that the amount requested would not be enough to achieve the desired objective and then encourage the applicant to ask for more money, which was likely awarded. Given the way that John D. Rockefeller had made his fortune, the ways in which he was giving it away—generously, empathetically, and, above all, ethically—was all the more amazing. It was said that the man, as founder of Standard Oil, had used "the methods of his time" in acquiring his billion or billions (few knew his real worth), a kind way to describe the often Draconian and Darwinian approach to commerce that he and his competitors considered business as usual in the late nineteenth century.[19]

Even the Rockefellers' donations of hundreds of millions of dollars could barely make a dent in the philanthropic frenzy of the 1920s, however. Many rich, and especially the super-rich, were, like the Rockefellers, regularly bombarded with requests for money, most arriving in the morning mail. Mrs. E. H. Harriman, widow of the legendary railroad executive, for example, received thousands of "begging letters" each year, and Henry Ford got an amazing 1,500 per day. (In each case, the total amount requested would quickly deplete their respective fortunes.) Many rich widows spent much of their time dictating letters "refusing to subscribe" to petitioners' requests, a fair share of them frauds. When a large gift, big inheritance, or sale of a multimillion dollar company was reported in the newspapers, letters poured into the lucky person's office or home, an unlucky consequence of his or her windfall. "Letters of appeal are a by-product of being known to be rich," wrote W. H. Allen in his 1912 book *Modern Philanthropy*, a full study of Mrs. Harriman's experience in fielding requests for money. Much worse than having to respond to each request or weed out the frauds was the occasional letter threatening physical harm or blackmail if the receiver didn't come up with the goods. Some wealthy people had their local police force working full-time on such cases or even hired their own private detectives to nip them in the bud. Needless to say, all these trials and tribulations drove many to support their causes secretly or anonymously as exposure of the American rich to the public and money mania among the masses increased exponentially in the twenties.[20]

The U.S. Postal Service wasn't the only way the wealthy got pinched by those looking for a handout. Relatives, friends, acquaintances, and business associates often put the squeeze on the rich, asking them to fork out everything from their kids' college tuition to a monthly allowance for dear old mother-in-law. It wasn't uncommon for complete strangers to make personal appeals to the famously rich, making the latter appear eccentric or socially phobic when they dared not venture out of their fortresslike Xanadus. Businesspeople who'd been promoted from vice president to president of their company were surprised to learn that they were expected to make donations to sometimes hundreds of charities as a symbol of goodwill, the practice viewed more as a fixed obligation, like taxes, than a voluntary one.[21] The most famous businessman in the world, Henry Ford could hardly go out in public without being peppered by face-to-face requests for money, all of them lost causes given that Ford was opposed to both the idea and practice of organized charity, thinking that it injured character. "I have no patience with professional charity or with any sort of commercial charity or with any sort of commercialized humanitarianism," Ford wrote in his 1922 book *My Life and Work* (the chapter in question sensibly called "Why Charity?"). Besides being on the opposite end of the spectrum when it came to giving away money, Ford also differed greatly from the only person on the planet who had more of it when it came to how much they kept around. Rockefeller reportedly never had more than a total of $50,000 in cash in his bank accounts. The majority of his fortune was continually reinvested, while Ford kept a few million liquid. This, if true, offers a neat metaphor for their contrasting personalities and general outlooks on life.[22]

In 1924, two new mega-philanthropists burst onto the scene, their gifts rivaling those of the reigning champions of charity, Rockefeller and Carnegie. George Eastman, the camera king, and James B. Duke, the tobacco titan, collectively gave away over $50 million on the very same day, up to that point probably the largest amount of money ever donated within a twenty-four-hour period. As with Rockefeller's gifts, most of the money went toward education, rather ironic given that neither man had gone to college. Also like Rockefeller and Carnegie, Eastman and Duke had made their fortunes according to the practices of their time, making their gifts a kind of penance for blatant price-fixing and their scorch-the-earth approach to competition. Most of Eastman's gift went to the University of Rochester; another chunk went to MIT (which for years had received sizable donations from a certain angel named "Mr. Smith"). Eastman also gave $1 million to Tuskegee Institute and Hampton Institute, two southern black colleges; this gift appeared to administrators at both schools like, as the *Boston Herald* described it, "a bolt from the blue." Duke's huge gift to Trinity College came with one big string attached—that the school be renamed Duke University (a condition deemed "regrettable" by most alumni and Durhamites but rhetorically justified by the administration as a sensible way to differentiate it from the three other Trinity Colleges scattered around the country). Eastman's and Duke's mother lodes resembled those of not just Rockefeller

FIGURE 1-2. Nine American, well-dressed captains of industry in New York in 1928. From left to right, they are Harvey Firestone (rubber), Julius Rosenwald (merchandising), Thomas Edison (inventions), Thomas Lipton (tea), Charles M. Schwab (iron and steel), Henry Ford (automobiles), Thomas E. Wilson (meat packing), George Eastman (photography), and Walter Chrysler (automobiles). *(American Stock/Getty Images)*

and Andrew Carnegie but of other captains of industry, like Henry Frick and Milton Hershey, who were also giving away tens of millions of dollars in a single shot. "Our rich men in increasing numbers are practicing the doctrine of stewardship of wealth," opined the *Pittsburgh Chronicle Telegraph*, recognizing that these tycoons turned activists were "exhibiting the same qualities of shrewdness and sound business sense that aided in the acquisition of their wealth."[23]

Some of the richest of the rich may have decided to devote their lives to full-time philanthropy, but most wealthy Americans were in fact not at all interested in retiring, least of all to give away most of what they had worked so hard to earn. Some, loyal to their businesses 'til the bitter end, could not bear the thought of seeing their companies fail should they leave, and they stayed on until they were pushed out the mahogany door. Bruce Barton, the famous advertising executive, had another theory about the reluctance of the American rich to retire. "Money is the score of the game," he argued in 1926, with wealthy Americans wanting to keep racking up points if only to beat their fellow players (not unlike the sentiment expressed in the 1980s bumper sticker: "He with the most toys wins"). Gentlemen in other parts of the world, notably Europe, typically moved to the country and dabbled in public affairs after a successful and lucrative career, but quitting the game just didn't seem to be in the American DNA. "The ambition of the European is to secure an independence early and then play or travel or just sit tight," Barton surmised, but "idleness has little attraction for us."[24]

A VAST CROP OF MILLIONAIRES

With big money to make in the midtwenties, idleness was the last thing many Americans were interested in. By 1924, the jitters that followed the Great War now largely gone, the time was ripe for many men's minds to turn to one of their favorite fancies: how to get rich or richer. Frederick Palmer, writing for *Harper's* that year, observed that at the resort hotel he had recently stayed, "the talk among the groups which gathered on the veranda after dinner was usually of money," when a few years back it might have been politics or those very unladylike suffragettes. "So it is wherever you go," Palmer added, noting that eight out of every ten people in the smoking room of a transatlantic ocean liner he had been on some months before were also talking money.[25] More importantly, wealth was not just on the minds and lips of the already wealthy but on those of ordinary folks as well. The first real "how to get rich" movement rolled across America in the midtwenties, infusing the idea of wealth with a heavy dose of populism and liberating it from the dark netherworld it had occupied for the last half century or so. Writing for *Collier's* in 1926, Rheta Childe Dorr revealed the secret to becoming wealthy to the magazine's readers, many of them women who no doubt wanted to turn their new independence into hard cash. "You do it by investing, letting the interest pile up, and finally live off the interest," Dorr advised; her own goal was to accumulate $100,000 in the next ten years so she could live on the $500 a month she'd earn from the money.[26]

The dream of becoming wealthy was not just wishful thinking. The country as a whole was in fact getting richer. The American standard of living in 1926 was "so high that the average family enjoys today luxuries and necessities that were formerly regarded as luxuries which only a few short years ago were the mark of the wealthy," according to the *Troy Record* in 1926. The *Pittsburgh Gazette Times* agreed, attributing this phenomenon to the trickle-down effect of the growing number of millionaires and suggesting that Americans should be thankful for the multiplying rich. "When the making of millionaires is accompanied by such an increase of general prosperity, the country may well pray for more of them," the newspaper's editor wrote, more or less saying that when it came to the American rich, if you can't beat 'em, join 'em. Part of the new lovefest for the nation's wealthy was its growing diversity; the rich were no longer just a small cabal of crusty men doing anything and everything they could to monopolize their particular industry. "We have railroad millionaires, and coal millionaires, and oil millionaires, electricity millionaires, and gas millionaires, and harvesting machinery and meat-packing and steel and publishing and real-estate millionaires," the *Philadelphia Evening Public Ledger* observed, the explosion of wealthy individuals a direct result of the nation's broad-based economic boom. The blossoming of American popular and consumer culture in the 1920s was also helping create a new generation of rich. "New fortunes are [being] made out of devices not heard of by our grandfathers," the Philadelphia newspaper continued, recognizing that "we are building up a group of radio millionaires just as we developed automobile millionaires and before them telephone millionaires."[27]

Hard data backed up the obvious fact that wealth was spreading like wildfire in the latter half of the twenties. Bank deposits were up, for one thing, with the four biggest banks in the country (National City, Chase, Guaranty Trust, and National Bank of Commerce, all in New York) holding more than $2.5 billion in combined deposits in 1926—two and a half times the $1 billion in total bank deposits in New York at the turn of the century. As well, sixty-three banks and trust companies across the United States each held deposits of more than $75 million, proof that not just New Yorkers were enjoying the prosperity. "New York, Boston, Philadelphia, Chicago, and San Francisco are no longer the exclusive habitat of the millionaires," observed Oswald Garrison Villard in *Harper's* in 1927; the nation's entrepreneurial climate and a more connected society allowed wealth to flourish pretty much everywhere.[28] Wall Street was also having a bull run ("millions of investment money is pouring into the market," reported the *Wall Street Journal* that year), another obvious sign of the economic boom.[29] Finally, in its analysis of estates, Guaranty Trust revealed that there were six times the number of millionaires in the United States in 1928 than in 1923—a huge increase in just five years. If it wasn't clear enough from the gobs of money being thrown around, financial evidence like this showed that, without a doubt, America and Americans were getting wealthier by the minute, its extreme upper reaches of course benefiting the most.[30]

By early 1929, the economic boom of the second half of the twenties had resulted in nothing less than "a vast new crop of millionaires," as Samuel Crowther described it that year. The vastness of the crop was making a millionaire—the standard benchmark for being rich—not what it used to be, however. "Within the last ten years no end of people have become rich," he observed, believing that "a man with a million dollars cannot, in these days, be counted as really rich." The paths to wealth were varied, but most eventually led to Wall Street. Many family businesses were going public to capitalize, literally, on investor demand. Upon the deaths of their founders (such as the Dodge brothers), other companies were promptly sold to bankers, their bricks and mortar converted into highly marketable stock certificates. The stock market, more than anything else, was democratizing wealth, spreading it from the coffers of a handful of super-rich into the swelling bank accounts of thousands of ordinary Americans. Many of the newly wealthy were women, some of whom dipped into their family's savings accounts and, unbeknownst to their more risk-averse husbands, turned their nest eggs into small fortunes by taking a flyer or two. "The fortunes of yesterday—the Astor, the Gould and the Vanderbilt—are not great today except as legends," Crowther continued, "but there are millionaires tucked away in every nook and cranny of this country that no one ever heard of." With a few speculators riding on the coattails of each professional investor who was doing the heavy lifting by helping manage a particular business, one hardly had to be an expert to see one's portfolio multiply five, ten, or even more times. And as buying on margin became increasingly common, the actual merit of a corporation in which one was investing was becoming almost irrelevant. "The public is in a mood to take shares in the enterprises which have a record of success and in some which have none," Crowther concluded, not aware of the inherent danger in "It may be possible to reap without sowing."[31]

Those shopping for holiday gifts in 1929 could find plenty of ways to spend the big bucks they earned that year, with the American marketplace brimming over with goodies for the wealthy consumer. Replacing that old upright piano with one of those new baby grands (actually called miniature grands at the time) was a popular choice, as was one of the latest radios, with more bells and whistles than ever before. "Motor attire" too was moving like hotcakes, with all the scarves one could ask for to complement a Rolls Phantom or Duesenberg J. Those looking for something more refined might opt for a smoking jacket, paisley robe (with matching slippers), or an ermine, sable, or silver fox coat or wrap (the best made with three to six skins). Women wanting to express their recently discovered sexuality (in public, anyway) were going for black hosiery in cobweb or "tango net" designs and, even more daring, corsets, girdles, and garters in silk, satin, and lace (the Victoria's Secret teddy of the late twenties). For the wee ones, there were electric trains and flying model planes or, if all else failed, "merchandise bonds" (gift certificates) to let that jaded boy or girl get whatever his or her little heart desired. Holiday shoppers hopefully got what they wanted that season as, for the next few years, Santa was going to be carrying a much lighter load down chimneys, even those of the rich.[32]

With such an abundance of millionaires by the end of the decade, those with real money felt the need to distance themselves from their lesser kin, with one particular possession—the private yacht—considered the best way to do that. "More than anything else, a big private yacht symbolizes money," Samuel G. Blythe stated—"big" meaning 200 feet or more. It was true that, with one possible exception—the marble swimming pool favored by the new Hollywood tycoons—an absurdly large boat was the tangible equivalent to the idea of wealth, largely because of how much money it took to operate the thing. Unfortunately, it was far easier for yacht owners to buy their boats than to get people actually on them. "The problem of getting a yacht full of congenial guests for a cruise of any length is one that most yacht owners give up in despair after a few tries," Blythe noted. Most rich people didn't know a bow from a stern or were prone to seasickness. Captains of industry were also not used to taking orders from other captains and dreaded the idea of having to sit next to a bore for hours or days with no escape possible. Having themselves been in the same position, yacht owners were fully aware of this and thus often invited only people who were somehow obligated to get on board, such as employees or those who wanted to borrow money. Even with this rather diabolical strategy, however, huge, beautiful yachts would often sit unused for years, their owners wishing they had not felt the need to display their great wealth so nautically.[33]

Although millionaires were popping up like daisies across the country, many of them with big yachts in dry dock, there was no doubt that New York City remained the national and world capital of wealth. More than a quarter of the nation's millionaires lived in New York in the twenties, with one particular avenue its home base. Park Avenue had "the most stupendous aggregation of multimillionaires which the world has ever seen," wrote Stuart Chase in 1927 for the *New Republic*, a claim backed up by a simple stroll down the avenue. One would encounter a steady stream of dowdy governesses, impeccably dressed children, and exotic dogs (Airedales being the pup of choice). While Fifth Avenue had a generation earlier unquestionably been the place to be, many of its mansions were being torn down, a sure sign that there was a new kind of plutocrat in town.[34]

Called "Croesus's sixty acres" by journalist Maurice Merney (after the rich fifth-century king of Lydia), Park Avenue, according to that writer "one of the phenomena of the American brand of civilization, a glittering world unto itself," fully deserved its status. Running three miles between Murray Hill and 96th Street on the Upper East Side, the avenue was home to 5,000 families and 20,000 people, one-third of one percent of the city's population. Despite its relatively few residents, Park Avenue hosted an aggregate fortune of $3 billion in early 1929, bigger than France's war debt to the United States. Four times as many millionaires lived on the avenue than in all of Great Britain; there were in fact more millionaires per square block than per square mile anywhere else in the world. Wide, flowery, and just steps from the city's smartest shops, the avenue was a realtor's dream, the perfect location for both Fifth Avenue refugees and the hordes of nouveau riche created over the past decade. "The avenue glitters before the eye in an atmosphere of gold," gushed Merney, a sentiment shared by the growing number of wealthy elite who believed that any other address on their stationary just wouldn't do.[35]

FIGURE 1-3. John Hertz Jr. (left), Helen Hertz, and friend Richard Busvine walking along Park Avenue on Easter Sunday, 1933. The two Hertzes were the children of John Hertz, founder of the Hertz Drive-Ur-Self System, now the Hertz Corporation. *(Morgan Collection/Getty Images)*

It was almost inevitable that Park Avenue would become, in Merney's smitten view, "the plumed, pearled lady with the beauty spot, much to be desired and costly to possess." Exactly a hundred years earlier, the *New York Mirror* described it as a "grand avenue," situated on "by far the most desirable position, and over much of the best ground on the island." Even as a dirt road, what would become Park Avenue somehow matched or even surpassed the grandeur of "any other thoroughfare in the world," according to the newspaper. A century later, it remained, in Merney's words, the "immigrant's conception of the Promised Land." By 1924, Park Avenue had its own publication, the *Social Review*, probably the only magazine published by and for a single street up to that point. Five years later, the monthly magazine (available to residents only) was a hundred pages long (half of it advertising), its primary editorial thrust an antinoise campaign to ban the kind of car-honking that was plaguing many fine neighborhoods in Paris.[36]

On the outside, Park Avenue may not have been as fashionable as its neighbor to the west once was, but on the inside it wore its wealth extremely well. Residents spent $280 million a year ($70,000 per family), according to the Park Avenue Association, much of that on furnishings for their apartments in old brownstones or the new boxy buildings. Wood paneling imported (piece by piece) from English manor houses was all the rage for urbanites with a sense of style and barrels of money in the twenties, complemented by a custom-built (and, remember, Prohibition-era) barroom complete with brass rails and beer taps. Park Avenuers typically gave their interior decorators carte blanche (along with a hundred grand) to turn their apartments—often duplexes or, best of all, triplexes complete with roof gardens—into masterpieces, with early English furniture, imported fireplaces, Lalique lamps, and beamed, frescoed ceilings. A new thing—the cooperative apartment house—was becoming very popular, with a classic six on Park Avenue going for (hold onto your hats) $75,000 in 1927. Rich bachelors were opting for rooms at the Ritz Tower, the premier apartment hotel on the avenue and in the city, which, because the house provided all services, was a convenient way around the pesky servant problem. "Here the American dollar reaches its dizziest point," Chase said about the avenue, concluding that, "If America has a heaven, this is it."[37]

A NEW KIND OF MAN

Thankfully for the American rich, there would also apparently be a heaven waiting for them when they were ultimately evicted from

Park Avenue. After a couple of thousands of years or so, Christians were coming around to the idea that the wealthy could indeed enter Paradise when their days on this mortal plane were over (discounting the well-known part of the Bible that stated that the average rich man had less chance of getting into Heaven than a camel had of passing through the eye of a needle). "So long as our American rich men and women are warm hearted and kind, as they are today," said Cardinal O'Connell of Boston in 1926, a mansion in the sky was waiting for them, good news for wealthy folks concerned that God might have a different view of privilege and social class. Although it was true that the wealthy were redeeming themselves through their good works, O'Connell and other leaders of the Catholic Church knew where their wafers were buttered and no doubt made a special effort to inform the pearled that they too could look forward to passing through the pearly gates. The Church was one of the biggest beneficiaries of rich men and women of that religious persuasion, making the Cardinal's blessing a smart way to keep the milk and honey flowing.[38]

Catholics weren't the only spiritually inclined to embrace the rich with open arms as the memory of their less than benevolent older kin faded. Besides becoming as American as apple pie, wealth was, not coincidently, becoming more Christian in general, no longer a servant of the devil. The devoutness of some of the nation's richest men accounted for some of this, of course, but it was much more than that. In explaining America's mass pursuit of wealth, Bruce Barton, who besides being one of the nation's top admen was author of the 1925 *The Man Nobody Knows* (in which Jesus Christ is portrayed as the ultimate salesman), made it clear that being rich was no sin. The Bible "does not say that *money* but the *love* of money is the root of all evil," wrote Barton for *Good Housekeeping* in 1926, an attempt to reconcile the era's mad quest for wealth against the moral values of Christianity.[39]

With the much-publicized return of multimillionaires' fortunes to the public and the spiritual reconciliation of the wealthy, the redemption of the American rich was virtually complete by the late

1920s. Millionaires were not necessarily all crooks, it seemed, a new and refreshing idea for most Americans who had witnessed how those of the last few generations had made and spent their money. As well, there was a growing recognition that the rich were largely responsible for the general prosperity (the "common wealth") of the nation, that they had raised the standards of living for all through their industriousness and leadership. One was still envious of the super-rich, of course, but it was more than possible that they had in fact given, via the fruits of their labor, more than they took (the best case being Ford's automobile and Rockefeller's gas that those wonderful machines ran on).[40] And rather than the dynastic kind of families that had served as the country's unofficial aristocracy for almost a century, as Cornelius Vanderbilt IV had pointed out, a different kind of monied or favored class was definitely emerging. This new plutocracy—simply rich versus super-rich— held values similar to those of the average American, rooted in Christianity and a solid work ethic. As well, the new American rich had fewer prodigal sons and was less likely to squander or bicker over their fortunes like many Old Guard families had famously done, which also contributed to the shrinking stigma of being a fat cat. The American rich had, it seemed, finally been awarded full citizenship by its less privileged citizens, something they hadn't enjoyed since the Civil War and rise of the robber barons.[41]

This huge shift in the composition of the wealthy elite did not go unnoticed by social critics. "A new kind of man has come to the top of the time," Samuel Strauss declared in *Atlantic Monthly* in 1927, relieved that it was not "the old-fashioned rich man, the money-makers, the profit-takers who would be in charge." Strauss firmly believed that the country had turned an important corner in the nation's history, no longer held prisoner by the "hydra-headed monster"—big business and trusts—that had dominated the economy through nefarious methods. It wasn't just that these men were too rich, too powerful, or even too corrupt; it was that the kinds of organizations these men had led violated the democratic principles that the Founding Fathers had imagined when they forged the nation. In less than a decade, the fear, hatred, and resentment held toward the rich had almost completely disappeared, replaced by a profound confidence in the workings of American-style capitalism.[42] "The wide diffusion of wealth has bred a great tolerance [for the rich]," agreed Albert C. Ritchie, governor of Maryland, his theory being that "the public . . . is rather enamored with the bigness of it all."[43]

The distribution of wealth—a millionaire might be living right next door rather than just in the big house on the hill—was perhaps the most remarkable thing about the complete turnaround of the American rich. Easy credit and investment bankers' creation of new corporations simply to get in on the action were helping spread wealth to the masses, an unprecedented phenomenon in American history. "They [millionaires] are not affluently isolated figures standing ostentatiously on rich, golden peaks above their fellows," said Blythe in 1929, observing that "nowadays they run in herds." The glut of millionaires in the late 1920s had much to do, of course, with the fact that it was infinitely easier to become rich than in the last two or three generations, when a select few ruled the roost and crushed those who got in their way. "It is no particular trick to get money in these times," Blythe observed, fully believing that "any man with fairly good qualifications as to business acumen, opportunity, environment and nerve can get it."[44] Wealth was, rather suddenly, not the exclusive province of a select few but something all Americans could realize if they played their cards right. "For the present no active hostility to the rich can be found," claimed Hoffman Nickerson that same year, recalling the days when muckraking journalists like James Gordon Bennett, Joseph Pulitzer, and William Randolph Hearst, as well as Presidents Roosevelt and Wilson, attacked the wealthiest Americans for their abuses of power.[45] "Some day the annalists are going to write a chapter to explain what happened between yesterday and today to cause the amazing reversal in our attitude toward great wealth," Strauss correctly prophesized, thinking this chapter "will be one of the most interesting and illuminating expositions in our history book."[46]

Even politics—a career in which being rich was considered at the very least a red flag—could now accommodate people of significant means. "Millionaires are in much better repute than they were a few years ago when politicians would have paled at the thought of nominating a millionaire for president," noted an editorial in the *Chicago Daily Tribune* in the fall of 1927 as elections approached, the slate peppered with men of great wealth. With the spread of prosperity and big business having cleaned up its act, wealth and political aspirations were no longer mutually exclusive; the public was now willing to place trust in a rich man or woman. In fact, being rich had turned from a liability into an asset when campaigning, wealth now considered solid evidence that one could be an effective leader. "Instead of wealth barring a man from public office . . . it stamps him as a man efficient in business and capable of successfully conducting public affairs," the editorial continued, a major shift in the popular imagination about the American rich.[47]

Herbert Hoover, the winner of the election, was exactly the new kind of man who had "come to the top." Hoover had made his modest fortune as a top mining engineer, entering public service during World War I when he became bored with making money. Like most of those who would occupy the White House after him, Hoover surrounded himself with men of equivalent or much greater wealth, taking advantage of the new admiration of the rich. "Herbert Hoover has undertaken to make American people look upon men of great riches as the natural material for leadership in government," said Laurence Todd in *The Nation* in 1929, noting that the president's cabinet was chock-full of millionaires, including Henry L. Stimson (Secretary of State), Andrew W. Mellon (head of the Treasury, rather fittingly, being the third or fourth richest man in the country), James W. Wood (Secretary of War), Charles Francis Adams (Secretary of the Navy), Robert P. Lamont (Secretary of Commerce), and James J. Davis (Secretary of Labor). This esteemed group was clearly the richest of what would come to be called a "Millionaire Cabinet," raising suspicion among more liberal critics that the president was stacking the deck toward business interests and the upper class.[48] Most, however, viewed politics as not just a sensible but an honorable realm for a wealthy man, a way to serve one's country after serving one's own interests. "No rich man, seeking useful and patriotic outlets for his abilities, can do better than undertake some form of public service," thought Blythe that same year, knowing that the relatively paltry salary of cabinet members ($15,000 in 1929) certainly wasn't driving the wealthy to politics.[49]

Whether it was for man or country or both, there was no doubt that there was a disproportionate number of rich men in politics at the tail end of the twenties. President Coolidge had also put together a cabinet of mostly wealthy men (including Mellon, who had also been a member of President Harding's cabinet), but Hoover's cadre of "men of property" seemed to be part and parcel of the era's unprecedented prosperity. The Senate had already long been nicknamed "the millionaire's club," with simply getting elected a pricey proposition even in these pretelevision days. Twenty of the ninety-six U.S. senators in 1929 were believed to be millionaires; in fact, their $10,000 salaries were hardly the incentive to put on hold (and often squash) what was typically a lucrative local law career to head to Washington. While the House was definitely not quite as well to do, it too had a fair number of ex-swells in its chamber, and the roster of ambassadors and those in foreign service was almost totally composed of men who could afford to entertain nobility and dignitaries in the style to which they were accustomed. Despite its democratic ideals, American politics were not very different from the European aristocracy, it seemed, each governing the people from a golden throne.[50]

A STRANGE AND FASCINATING NEW GENERATION

The pronounced work ethic among the new generation of rich that emerged after the Great War was yet another characteristic that distinguished them from their fathers' and grandfathers' million-aires. Gloria Gould, the daughter of industrialist George Jay Gould, was running a theater on Broadway in the midtwenties, for exam-ple, while fellow socialite Sarah Parker Conover had an antique shop in Manhattan, and both William Averill Harrison and Junius Morgan had entered their respective family businesses as the sons of extremely wealthy men. Vincent Astor was a successful, hard-working real estate developer, suddenly thrust into the limelight and the business world in 1912 when, as a Harvard freshman, his father, John Jacob Astor IV, went down on the *Titanic*.[51] Cornelius Vanderbilt IV was also working nine to five, although he could obvi-ously have chosen to do other things, like spend some of his fami-ly's hundreds of millions. After serving in France as a buck private in the war, Vanderbilt returned home, not to enter Yale as planned before going into the family business but to look for a job. Knowing that Vanderbilt liked to write, Teddy Roosevelt, a good friend, sug-gested he become a journalist, and soon the scion was working at the *New York Herald* as a cub reporter at $30 a week.[52]

Unfortunately, the Colonel caused more havoc with his advice to Vanderbilt than he did charging San Juan Hill. Vanderbilt's par-ents were shocked to learn of their son's decision to enter the Fourth Estate rather than manage the family fortune and remain a "gentleman" as was his destiny; they gave him twenty-four hours to quit his job (in part because the Vanderbilts had long been painted by the press, as Vanderbilt described it, "in garish hue"). Much to Mom and Dad's displeasure, IV kept his job, earning him the public designation as a "parlor pink," the term for a rich man's son who breaks away from family ties or traditions and is conse-quently presumed to be a Communist. "Members of society . . . have an idea that one must be socialistic if one desires to get out with the rest of mankind and hustle for an existence," the twenty-eight-year-old complained in 1926 in his article in the *Saturday Evening Post* plainly titled, "It is Hard to Be a Rich Man's Son." Such rumors no doubt made people think that Vanderbilt might want to divest himself of his family's wealth, accounting for the

21,456 "begging letters" he received in 1925, which added up to exactly $8,345,676 in requests. (Interestingly, Vanderbilt also received 19,000 "mash notes"—11,000 with photos—that year, making one think that women were fine with his possibly being a Bolshevik as long as he was still rich.) Vanderbilt soon moved from the *Herald* to the *New York Times*; he wrote articles for other publications under an assumed name (not cashing his paychecks) and eventually started a few newspapers and magazines of his own (following in the journalistic footsteps of another scion, William Randolph Hearst's doppelganger Charles Foster Kane). "My best recreation is my typewriter and something interesting to write," Vanderbilt insisted, this despite friends (like the boxer Gene Tunney) urging him to put the typewriter away and have more fun with his father's enormous pile of dough.[53]

Along with the emergence of the modern American rich in the 1920s came nothing less than a total overhaul of high society. By 1927, the "Four Hundred" had become at least four thousand—the standards for New York Society (the size of Mrs. Astor's ballroom, most famously) considerably diluted. Most of the Old Guard not surprisingly longed for the good old days when the barriers to society held back every Tom, Dick, and Harry with a million or two. Some, however, welcomed the new blood, bored with the same old people on the incestuous New York to Newport to Hot Springs to country house circuit. The end of the "Four Hundred" era also meant the end of their grand parties, now viewed as anachronistic white elephants too formal (and costly) to consider staging. Entertaining in the 1920s was much more modest, the over-the-top style of dinner parties adored (and expected) by the previous generation of society now distinctly out of favor. Parties were now usually catered rather than home-cooked, with much less food served (rather than the ten courses of a better turn-of-the-century dinner—oysters, soup, fish, entréc, roast, second entrée, salad, dessert, fruit, and candy—only five or six courses were being ladled out). The kind of conversation served up at the lavish dinners of the past was also kaput, replaced by bridge games or professional entertainment brought in by the hostess (often intentionally loud to drown out any ill-advised attempts to engage in witty banter). As well, the big dinner parties of the past had shrunk to more intimate affairs; these smaller soirees had less need for social secretaries. Handwritten invitations—a time-consuming process, to say the least, when hundreds were needed—were replaced by invites sent by telegraph, a nod to modern technology and the accelerated pace of society.[54]

Another thing rocking society's boat was, in a word, women. "There is a strange and fascinating new generation in society, wiry, husky-voiced fox-hunting young women who are full of fire and adventure—flippant, kind-hearted, imperturbably good natured and brave," wrote Elizabeth Barbour in 1927; this was a much different breed than the ladies who had flitted through society a generation earlier. Maybe because they were eating only five or six courses at dinner parties instead of ten, these women were appreciably thinner than their turn-of-the-century sisters and left their long white gloves, tiaras, and jewels at home when they went out. And, like women from all classes, society girls were wearing rouge and lipstick, smoking cigarettes, carrying flasks, canoodling with men, and driving automobiles, all things that ladies (and men) of the Gilded Age would have found shocking at the very least.[55]

As traditional gender roles went up in smoke, another social phenomenon of the twenties—the nation's skyrocketing divorce rate—also struck high society with a vengeance. Cornelius Vanderbilt IV claimed that forty-one of the forty-seven couples he knew who had been married in the past six or seven years were divorced, legally separated, or in Reno or Paris pursuing one or the other. "It is well said that nearly every time the wedding march is played in society realms another case is being made for the international divorce lawyers," he quipped in 1927, with love seemingly "a luxury that only the less prosperous can afford." Vanderbilt wasn't exactly sure why divorces had rather suddenly become so popular, particularly among the upper crust, thinking that the war, women going off to college, greater mobility, and the "fast living" of the twenties all might have something to do with it. The society expat had no doubt that the American rich were now less concerned with what others thought about them and had developed much more of a "damn the torpedoes," even reckless, attitude since the Great War, each of these also possibly wreaking havoc with the institution of marriage. The wealthy had also abandoned much of their sense of duty, Vanderbilt believed, acquiring in its place a strong taste for pleasure and thrill-seeking, which often made couples' honeymoons over as soon as, well, the honeymoon. "There is a general change throughout the world in the order of things," Vanderbilt concluded, this seismic shift shaking the very foundation of the affluent class.[56]

A related ripple in this shifting of the plates of the American rich was husbands' appropriation of the social sphere from their wives. Since the Civil War, "society" had been a decidedly feminine domain, ruled over and managed by women like Mrs. Astor and Mrs. Fish. ("The absorption of men in business . . . allowed women a somewhat undue authority over other than money getting activities," as Nickerson explained it.)[57] But as socializing and business became indelibly entwined in the late twenties, increasingly men were the ones to draw up guest lists for dinner parties, changing the tenor of entertaining considerably toward "money getting," much to the displeasure of anyone expecting the kind of verbal gamesmanship of yesteryear.[58]

This new generation of American rich was also prone, as Maude Parker put it in 1929, to a "vagrant existence" or "de-luxe nomadism," making society much more cosmopolitan. The rich "lived like gypsies," she observed, "but on a scale which for luxury had never been equaled in the history of the world." It was true that many of the New York wealthy were spending just a quarter of their time at "home," the rest of the year spent not just at their Long Island country houses or in Newport but in Biarritz, St. Moritz, Le Touquet, or places as far-flung as Egypt or Honolulu. One entrepreneurial New Yorker opened up what was probably the first luxury time-share operation, renting out English manor houses, villas in Lake Como, and castles in Ireland to the emerging "International

Set." More adventurous moneybags from New York, Hollywood, San Francisco, and Chicago found themselves in Europe rubbing tweed or linen shoulders with Russian grand dukes, Italian princesses, and English lords, expanding the boundaries of society in the process. "Americans have taken the world for their playground and their playmates are gathered from almost every country," said one young lady of privilege in the international swim. The only requirement for joining the fun was "the ability to pay."[59]

WHERE ARE THE IDLE RICH?

Given free rein in this bigger playground, American society would never be quite the same, its manners deeply affected by its more wandering ways. Overseas travelers adopted a new kind of casualness, with rich globe-trotters viewing recent acquaintances not as good friends in the making but as ships passing in the night, there for temporary amusement before setting sail for the next port. In just a few weeks, members of the International Set who had not met before were finding themselves calling each other by their first names, or even nicknames, a practice previous generations of wealthy peripatetics would have found in rather bad form. Americans would bring this informality home with them from their travels, as well as other Euro-customs, such as dining much later than even New Yorkers were used to, making the highly structured and to-the-minute synchronized dinner parties of the Old Guard seem like military maneuvers. Having spent time in Biarritz, Spain, or the Lido, the smartest of the smart set now weren't serving dinner until 11 P.M., again something the wealthy elite of the turn of the century would have considered in horrific taste.[60]

Younger members of society coming to age in this new, much more cosmopolitan scene were naturally most influenced by being thrust on a global stage. To be a real success, for example, debutantes now had to be internationally known; it was no longer enough to come out only in one's hometown or even in other cities around the country. Parents of aspiring debs in the United States were having their social secretaries send photos of their daughters to magazines in England, France, and Italy that covered the international society beat; their publication was a signal that the girl was open to consideration from European wooers (hopefully one with a title). More than a few European young men, meanwhile, were on the hunt for a rich American heiress who could replenish his family's depleted fortune, making this new transatlantic love connection a good opportunity for each to find the perfect match.[61] Indeed, minor nobility who were "pecuniarily embarrassed," i.e., broke, seemed to be roaming Europe in the late twenties, encouraged by their families or eager themselves to swap their depreciated titles for American greenbacks. Such men were especially popular among American parents whose daughter's friends had landed big fish—the title by marriage a way to keep up with the proverbial Joneses.[62]

It was spending money, however, that this strange and fascinating new generation spent most of their time reinventing. Drinking lime rickeys at the Ritz bar in Paris, ground zero for the rich in the late twenties, was a virtual requirement for being considered part of the A-list, and didn't come cheap, after all. The idea that the wealthy elite were America's version of aristocracy—something previous generations had spent so much time and so much money nurturing—was largely shelved by young adults, replaced by the simpler question of how much cash one had at one's disposal. (Some women, anxious to get some extra pocket money, had taken to selling their slightly used evening gowns to secondhand stores for $15 a pop.)[63] Pure and simple, popularity was expensive, especially since gambling had also become one of the favorite pastimes of the young rich, specifically playing cards for money (the Texas Hold 'Em of its day) and betting on horses at the racetrack.[64]

Even more noticeable than the pronouncement of cash as king was an acute restlessness among privileged youth. They were no longer willing to sit at dinner tables in their tuxes while the soup to nuts were served over the course of an entire evening at glacial

FIGURE 1-4. The lobby of the Ritz Hotel in Paris circa 1920. The Ritz, with its famous bar, was the destination of choice for many heirs of the American rich through the decade. (*H. C. Ellis/Hulton Archive/Getty Images*)

speed. Much like their own countercultural grandchildren would, twentysomethings of the 1920s broke free from the formality and conventions that their parents had so embraced, seizing the day's tolerance for spontaneity, hedonism, and iconoclasm. Fun-seekers were ready to jump to another party or nightclub at a moment's notice if the one they were at was a dud. The best private bashes were not the most elaborate but those that allowed the freedom of a public place, like a cocktail lounge. If dinner was served, guests would plop down at the table in seats of their own choosing, rearranging the name cards to suit their liking. Criticizing food, service, or accommodations became accepted practice among this worldly crowd, not considered oh-so-rude as Mom and Dad would have whispered if one of their own had done such a thing. Even within the normally staid universe of the American rich, the times they were a'changin'.[65]

It wasn't just the International Set who brought European sophistication to the American scene in the twenties. The opening up of global markets after the Great War also helped make the American rich more cosmopolitan, as business executives regularly headed across the pond to compete on a bigger playing field. Even if the primary reason to set sail (often on the *Leviathan, Majestic,* or *Ile de France*—the *Nina, Pinta,* and *Santa Maria* of wealthy explorers in the late 1920s) was for business, Americans going over to Europe made sure to set aside time to boost the local economy. Rich couples would typically bring along a servant or two, sometimes making them learn French if France was on the itinerary so that one wouldn't have to "rent" one (who could, it was feared, spill gossip to newspapers and magazines or give confidential business information to competitors) over there. [66]

Once in Paris, while the men attended their meetings, wives (or mistresses) would go shopping, heading first to their favorite dressmaker to see the latest collections. There, like at Madame Callonet's, they would be whisked to a private room upstairs, where women with the same figure (and, rather amazingly, similar coloring) as the buyer would model the gowns. With measurements on file, there was no reason to put the lady through a preliminary fitting, although there would be a final fitting just in case the fashionista had added or subtracted a few pounds since the last visit. (In such a rare case, a gang of seamstresses would be brought in to resize the dress, often working all night.) It wasn't unusual for a woman of wealth to choose as many as a dozen gowns for the coming season, along with five or six coats and an armoire full of lingerie. Once the gowns were selected, it was off to the milliner for matching hats, with the shopkeeper somehow able to simply discern which would go best with each outfit and the lady's hairstyle. Not only was this kind of customer service impossible to find anywhere in the United States, but "buying direct," if you will, spared clotheshorses the hefty retailer markup on couture (typically 100 percent). Such big savings made it worth waiting a month for the clothes to be made and shipped overseas and somewhat cushioned the blow when the enormous bill arrived.[67]

Haute couture wasn't the only thing rich Americans were on the prowl for on their European business jaunts. Decorators had already scouted out which antique chairs and sofas their clients should have a look at when redoing a parlor or drawing room, and shop owners were warned in advance by telephone when the woman of the house would appear to assess the furniture, swatches of new carpet, and curtains on hand. Porcelain manufacturers and rare book dealers too were placed on full alert when more discriminating shoppers were in town looking for new (or old) items to add to their collections; sellers often went over to the buyer's hotel room to show off their wares, for discretion and to save the latter time. Husbands in London were just as excited to pick up an eighteenth-century first edition or a letter in Byron's, Shelley's, or Keats's own hand as wives in Paris were upon finding the perfect dress, which would impress the most critical good friend. Time spent in London might include a search for a new head gardener, ideally someone who could produce a first prize in the dog-eat-dog world of flower shows. If time allowed a side trip to the Isle of Guernsey, men might also score a few dozen head of cattle for their Vermont hobby farms, something which would make the boys from the club green (or, in this case, brown and white) with envy.[68]

Wealthy Europeans, on the other hand, were far less excited to head west, and not just because it was slimmer pickins' when it came to shopping. The relentless pace of the late twenties, fueled by Americans' intense desire to both work hard and play hard (much like the go-go 1980s six decades hence) was something most Europeans found too chaotic (and vulgar) to be to their liking, the kind of grounding their cherished Old World traditions provided wholly absent. While upper-class English or French could be found in salons, passionately chatting about Salvador Dali's joining the surrealists or Jean Cocteau's *Les Enfants Terribles*, their American cousins were typically engaged in highly organized and structured activities such as playing sports, taking language lessons, or going to lectures. While their husbands put in long hours at work, wealthy women were equally busy hitting golf balls, breeding dogs or horses, writing poetry, making sculptures, or even learning to fly "aeroplanes." Knowing how occupied rich women were in what was called "creative leisure," in addition to managing their houses, socializing, and mothering, leaders of charity organizations sought out the merely well-to-do, who would have more time at their disposal, to serve on committees. Department store managers understood the same thing, considering upper-middle-class women their best shoppers because they had time to browse, unlike their wealthier sisters, who came in to buy a specific item and then left in a jiffy.[69]

The vigorous, even frenetic, lifestyle of the American rich was a far cry from the sedentary stereotype of the wealthy. "Where are the idle rich?" Maude Parker wondered in 1929 shortly before the Crash, seconded by an anonymous woman who had taken on at least her share of responsibilities and obligations. "Being rich seems to be a job in itself and such a strenuous one," the latter declared, explaining that this "arises in part from the old Puritan tradition that wealth is somehow evil and in order to offset its curse one must spend it wisely." And in keeping with industrial advances of the day, such as the assembly line and time-motion studies, the everyday lives of the American rich were increasingly geared toward efficiency, to making the most out of what was increasingly viewed as the most valuable commodity of all—time.

As the end of the decade approached, the system, pushed to the limit, showed signs of crashing, and not just financially. Going full throttle was believed to be the reason so many rich men and women were suffering what were believed to be "nervous breakdowns" and leaving town for "rest cures," while others sought help from the new varieties of psychiatry washing up on American shores direct from Vienna. Soon, much more than a month in the country or a series of sessions with a Freudian analyst would be needed to soothe the jangled nerves of the American rich.[70]

CHAPTER 2

BROTHER, CAN YOU SPARE A DIME?

1930–1945

"They were born on the ticker-tape,
and there they have died."
—*ST. PAUL PIONEER PRESS*,
SPEAKING OF NEW MILLIONAIRES IN 1930

IN 1935, CROSWELL BOWEN, A SELF-PROCLAIMED TWENTY-eight-year-old son of a rich man working as a furniture sales-man, looked back on the unexpected events of the past six years. Like his peers, Bowen was taught and fully believed that the world would be his oyster on the half-shell when he graduated from Yale in 1929. Bowen was crushed, however, when he returned from his obligatory post-college Grand Tour to find the job he had been offered by a prominent Wall Street broker existed no more because of the market crash. Worse news arrived when Bowen's father's bank loans were called in, which meant that Croswell would have to fully support himself from now on. After floundering for a few years, Bowen landed a job selling furniture and by 1935 was making $22 a week. Although bitter about the way things turned out, Bowen considered himself lucky to have a job at all and one, as it turned out, he actually enjoyed and was quite good at. Other Ivy League men he knew were spending much of their time drinking in bars, waiting for something to turn up or for times to get better. "It is tragic to see some of them, educated, charming, and eager," Bowen rather ironically reflected, thinking, "their principal fault seems to be that they were brought up the sons of rich and influential parents." Bowen compared his cohorts to the Lost Generation of the twenties who had returned from World War I a decade and a half ago alienated and directionless. "Whereas its members were shell-shocked, we have been depression-shocked," he thought, "react[ing] to the economic upheaval with despair, loss of faith in our economic organization, and generally chaotic thinking."[1]

Sons of wealthy men, who not that long ago thought their futures would be limitless, were not the only ones to find themselves bewildered, to say the least, when the economy imploded. American wealth culture of the 1930s and early 1940s was unlike anything that preceded (or followed) it, an especially traumatic experience for the rich who had ridden the wild ride of the 1920s. For many of the surviving Old Guard, the Depression and war years would prove to be a knockout blow, now that the iconic trappings of wealth were viewed as in bad taste and, for the moment at least, un-American. Others would embrace a "frugal chic" lifestyle, this era's "middle-class millionaires" pinching their pennies until the dollars started rolling in again.

Blamed in large part for bringing on hard times for all Americans, the rich would enter the crosshairs of the FDR Administration, even their assets up for grabs in the common pursuit of a more democratic and equitable society. Much of their fortunes wiped out by the Crash and now attacked by a president who stated his clear intention to "weed out the overprivileged," the American rich were faced with nothing short of the possibility of extinction. The thirties were indeed a New Deal for the American rich, the decade's pinkish tint in direct contradiction to the very concept of elitism. Right on cue, however, American wealth culture would come roaring back in the late thirties and early forties, when laissez-faire capitalism once again became an integral part of our national ethos. In fact, a new generation of rich would emerge out of the turmoil of this decade and a half, something that few people could imagine in the midst of the nation's worst economic crisis.

WHO WILL BE THE NEW RICH?

Indeed, in the months after the market crash, many wondered what would become of the American rich or, more accurately, the once-rich Americans. "Where are all the new millionaires of 1928?" asked *Literary Digest* in 1930, noting that they may have been "kings for a day, or a year, but now they are unthroned." Indeed, many, if not most, of those who had made millions in the stock market in the late twenties had "lost everything but their fountain-pens and their bright illusions," as the *Philadelphia Evening Public Ledger* put it. Some of them were now living with their parents-in-law and trying to borrow money to get back in the game. A popular rumor at the time was that many professional investors had not only exited the market in 1928 but actually forced it to crash, making themselves that much richer, relatively speaking. The hard truth, however, was that 75 percent of both amateurs and pros kept their fingers in the cookie jar through Black Tuesday and were now paying the high price for it.[2]

The almost-overnight sea change for the American rich not surprisingly had a major effect on how the remaining wealthy were perceived by others. "A new quality, it seems to me, is detectable in the attitude of the so-called average person toward the men of wealth," noted an anonymous millionaire writing in the *Saturday Evening Post* in 1930. The old (sinful) standbys—envy and covetness—were now less in play, he believed, replaced by a greater interest in how a wealthy person was using his money. The economic crisis had, it seemed, created the climate for a less emotional but more critical view of the rich among the 99 or so percent of the population who weren't.[3] "What we seem to need is more adult education for millionaires," argued *The Nation* that same year, suggesting that "there are too many books on how to be successful and too few on what to do after that."[4]

Suddenly enrolled in the school of hard knocks, the rich were actually learning something radically new—how not to spend money. "Economy is now the spice of life even in Park Avenue," Nancy Hill observed in 1931, as the wealthy embraced the rather unfamiliar values of frugality and thrift. More than a few rich New Yorkers were overheard boasting about how much they had saved by not buying a luxury item or expensive meal, suddenly proud of their restraint and common sense when it came to spending money. Cutting back on the lavish lifestyles they enjoyed in the twenties was the first order of business for most, an action that, while certainly painful, was at the same time rather au courant among the smart set. Footmen were typically the first to go; quickly followed by the tough decision to release the rest of the servants and chauffeur (many of whom agreed to stay on at half the salary they had been making). Closing one's country place and dismissing the gardeners there was often next, but here too the staff often asked to remain in their cottages and grow food on the grounds in order to avoid becoming destitute. Interestingly, even those who somehow weathered the Crash frequently made it a point to make it appear as if they too had to scrimp to save money. Draining one's swimming pool, for example, was an excellent way to let others think that one was part of the new, less ostentatious club and avoid the rather ironic public embarrassment of being very well off.[5]

Bankers, for whom belonging to eight or nine private clubs in town and in the country was not unusual, resigned from the three or four they hardly used, sometimes to the chagrin of their wives, who relied upon those memberships to keep their high profile in society. Pawnshops, having discovered an entirely new customer base, found themselves having to accommodate wealthy patrons' desire for discretion when they hawked the family jewels. Side doors were built for customers to get in and out without being seen, and managers of the shops prepared to make a deal in a hurry by having more cash on hand than usual. Still, friends and acquaintances would occasionally run into one another in the shops, almost always an awkward moment for all parties involved. It being a buyers' market, pawners selling grandma's cameo brooch or engagement ring often received just 10 percent of its insured value, another bit of humiliation for the once high and mighty. Dining at fancy restaurants, only recently an everyday occurrence, was now a special event; splitting checks and examining bills for accuracy were new but necessary steps to ensure staying in the budget. Even taxis were out for some, the subway or el an adventure for those who had not experienced the pleasure of New York's efficient but sometimes unpredictable mass transportation system. Others were taking more extreme measures to save a penny here and there by using paper napkins instead of linen, ordering unsliced bacon from the grocer, and making sure the lights were off in rooms not in use.[6]

With the wealthy's eagerness to save money whenever and wherever possible going from the sublime to the ridiculous, some could not help but imagine even more absurd scenarios. "Just where all of this economy will end and how far spread it will go is difficult to judge," Nancy Hill wrote in *Outlook*, suggesting that rules such as the following might one day be pasted on a guest-house wall for visitors to observe:

> Guests are requested to turn off all lights before leaving room. Failure to do so forfeits your privileges as a guest and you will be expected to catch the next train back to town. Guests will please use only one hand towel and one bath towel during the weekend. If you forget to bring your own cold cream tissue, wash your face with soap and water. It will probably be a pleasant surprise to your face. Don't make passes at the maids. It distracts their minds from their work, and God knows they have enough of it since we've had to cut down. I don't suppose you have any jewels left, but in case you have, hang on to them.[7]

Despite all this frugality, there seemed to be no scrimping on alcohol among the rich (and lots of non-rich, of course), with both bootleggers and speakeasies booming during those days of prohibition in the early 1930s. Cocktails and highballs were more often than not at the ready, compensation perhaps for all the other lost pleasures. The upper crust had also picked up the habit of not only drinking at "speaks" but also dining there, something owners of chic restaurants were not at all happy about.[8]

Perhaps the hardest hit but least penny-wise rich were those who had been living a life of luxury purely off the interest and dividends from their securities. Having no job, their equity reduced by a third or sometimes much more (an 80 percent loss wasn't unusual, in fact), these men often went into a state of denial as their monthly allowance shrank to a fraction of what it had been. These were the "poor rich" (or perhaps "rich poor"), folks trying to maintain their cushy lifestyles out of hubris but secretly quite terrified as their nest eggs evaporated and debts ballooned. Rather than simply lower their standards of living by, say, moving to a less expensive apartment, dismissing the chauffer and discarding the limo, and nixing the months-long trips to Europe, these rich— afraid to lose their friends or admit to themselves they were now, dare it be said, middle class—stuck their heads in the sand, existing in a constant state of anxiety. Many poor people were, it could be argued, substantially richer than these supposedly wealthy individuals imprisoned in a kind of financial purgatory, a theme that might sound pretty familiar today.[9]

With the once-wealthy now slicing their own bacon to save a few cents, it was vividly clear that an era in American history had ended. Charles M. Schwab, chair of Bethlehem Steel, went as far as to insist that "there are no rich men in America today," the entire species that had thrived the previous decade having "practically vanished." "Men are afraid to look at their ledgers to see if they are worth anything or not," he told a group in New York in 1932, accurately predicting that this sorry state of affairs would continue for another five or six years.[10] Although he must have been speaking metaphorically—there were undoubtedly thousands of millionaires left in the United States—Schwab's comment was widely jeered by newspaper editors, who had little sympathy for those whose fortunes had diminished. The *Philadelphia Record*, for example, offered to draw up "a new list of worthy recipients" of $1 million, going further by proposing that Andrew Mellon, J. P. Morgan II, and Schwab himself be included in this group of deserving individuals. "Won't somebody please chip in to finance a cup of coffee and a sandwich for these needy gentlemen?" the paper humorously appealed to readers.[11]

Some people, however, rather than being angry toward the rich for crashing the system out of greed, actually felt sorry for them. Those most fully vested (and invested) in the workings of capitalism had, after all, not only lost a good chunk of their material assets but a lot of faith in the institution itself, a double whammy that was too much for some to bear. The majority of Americans with smaller bank accounts were in a sense better off, simply because they hadn't dedicated most of their waking hours to making and spending money, as a fair share of high rollers had done in the twenties. Those whose passions resided in the intellectual or natural world had lost nothing, while those living in the financial world may very well have lost everything.[12]

Clarence Darrow, already considered a legend in 1934, felt little empathy for the rich and their plight, however, believing that the inequities of capitalism were leading to nothing less than the end of civilization. "Civilization has been destroyed by those who own it, by the people who have the vast wealth, the masters of the world who will not permit a fair distribution of its products," the seventy-seven-year-old lawyer told an audience of two thousand in New York, characterizing the present age as one of "economic slavery." Darrow's appearance was billed as a debate with John Hayne Holmes, but Holmes, a prominent minister, found he had little to disagree with his opponent about. Tickets for the event, which originally cost a quarter, were going for a dollar in the street, many people apparently very interested in what the best minds of the day had to say about the division of wealth in the country.[13]

With once great fortunes destroyed by the market crash and tax rates for anyone with real money that were nothing less than cruel, speculation was rife about who would emerge from the ashes to become part of a new wealthy elite. "Who will be the new rich?" asked Howard Wood of the *Chicago Daily Tribune* in 1932, struck by the tremendous shift in the affluent class since 1929. Presidents and vice presidents of companies gone belly-up were pounding the pavement looking for jobs or, if lucky, living off their pensions in relative comfort. Real estate in nicer neighborhoods was selling for half what it had a few years back, and golf clubs that had waiting lists in the twenties were giving away memberships to all comers, some even deferring dues.[14] Rather than make those who had lost it all in the market never want to hear the words "Wall Street" again, however, the Crash made some investors, recognizing a bargain when they saw one, more eager than ever to speculate. Most of those in the industry, no doubt also wanting to stir up business, remained bullish in the early thirties, advising those wanting to make their next fortune to get in now. One prominent banker thought in 1932 that the next crop of millionaires would be "those who have had money to buy [stocks] at the absurdly low prices which rule this year," this bountiful harvest ready to be picked in about five years. Anyone familiar with the roller-coaster history of the stock market believed the same thing and scrounged up whatever they could, ignoring those convinced that good money was being thrown after bad.[15]

The rich themselves, like Americans as a whole, seemed to be split about what the future had in store. Wealthy businessmen especially were experiencing a crisis of faith, wondering if the good old days were over, never to return again, at least during their lifetime. Driving Buicks instead of Lincolns, their yachts in dry dock, these men thought long and hard over whether they had killed the goose that laid the golden egg. In retreat, cutting their losses and selling short, for those believing they were morally entitled to pursue the common but great enterprise of creating wealth it was definitely not business as usual. Others, however, did not feel like they had been tossed out of the Garden of Eden on their ear; some believed they remained the natural leaders of American society and that the rules of the game would prevail in the long run. The economic crisis and New Dealers were just the latest in a long line of threats they had faced and would continue to face, threats that would ultimately be overcome as the values of achievement and success came back into favor. The American rich, they insisted, would be back.[16]

SOAK THE RICH

Others, however, had different ideas. The travails of the Depression, combined with FDR's socialist leanings, created a perfect storm for those morally opposed to both capitalism and, especially, the passing down of great wealth; their voices were heard and occasionally heeded. Many were beginning to think the inequities of our Darwinian economic system were fine, perhaps, when it was chugging along like Henry Ford's assembly line, but not when the machine had clearly broken down. Refilling the Treasury's coffers with rich people's money could help the nation recover from the Depression, the Roosevelt administration proposed, by paying for social services for the needy and funding a great public works program that would put less advantaged Americans back to work. "Soaking the rich," as this idea became popularly known, was the answer to helping the poor.

More important than the economic aspects of heavily taxing the rich, however, were the social implications. The Depression was vivid proof that a more even playing field was needed in America, leftish proponents argued, with a wider distribution of wealth likely to ease social unrest between the classes and make a revolution less likely. (The top IRS official admitted that part of the rationale for an overhauled tax policy was to "protect the social order," not that crazy an idea given that more than a few Americans were keeping canned food in their pantries in case the masses decided to literally throw the bums out.)[17] The game was fixed and the dice were loaded, proponents of a "share the wealth" plan that emerged in the early 1930s heatedly pointed out, with heads of corporations using their power to gain an unfair advantage to favor themselves and their buddies; i.e., the "ownership" or "leisure" class. By putting excess profits back into the system rather than allowing them to just sit in a few thousand individuals' bank accounts, the theory went, America's out-of-whack economic situation would be brought back into balance.

Even the very idea that rich Americans had, upon their death, the inherent right to bestow their fortunes to their children was challenged in the mid-1930s, something that probably never could and never would have happened during more bullish times. "Three generations from shirtsleeves to shirtsleeves," went the popular and often true adage. But great fortunes often ballooned to herculean proportions, their sheer size making them resistant to the standard kind of squandering that destroyed a family's wealth.[18] Senator George W. Norris, a radical from Nebraska, was one of the earliest and firmest advocates of a progressive inheritance tax that would make the passing down of enormous wealth from one generation to another all but impossible. He was of the belief that "swollen fortunes" should promptly be given back to the people. "The man who has accumulated great wealth ought not to object if, when he is dead and when it is impossible for him to any longer use or enjoy his money, a portion of his great fortune should be turned over to the government under whose laws he has been protected in its accumulation," Norris told a group in Illinois in 1933, proposing such a plan as the best way to bring the country out of the Depression. Norris was not against wealth per se and didn't object to beneficiaries living a "life in luxury," but he saw the perpetuation of family fortunes as contrary to the nation's best interests. Norris even considered the turning over of one's wealth to the people rather than one's children "a blessing to humanity," something that would help create a more just society by reducing taxes for less prosperous citizens.[19]

Attacks on the rich seemed to come from all directions in the midthirties, as politicians looked for likely suspects to assign blame for the country's economic collapse. Because they remained better off than most, the wealthy were a convenient target—not just the problem but perhaps the solution. FDR made his point of view about the rich quite clear in his 1935 State of the Union address to Congress, when he said it was his intention to "weed out the overprivileged" in order to "lift up the underprivileged." If Huey Long had his way, the American rich wouldn't exist at all; his "share the wealth" plan was the most extreme assault on our to-the-victor-goes-the-spoils system. Although he hadn't quite figured out all the details, the Democratic senator from Louisiana was campaigning that the federal government seize and redistribute not just money from the wealthy but their cars, houses, and stocks as well. "We are going to redistribute in kind so the poor devil who needs a house can get one from some rich bird who has too many," Long said in 1935, adding, "We may even give a poor man a block of stock in some business corporation, having taken it from some man who has more than the limit." Interestingly, Long, who would be shot dead at the state capitol six months later, virulently maintained that not only was his plan not communistic, but it was the best chance to defend the country against encroaching Communism, because the masses were likely to revolt if things stayed the way they were.[20] The famous, or infamous, Detroit uberpriest Father Coughlin was nearly as antagonistic toward what he called "entrenched wealth" as Long. Coughlin attacked Wall Street and specifically the super-rich in his weekly radio sermons, preaching for a world in which one would not have to covet one's neighbor's possessions.

Less vitriolic but more convincing were proposals from progressives such as Governor Philip Lafollete of Wisconsin, who believed that wealth redistribution was the answer to the nation's "relief" problem. "What we'd like to see the government do is consciously assume responsibility for the distribution of income," he said plainly enough in 1935, thinking, much like FDR, that "the little guy" needed some help in order to stand up to big business, which not only had an advantage in the marketplace but found ways to avoid paying taxes.[21] (Only 16 percent of corporations that had filed tax returns in 1932—admittedly a terrible year for business— reported any income at all, and J. P. Morgan himself paid no income taxes at all that year or the previous one.)[22] It was apparent that unlike many people, especially those of the Republican persuasion, who put an individual's rights at the very top of the nation's creed, Lafollete and his ilk viewed American democracy as an extended family, its collective wealth belonging to the members of that family. Among this group, social justice was simply higher up on the morality scale than those of individual property rights, a premise that demanded, as the saying went, "the greatest good for the greatest number." These fundamentally oppositional points of view created a tension that tested the very idea of what the nation was and should be all about, with the American rich directly in the crosshairs of the debate.[23]

What the odd trio of Huey Long, Father Coughlin, and Franklin Roosevelt failed to see, as the more informed pointed out at the time, was that the nation's millionaires were simply not numerous or rich enough in the 1930s to make much of a dent in the American economy, even if most of their wealth were grabbed by the government. Only 2,000 to 3,000 taxpayers would be affected by the new laws, it was estimated: much too small a pool to generate enough money to achieve the administration's lofty goals.[24] Only forty-six Americans earned $1 million or more in 1933, and even appropriating the total wealth of the richest of the lot—Mellon, Morgan, Ford, Hearst, and Rockefeller—would yield only $1 billion, or $8.35 per citizen if redistributed.[25] Ideally, it could be argued, great fortunes would more or less self-destruct, their owners taking full advantage of the fact that, as the 1936 Moss & Hart play told it, "You can't take it with you." Andrew Carnegie had famously believed that it was a crime to die rich, giving away $350 million before he went to the big steel mill in the sky, which left a mere $50 million for himself and his family (a sum apparently not qualifying them as "rich"). The government should be encouraging this kind of philanthropy rather than taking and using outrageous fortunes for not precisely clear purposes, some—especially devout Christians—believed. The reality was that few, if any, multimillionaires in the 1930s had Mr. Carnegie's resources or generosity.[26]

Besides that, these men, and most other millionaires, had already transferred most of their estates to their sons (before passage of the 1932 gift tax and the increased estate, or "death," tax, in fact), making the government's expected windfall from a "share the wealth" plan greatly exaggerated. Others scrambled before the new law was passed, most notably John D. Rockefeller Jr., who was giving away securities like he gave away dimes, as an escape from the proposed plan. J. P. Morgan was reportedly selling much of his art collection to pay for his own death tax just in case, while ordinary millionaires were buying life insurance to pay the bill should it arrive (although that too would be taxed).[27] Add the given that the wealthy would employ their usual tricks of the trade to find ways around having their pockets picked, and anyone with a modicum of common sense could see that soaking the rich did not carry a lot of bite behind its loud bark. "All share-the-wealthers possess an extreme facility with prodigious statistics and a corresponding infirmity with arithmetic," Garet Garrett, one of a growing number of conservatives trying to stop the scheme in its tracks, wrote in 1935.[28]

As FDR's plan emerged as a touchstone of his administration's controversial, even radical, proposals, the trickle of opposition soon became a flood. Dislike them if you must (or perhaps should), some suggested, but destroying the American rich could have long-term consequences throughout society. "If all wealth above a poverty level were to be conscripted, it might be possible to finance the Government for a year or two," the Saturday Evening Post opined in 1933, "but what of the future—is the seed corn to be eaten and destroyed?"[29] Others feared that a wealth distribution program would come at the expense of philanthropy; directors of arts organizations, universities, and hospitals were nervous that their sugar daddies, already pinched by the Depression, would soon be tapped out.[30] Soaking the rich would also hurt those in the "luxury trades," still others argued, taking jobs away from ordinary folk in a wide variety of industries as the wealthy's ability to pay for expensive products and services fell.[31] And "poor relations," dependent on their rich relatives for a handout now and then, or much more, would also likely suffer if the plan became reality. Besides all this, who was to say that the government would be any wiser in the way that it gave away wealthy people's money than the wealthy people were themselves?

The business aspects of the "soak the rich" proposal were considered its Achilles' heel by those actually in business. Although FDR's plan was primarily intended to wipe out old fortunes (specifically the "disturbing effects upon our national life that come from great inheritances of wealth," in his own words), industry professionals advised that, because of tax shelters, more new fortunes would be destroyed than old ones. Allowing the Feds to claim two-thirds of the profits from a business—a bigger cut than Al Capone was grabbing in his own soaking schemes—would kill new enterprises even before they were hatched, businessmen maintained, not exactly a good recipe for bringing the nation out of the Depression.[32] And as Henry Ford, the poster child for the wealth redistribution plan, readily pointed out, owners of existing businesses might just choose to close shop if they knew most of their assets would be seized when they died, which was hardly an initiative to keep the wheels of capitalism turning.[33] As the coup de grace, administration officials, especially Secretary of the Interior Harold Ickes, appeared to be confusing the wealthy elite with big business—two overlapping but hardly identical entities—a blunder that could very well result in a law that would worsen the economy rather than improve it.[34] "Not often have so many goofy crackpots preached so much nonsense to so many people," concluded the editors of *Collier's* in 1935, making a strong case that the nation should simply stay the course as the economy slowly improved.[35]

Although the administration's plan was considered "middle-class radicalism" by its kinder critics, more outspoken critics viewed

it as "downright fascism." "Who has not observed the agony en-
dured by wealthy persons who see 50, 65, or even 77 percent of
their comfortable incomes wrung from them by a socialist state
masquerading as the very stronghold of capitalism?" *Atlantic
Monthly* had asked in 1931, before FDR had even stepped into
the White House. The general population, meanwhile, was running
about fifty/fifty in its own assessment of whether or not the rich
should be soaked.[36] Many wealthy Americans, not surprisingly, considered not John Dillinger but FDR "Public Enemy #1," fearing
they would essentially be blackmailed into handing over much of
their money, or else. E. F. Hutton declared himself only 30 percent
"free" in 1935, his other 70 percent was a "slave," based on the
taxes he currently had to pay.[37] Hardcore Republicans thought the
president must certainly be crazy; his plan seemed more likely to
hurt the poor by destroying their initiative to climb the ladder than
help them. The paranoid rich were convinced that the administration's aim was not actually to redistribute wealth but to punish
them for abusing their economic privilege, a literal payback for
their previous sins. As usual, the only ones who seemed to be bene-
fiting from the clash were lawyers, who were doing quite brisk business reshuffling estates and looking for any and all loopholes should
the tax man or tax men come a'knockin'.[38]

Despite all this opposition, the "wealth confiscation bill" as it
was being called, moved forward. FDR was plainly using the bill as
an extension of his New Deal "anti-bigness" policy and as a way to
deflect Long as a third-party threat in the 1936 election. Congress,
shaking in its boots about being perceived as aligned with the "overprivileged," endorsed the bill that year, stirring a new round of passionate argument against it. Some critics now opined that it would
not be the rich who would get soaked but the moderately well-to-
do, caught in the cross fire of corporate cutbacks and liquidations.
Former senator from Missouri Jim Reed exposed the pure un-
Americanness of the idea, going as far as to say that the bill was
"violative [sic] of the principles of the declaration of independence" and something that "might be entertained in Russia." Busi-

nesspeople, predictably, huddled together to forge their own counterattack. Captains of industry chose not even to attend a House Ways and Means Committee hearing on the issue, opting to wait until a bill was drafted and then to launch a full-scale assault before a Senate committee. Before that could happen, however, both the House and Senate passed bills levying roughly $250 million in new taxes on large estates and income. With the president's signature (executed somewhat surreptitiously and without an iota of ceremony), soaking the rich became law.[39] With the ink barely dried, the demise of the American rich was proclaimed. "The death knell of wealth has already sounded," William Pearson Tolley, chancellor of Syracuse University, ominously declared, while J. P. Morgan predicted that in thirty years no great fortune would remain. Would the American rich perish, as these men believed, or had it already?[40]

While today he is one of our most beloved presidents, Roosevelt was then vehemently detested by much of the upper class, at least during his first two terms. His wealth confiscation bill was tantamount to a declaration of war. One Park Avenue resident publicly threatened to physically harm the wheelchair-bound man, winding up in the pokey for it. "It permeates the whole upper stratum of American society," wrote Marquis W. Childs for *Reader's Digest* in 1936, describing a "consuming personal hatred" of FDR and noting the irony, given that most wealthy Americans had by then already bounced back nicely after the economy hit rock bottom in 1933. Despite being little affected by the changes in tax laws, "There is a widespread conviction among the wealthy that they are being butchered to make a Roman holiday for the less fortunate," Childs went on, something that he admitted he was at a loss to precisely explain. The most likely reason for this intense, personal dislike of the president seemed to be that he was, as a rich Philadelphia widow put it, "a traitor to his class," a situation made even worse by his "liv[ing] off his mother's income." Acts of hostility from the enemy could be expected, in other words, but not from one of their own kind.

The Roosevelt family had in fact been landowners in this country before it was one, making his administration's policies appear to be disloyal and a betrayal of those of similar backgrounds. Given his elitist upbringing and plush lifestyle, to some FDR's antipathy toward the rich seemed not only contradictory but contrived. "His education at Groton and Harvard, the verdant acres of Hyde Park, and the vacations on the *Nourmahal* [William Vincent Astor's boat, which happened to be the biggest oil-burning yacht in the world at the time] make his inveighing against economic privilege sound a little hollow," Robert Hale told readers of *Harper's Magazine*.[41] Roosevelt seemed to be following in the dubious footsteps of Grover Cleveland, Theodore Roosevelt, and Woodrow Wilson, presidents who were similarly disliked by many of the wealthy elite of their respective day (the latter redeemed only by his tenure during a world war, something that would also ensure FDR's legacy).[42]

Just as critics of Roosevelt's bill had predicted, the wealthy did everything they could in the late thirties to avoid being financially butchered. Even more so than before, millionaires increasingly disposed of their estates before they died so that most of it would not end up in the government's greedy hands. Giving away the bulk of one's money to relatives and friends and establishing irrevocable trusts for successive generations became popular ways to avoid the onerous "death tax," something the rich of this era came to dread almost as much as the Grim Reaper himself. "In this New Deal era, a man interested in arranging his affairs economically and to the greatest advantage of his dependents can no longer afford to die with a large estate," said Milton R. Stahl, a St. Louis banker, in 1938, not at all happy that "men of wealth are now taking steps to avoid large inheritance and estate taxes by passing on their property by other methods than testamentary disposition." As wealthy customers' estates got smaller, bankers like Stahl, less likely to be asked to oversee the disposition of sizable wills and management of heirs' money, were losing a lot of business. Whether FDR's grand plans were bailing the nation out of the Depression or rescuing the poor at the wealthy's expense were debatable at best, but they were taking money out of the deep pockets of well-to-do bankers who made their living off of even more well-to-do clients, hardly the war on the rich its worst critics imagined.[43]

MILLIONAIRE TOWN

Although any kind of grand "wealth redistribution" plan was probably doomed from the start, it was understandable that elected officials had major concerns about class divisions in Depression-era America. The economic crisis made the gulf between the wealthy and the poor deeper and wider, causing sparks to fly when the two groups unexpectedly collided. Such was the case in 1931, when a profligate debutante party was thrown on the same Washington, DC, block where a breadline had been set up. The extreme juxtaposition triggered a national debate over whether the wealthy should have the right to spend their money so freely when many were hungry and even starving. Henry L. Doherty's bash for his daughter, Helen Lee Eames Doherty, cost anywhere between $50,000 and $1 million—nobody seemed to know except Doherty—but its extravagance was unquestioned. A thousand guests (including Vice President Charles Curtis) took up two floors of the hotel in which the function was held, and two twenty-two-piece orchestras, the Cavaliers (a popular quartet from New York), and Jessica Dragonette (a well-known radio star of the day) provided the entertainment. Besides the full dinner before the dancing, a five-course supper at midnight and breakfast at 4 A.M. were served. The sheer plentitude was made all the more obvious by the hundred unemployed people who had gathered for a free handout in a garage just steps away from the hotel. Smelling a good story (besides the beef Wellington) in the air, a smart reporter for the *Washington Post* captured the scene; after the story hit the wires, editors from newspapers across the country weighed in, often passionately so. Some not only defended Doherty's right to toss his money around however he liked but argued that such lavishness was good for the economy, providing much-needed work for many in the struggling hospitality business. Others, however, felt that besides stirring the pot of Communism, the party was selfish and even cruel given the hard times and that much of the money spent on it should have been donated to those in need.[44]

This questioning of the wealthy's right to use their money as they like reflected the ambivalent feelings the non-rich held toward the rich during the 1930s. "The rich like the rich, the near-rich like the rich but not so well, the less-rich dislike the rich but not so much, and the poor dislike the rich heartily," *Fortune* found in a 1935 survey, but anecdotal evidence suggested that it wasn't so cut-and-dried.[45] The most famous rich person in the world, Henry Ford, was in fact well-liked by Americans from all classes (if not religions), despite his workers striking his plants every chance they could (business was business). Born on a farm and at heart a machine tinkerer, Ford embodied personal achievement and thus was able to transcend much of the negative feelings that flowed toward other, more elitist people of great wealth, who had made their money like warriors conquering nations.[46] Other rich people, the air of American royalty about them, were generally immune to the kind of acrimony directed at your average Rich Uncle Moneybags (the bearer of good and bad financial news in Monopoly, a game not coincidentally introduced in 1934).

Doris Duke, considered the nation's communal heiress, scored extra points with the public when she told reporters on the eve of her wedding to James Cromwell in 1935 that the bathing suit she was wearing was three years old.[47] Indeed, judging by the popular culture of the decade, interest in and perhaps even admiration of the rich had never been higher, despite the Marx Brothers' constant cinematic abuse of society matron Margaret Dumont and the Three Stooges' equally bad behavior toward the tuxedo crowd. Minute details of the lives of movie stars, much of it fabricated of course, filled the dozens of magazines devoted to such news. Many even viewed gangsters as popular folk heroes of the day, as they beat the system in their own particular ways. Advertisers seized on the public's fascination with wealthy celebrities, putting the rich and famous in their print ads and radio programs every chance they could to leverage their populist appeal and link it to their brands.[48]

Not only were certain people admired by the general public but certain places, too, simply because they were associated with wealth. Pasadena, California, commanded an almost celebrity-like status, considered perhaps the embodiment of the American dream. Known both as "the richest town in America" and "Millionaire Town" (nicknames that scared away the more reserved to other L.A. suburbs like Whittier, Monrovia, and Glendale and made flashier types head to Beverly Hills, Hollywood, and Malibu), Pasadena could indeed claim hundreds of full-time millionaire residents and thousands more during the season. The city had no real industry, which was exactly why so many wealthy people chose to live there (people actually joined the Chamber of Commerce to keep industry out rather than bring it in). Wealthy matrons married to retired plutocrats were a particularly visible presence in Millionaire Town. They spent much of their time, when not at the community playhouse or the Art Institute, with "chiropractors, osteopaths, fortune tellers, swamis, and purveyors of electronic vibrations," as one visitor put it in 1932. It was true that "quacks," as the reporter called them, especially appealed to the affluent ladies of Pasadena, a sign perhaps that things couldn't be too bad there if they could spend money on such less than necessary services. When a Hindu snake charmer in flowing robes set up shop in an across-the-tracks part of town, limousines were soon making their way there en masse, "loaded with vivacious ladies anxious to know if the seer could glimpse their husbands going on long journeys, or tall dark men appearing on the horizon."[49]

Wealthy matrons hoping their husbands would go out for a smoke and never come back might have had second thoughts if they knew what some of their sisters were going through when they became widows of rich men. Many women left large fortunes by their dead husbands found themselves held essentially captive by their money, totally unprepared to deal with the myriad of responsibilities that came with being rich, especially in the worst days of the Depression. "My fortune in these times is almost driving me crazy and is making life something less than pleasant," said one such anonymous wealthy widow in 1933, comparing it to "being on sentry duty twenty-four hours a day in the face of the enemy." Trying to make decisions about investments kept this woman up all night as she struggled with issues that used to fall exclusively within her husband's domain. "It is just plain hard work being a rich woman in these unsettled years," she said, considering herself a nuisance to her husband's friends and her bankers and brokers, who constantly demanded answers to their many finance-related questions in those days before mutual funds and IRAs. Not belonging to the Old Boys Club, this less-than-merry widow recognized she was at a disadvantage compared to men who freely traded news and advice on the links and in the barroom. The woman was actually using four banks so she could spread her many questions around and be less of a pest, an unfortunate situation that came with the gender territory of the day (and, to a lesser extent, today). Feeling "quite positively that a girl's education should include some knowledge of business," she planned to send her daughter to the Wharton School or Columbia School of Business so that she could have an easier time managing her own money when it was passed down. For all her worrying and self-doubt, however, this wise widow seemed to master the golden rule of investing. "I cannot help knowing that the best and richest men have no magic formula to guide them," she stated. "They make mistakes for themselves and would as quickly make them for me, so I might just as well make my own mistakes."[50]

This woman's frustrations in making her way through the complex world of investing, made all the more difficult because she was not a man, were doubly unfair, given that, according to one organization at least, women owned three-fourths of American wealth. Add up their savings accounts, securities, real estate holdings, and, most important, the value of life insurance policies of which they were the beneficiaries, figured the Women Investors in America, and women owned a significantly bigger share of the financial pie than men. Catherine Curtis, head of the organization, correctly believed that as women gained greater interest and clout in political affairs, they would leverage this power into more control of their own destinies when it came to investing.[51] "The great U.S. financial combine is not a group of mighty industrialists or Wall Street magnates but a vast framework of comfortably off, well-to-do, and really rich widows," *Fortune* agreed in 1936, concluding "the country's wealth is in the hands not of an oligarchy but of a matriarchy."[52]

Some women, not about to wait for their husband's life insurance ship to come in, went west to find fulfillment, fortune, and fame. With "the pictures" one of the most lucrative professions in the thirties, a rash of wealthy women made a beeline to Hollywood, hoping they could cash in on their social position. By 1934, the most successful of these socialites looking for a new challenge, not to mention a six-figure salary and international renown, was Virginia Peine-Lehmann, heiress to a clothing fortune and recently separated from her rich Chicago husband. While visiting Tinseltown, Peine-Lehmann was asked by a friend to play an extra in a film and, before you could say "Schwab's counter," had four screen tests, each resulting in a studio contract offer. The ex-socialite promptly signed one, changed her name to Virginia Pine, and started learning her lines. Less successful, and not just because her name wouldn't fit on a marquee, was another Chicagoan, Merry Fahrney Pickering Van Eizner. She decided she could "use a movie salary" after her father cut her allowance to one-tenth of what it had been. Kitty O'Dare, daughter of a turpentine tycoon, was given six months to land a part or else give up her Hollywood dreams. With the clock ticking and no offers forthcoming, O'Dare threw wild cocktail bashes and started dancing in a nightclub, hoping to attract the attention of a studio bigwig.

Although a long shot for wealthy young women, there were precedents for beating the odds and getting onto the big screen, most notably Elizabeth Young, an ex–Long Island debutante, as well as Adrienne Ames and June Collyer, each having previously been part of New York's social whirl.[53] More entertainers were in fact earning six figures in the late 1930s as top actors and actresses reaped the rewards of the huge popularity of the movies, making some wonder if comedians were becoming the robber barons of the day. "Possibly our future Rockefellers, Morgans, Fords and Carnegies will be men and women who make us laugh instead of those who sell us steel, bonds or automobiles," the *New York Times* half joked in 1940, suggesting that perhaps "the ruling class in America some day will be the house of mirth."[54]

THE VANASTORBILTS

Judging by the findings from a 1939 survey by *Town & Country*, there was no doubt that the ruling class in America already had a lot of mirth in their houses. Perhaps the first real quantitative study of wealthy Americans, the magazine's research revealed that the rich really were different when it came to how they lived and spent their money. Frustrated because they simply couldn't ring doorbells and start asking questions as researchers then could and did among middle-class consumers, *Town & Country* came up with the clever idea of sending a questionnaire to the two thousand subscribers to *Staff Magazine*, all of whom were butlers. Just 5 percent, or a hundred, of the Jeeveses completed and returned the questionnaire, but going in through the back door revealed a mother lode of insights related to rich people's buying habits. Nicknamed the "Vanastorbilts" by the magazine, the average household employing a butler kept no less than eleven servants on staff, extravagant sounding, perhaps, but not surprising, given that almost all the families owned both a city townhouse and country house, with a total of forty rooms. Most families also maintained working stables at their place in the country.

But entertaining was where the rich really stood out from the crowd. The Vanastorbilts hosted an average of 181 people a *month* during the summer and 138 during the winter, which worked out to a rather astonishing five guests per day. And how did these guests spend their time at their gracious hosts' spreads? Drinking, it turned out, at least judging by the reported quantity of alcoholic beverages consumed every year. The average family bought no less than 1,663 bottles of booze annually, going through 193 bottles of wine, 214 of rye, 242 of scotch, 60 of bourbon, 48 of Irish whiskey, 47 of brandy, 289 of gin, 24 of cordials, 157 of champagne, and 389 bottles of beer on the wall. Liquor advertisers in *Town & Country* were no doubt pleased to learn that they were not wasting their media dollars.[55]

While some of the particulars of the Vanastorbilts' lifestyles might have come as a surprise (like how they survived consuming almost five bottles of hooch a day), many of the more fabulous goings-on of the rich could be read about in the daily paper. As the wealthy regained their confidence in the late thirties, newspaper society pages and Lucius Beebe's syndicated column were filled with juicy details about the smart set. Having buried their heads in the sand for almost a decade, afraid to be recognized as a member of the ownership class or, even worse, have their money snatched away because they were part of that elite group, the rich were ready again to display their peacock feathers. One of the first volleys marking the return of the American rich to be fired was the 1937 debut of Lesley Hyde Ripley in Newport, when the girl's parents built an addition to their home to hold the party at a cost of somewhere between $10,000 and $25,000, only to tear it down the very next morning. The following season, Brenda Diana Duff Frazier was named the brightest rising star of New York society, her own debut party at the Ritz-Carlton recalling those held there before the wealthy went on hiatus. In addition to $5,000 for about two thousand calla lilies, poinsettias, and chrysanthemums, the $23,000 bill included a grand for "breakage," just the kind of extravagance that the wealthy were known (and hated) for in the good old days.

Eight years earlier, in fact, Barbara Hutton's debut party was held in the very same ballroom, that event having earned a solid place within the pantheon of legendary society soirees.[56] Under a blue-sky painted ceiling, with a papier-mâché moon floating above, Babs's party was a cornucopia of conspicuous consumption, as poetically captured by Helen Worden:

> One thousand guests, four orchestras, one hundred musicians, two hundred waiters, ten thousand American Beauty roses, Rudy Vallee, twenty thousand white violets, Joseph Urban, one thousand five-course midnight suppers, Mme. Argentina, one thousand breakfasts, fifty thousand dollars, and all the silver birch trees, scarlet poinsettias, mountain heather and tropical greens that could be rushed from California and Florida.[57]

Besides being absurdly expensive and grossly wasteful, borrowing a page from real-life Jay Gatsbys from a decade past, parties of the late 1930s were also frequently themed, another throwback to the wild and wooly twenties. C. Henry Buhl of Detroit adopted Sing Sing, the notorious prison, as the theme for his birthday party, an ironic turning upside down of class and social status. Invitations to the party were fake summonses, demanding guests appear in court (the location being "In the State of Inebriation, County of Fun") wearing striped and denim clothes. Staged under the stars by beautiful Lake St. Clair, Detroit's best were served gourmet food on paper plates and drinks in tin cups by waiters dressed as, of course, prison guards. This was amateur stuff compared to some other parties, however. Beebe, perhaps the definitive authority in such things, considered Alfred E. Barton, manager of the ritzy Surf Club in Miami Beach, the best party thrower in the country in the late thirties, his specialty also of the let's-pretend-we're-not-rich-and-sophisticated type. For one soiree, Barton wrangled twenty old, beat-up cars that guests were invited to drive in the club itself; guests were actually encouraged to knock over tables and the occasional dowager. Another party at the Atlantic Beach Club on Long

Island was a "barn dance," where city mice got the chance to participate in a spelling bee, watch a wrestling match between one of their own and a greased pig, and, as a fitting finale, join in for a spitting contest. The American rich, victorious over both their financial follies and New Dealers' attempts to ruin them, were back in business.[58]

Late thirties cocktail parties were less offensive but often equally entertaining opportunities for wealthy urbanites to engage in "Anything Goes" hijinks. John Joseph O'Donahue III's shindigs in his Park Avenue apartment were especially wild. The police were called there so often that the host had a prepared press release at the ready, beginning, "Among those arrested were . . ." Ronald Belcom's drinkfests at New York's Hampshire House included not only a gentlemen with a gay-nineties handlebar mustache on a period bicycle riding around the Cottage Suite but a "drunken waiter" hired to be at least as disruptive. Serving the wrong drinks, taking forks out of hungry guests' hands, and removing full plates of food, the waiter had the room in swells in hysterics. The waiter, it turned out, was one Frank Libuse, an entertainer frequently hired by top society hostesses. (Even society's queen mum, Mrs. Vincent Astor, used Libuse to, as she put it, "worry her guests.") Private dinners, usually held in a club or hotel, were much more dignified affairs, of course, with anywhere from twenty to one hundred people celebrating some sort of special occasion, such as a visit from a member of European royalty, with nary a drunken waiter (at least one pretending to be).[59]

Charity luncheons, typically populated by the same segment of society as the cocktail set, were also back in a big way. During the season in New York, three or four luncheons a week were not unusual, after which a string of chauffeurs would drive piles of collected rummage to the cause du jour. Fashion and jewelry shows often preceded or followed lunch, the more fabulous of which drew the attention of newsreelers, who splashed scenes of the rich and famous before envious moviegoers around the world. Society fashionistas had taken to wearing hats bearing a strong resemblance to birds (one described by a critic from the *New York Post* as "a whole white dove perched on a bit of black velvet") and vegetables ("a black felt funnel filled with a large green velvet cabbage"); some were simply incredibly large ("so enormous it makes a sombrero look like a child's beret," the fashion critic remarked about an especially sizable one). Even men occasionally put up with a lunchtime fashion preview for a good cause and to rub elbows with the boys, the more adventurous plunking down a grand or two for a plum-colored suit, canary yellow dinner jacket (for wear in the tropics, naturally), or blue cashmere overcoat with mink lining. Having weathered the storms of the 1930s, the rich were now proudly and literally wearing their wealth on their sleeves.[60]

Accessorizing had perhaps reached a high point of over-the-topness among the wealthy, gossip columnists' reports from the field confirm. "Mrs. Wanamaker Munn showed up the other evening with no less than eighteen gold bracelets on one arm," observed one society page critic, proof positive that flashier society women went out on the town not to see but to be seen. Broadway openings were particularly fecund opportunities for showing off one's plumage. "Lillie Harriman Havermayer [was] weighted down to her seat by the most opulent silver fox 'farm' any human being ever attempted to carry about," Cholly Knickerbocker of the *Journal and American* (a Hearst paper popular with New Yorkers of all income levels) wrote after attending the first night of *Dear Octopus*. Dixie Tighe of the perennially gossipy *New York Post* made note that Mrs. Jessie Donahue wore not only *two* strings of pearls to the opening of Noel Coward's *Set to Music* but also "a string of emeralds so large she gave the appearance of being marked 'GO,'" the image of gems apparently as big as traffic lights a luscious one for readers of all classes. [61]

Underneath their finery and bling, some of the rich of the late 1930s sported another kind of adornment associated more with the working class and sailors: tattoos. "Members of our best-advertised families are known to be colorfully embellished on limbs and torso with lovers' knots, anchors, and what-have-you," Lundberg reported, the American "snobacracy" having lifted the look from British ladies and gentlemen. A little investigative work by *Town & Country* revealed that quite a few of the upper crust of seventy years ago in fact had body art, making today's inked seem perhaps a little less hip and edgy. Mrs. Paul Abbott and Mrs. Arthur White each had butterflies on their knees, for example; Caresse Crosby Young had a cross on the sole of her foot, and Haydie Eames Yates had, rather daringly, a kewpie on her thigh. A full half of the hunting crowd in Maryland had fox heads somewhere on their skin, the magazine discovered, and quite a few men had also been "tooed," notably Alfred Victor Du Pont (serpent on his left arm) and E. B. Condon (cockfight on his shoulder). No instance of piercing among the moneyed class was reported, however.[62]

Even before the age of paparazzi, photography played a key role in generating the kind of publicity that the more socially conscious rich relied on heavily to advance their cause. "Getting a picture of your face or your place in the papers is virtually the *sine qua non* of survival in the plushier circles," wrote Isabel Lundberg in 1939, noting that New York's socially ambitious would often design their entire evenings around having a photo taken of them in hopes it would appear in the society pages. Considering the whole practice tacky, the *New Yorker* proposed that the city's nightclubs dispense with their resident photographers hired specifically to bring in the social set and their deep pockets.[63] Lucius Beebe, the syndicated columnist, thought doing so would be lunacy and prove disastrous for nightclub owners if taken seriously:

> The thought itself is enough to give Fefe Ferry (Monte Carlo), John Perona (El Morocco), Sherman Billingsley (Stork Club) and other white-tie entrepreneurs vertigo, as it is a suggestion, not only in the direction of sheer madness, but of immediate and certain bankruptcy for any establishment that might act on it. Toss out the floorshow, throw away the band, tear up the decorations and bring in for waiter-captains the familiar gorillas of Prohibition, and a night club might still be a success. But dispense with the photographers

and the establishment's number is up, the bell is tolled at Lloyd's and the rented waiter's jackets can go back. The cameraman is about the only fixture in contemporary social existence that is absolutely indispensable and without whose presence no proprietor can hope to open for business a second night.[64]

Another way plushier circles conveyed their plushiness was by adopting the latest and greatest when it came to travel—the private plane. By the end of the thirties, some of the trendier rich were ditching private railroad cars—a major status symbol for the past half century—for something a lot faster and decidedly more modern. Filling a chartered train to go from New York to Miami or Chicago and all points in between had been de rigueur for those wanting to travel in style, but now the airplane was eclipsing the iron horse as the preferred mode of transportation. When a notable Robinson married an equally notable Peabody in the spring of 1939, for instance, the whole bridal party, ushers and all, boarded a transport plane from New York to Bermuda, considered the only way to fly among the pre-jet-set set. The private plane arguably became an official marker of the American rich the summer of 1939, when Mrs. Andrew Carnegie's oldest daughter, Louise, got hitched to a Scottish lawyer, and their whole gang (including the minister of the Brick Presbyterian Church and his wife) flew off to the Highlands for the big event.[65]

YOUR IMPERIAL HIGHNESS

Many more Europeans, their countries overrun by the Nazis, headed the other way across the Atlantic during the late thirties and early forties, infusing the American rich with some new and exotic energy. These émigrés were hardly huddled masses yearning to be free; they were attracted to the United States not just as a political haven but as a safe place for their piles of cash and valuables. To guarantee the money would be there when they walked off the plane or ship, bank deposits often preceded the arrival of their owners, although jewels and artworks were typically carried by hand or secretly stowed in storage. European banks were also sending their currency and gold west, opening up U.S. branches to ensure their wealthy depositors' assets would not fall into German hands. This huge outflow of wealth from Europe to the United States in the late thirties and early forties was without precedent, Paris having historically been the go-to place for rich on the run.[66] With Nazis drinking champagne on the Champs Elysées, however, the land of liberty an ocean away looked like a pretty good alternative. This created what was probably "the greatest flood of wealth that ever poured from one continent to another," as S. F. Porter of *American Magazine* claimed in 1942. Over $5 billion traveled from Europe to the States between 1935 and 1942, Porter believed, a sum that shifted not just the economic and social landscape of the affluent class but of the world.[67]

Although much of this migration of wealth from Old World to New World was legally transferred to elite private banks like JP Morgan, Lazard Freres, Brown Brothers, and Harriman & Company, a fair share came in much less officially, under the radar of both large financial institutions and the government. (Between 1939 and 1942, rentals of safe deposit boxes reportedly shot up 1,000 percent, the place of choice for émigrés to store not just their valuables but also their cash, both for extra safety and to keep their net worth private.) Amazing stories of how rich Europeans escaped with their valuables or converted them into cash to be smuggled into the United States abounded, some of them probably even true. One man reportedly fed his jewels to his cattle, shipped them to a safer country, and then had them slaughtered, leaving the steaks but taking the gems to America. Another involved a man who melted down his gold, shaped the metal into a car fender that he painted black, and drove across the border to freedom. Getting automobiles themselves or other valuable property from Europe to the States did not have to be as ingenious as long as one could afford it. In 1940 alone, eighty Rolls-Royces were shipped across the Atlantic, as well as quite a few racehorses—luxuries for which some Europeans apparently felt there were no American substitutes.[68]

Along with as much of their stash as they could get out, three different types of rich refugees washed up on American shores during the war: exiled royalty (European ex-empresses, crown princesses, archdukes, and counts, plus a few Indian maharajas and Asian potentates, finding themselves without a kingdom to rule over); European bankers and businessmen who wisely decided to put their careers on hold for awhile; and American society expats who came to the conclusion that the United States, despite its glaring lack of taste, wasn't so bad after all. Wealthy Jews and Germans—careful to speak English in public—were of course part of this diaspora, as were French socialites, who for some reason or another opted for America instead of Northern Africa as a sanctuary. Rather than join the resistance and drink in the real-life equivalents of Rick's American Café, these Frenchmen and Frenchwomen were likely to be found mixing it up with the Park Avenue crowd in New York and rooting for de Gaulle's rebel movement from a chic boîte.[69]

Not surprisingly, the influx of titled characters was a windfall for society writers like Cholly Knickerbocker (a.k.a. Maury Henry Biddle Paul; his acerbic reports about the rich were considered the "Page Six" of the day). More than twenty Rothschilds arrived from Paris and Vienna by 1942, the legendary banking family providing prime fodder for inquiring minds wanting to know more about the everyday lives of barons and baronesses.[70] Already familiar with various lesser European royalty from the pages of *Vogue* and *Harper's Bazaar*, readers were suddenly learning much more about people like Archduke Otto, who'd taken up fancy digs in the Essex House on Central Park South. Part of the Habsburg Dynasty that had collapsed at the end of World War I, the Archduke was still called "Your Imperial Highness" by his entourage, despite having no empire to speak of. The Apostolic King of Hungary had also landed in New York, but being a B-list royal and a little strapped for cash, he was living rather modestly in an apartment house. Still, the oldest son of the late emperor of Austria remained confident that he would one day rule not only Austria and Hungary but the rest of Central Europe, as he and his followers believed he rightfully should. Another royal in exile, the Crown Princess of Norway, could often be found shopping on Fifth Avenue during the war, but she lived in, of all places, Pook's Hill, Maryland, in a rented house that FDR had personally helped pick out for her.[71]

Most European businessmen who had rescued themselves and their fortunes by coming to the States were more or less just waiting the war out, dabbling in the stock market but not undertaking new enterprises. One notable exception was Fritz von Opel, the German automaker who GM had bought out in 1929. Opel arrived in the United States in 1940, $8 million in tow, and promptly began running an oil company in Tennessee, as well as the Harvard Brewery in Lowell, Massachusetts. Like any rich person worth his salt, Opel was house hunting on Nantucket, the landscape there reminding his wife of her youth on the isle of Sylt.

Sometimes not just a businessman but his entire business exported itself to the United States during the war. Such was the case in the diamond business, when dealers from the Netherlands and Belgium arrived in New York en masse, their pockets filled with stones. The men carrying the tools of the trade—diamond cutters—were not as lucky getting out of war-torn countries, however, and the uncut rocks waited in safe deposit boxes in Rockefeller Center. Many diamond cutters would arrive after the war, further shifting the industry from Amsterdam and Brussels to New York.[72]

Rich refugees' wartime presence could be felt most strongly in the marketplace, to both the delight and chagrin of many a shopkeeper and those in the hospitality business. The International Set, as they came to be called, went on a buying spree during the war that natives had never witnessed. The way they spent their money and the sheer amount of it was shocking to a nation trained during the last decade and change to be thrifty. In swanky New York nightclubs, Eurotrash circa the early 1940s threw $100 and $500 bills around like they were confetti; the bills were too large sometimes for the managers to make change. In Hollywood, owners of boutiques had taken to hiring only shopgirls who could speak French in order to cater to the "refugee trade." And in Chicago, the fur was indeed flying. European baronesses and countesses, as well as American heiresses who had returned to the States, collected mink, fox, and ermine coats and stoles like they were going out of style.[73]

Wealthy war refugees were also determined to see (and buy) all that this big country could offer, hitting the road when they felt like leaving their lavish apartments (sometimes, ironically, sublet from well-to-do Americans serving overseas). Rooms in luxury hotels and resorts were leased not by the day or week but often for months, especially as it became clear the war would last for years. Ski resorts like Sun Valley and Lake Placid were littered with the International Set, as were Palm Beach and Palm Springs, permanently making "the circuit" much more cosmopolitan. This was before Las Vegas appeared like a mirage in the desert, so the set frequently headed to Reno to get their gambling fixes, as well as to the Kentucky Derby in May, no doubt enchanted by the latter's pomp and circumstance (not to mention mint juleps). Rather than mingle with the natives to learn and possibly embrace local customs, however, these Europeans were known to prefer to keep together, not something that pluralistic Americans, even rich ones, liked to see.[74]

This herdlike tendency was, unfortunately, the internationals' least offensive characteristic, at least according to many of those who encountered them on the homefront. Their showy jewelry, propensity to burst into song in their native tongue, even their strange ways of eating were just a few of the things that annoyed the average man or woman, who believed that foreigners should remain as inconspicuous as possible while we were at war. Waiters and salespeople generally despised rich refugees, thinking them rude, arrogant, and, worst of all, poor tippers. Conditioned to haggle over everything, with asking prices always viewed as negotiable, Europeans were considered cheapskates by merchants not used to bargaining sessions that sometimes lasted for hours. Refugees' perceived tendencies to act like they owned the place rather than being grateful for their safe harbor was deemed their worst offense, along with their occasional practice of insulting Americans right in front of Americans. Given all we were doing to save these people and their countries, some reasonably asked, couldn't they behave more like us?[75]

Children of rich refugees, apparently on much better behavior than their parents, were happily received by the natives and often placed among their American counterparts in the city's best private schools. A gaggle of English kids found their way to Dalton and Spence early in the war, for example, much to the delight of their classmates' parents, who considered them a good influence, in part because they spoke the way rich people were supposed to sound. "If a young Morgan or a young Phipps learns to imitate the accent of young Lord Primrose or John Julius Cooper, no one is going to object," remarked *Fortune* in 1941. The British lads and lasses of privilege, meanwhile, were less interested in American accents than American plumbing, which they found far superior to their own leaky and clangy pipes across the pond. The English knew a thing or two about how to act properly rich, it seemed, but American sinks and toilets were clearly first class.[76]

Go Boating and Help Win the War

Even the International Set, with all their converted currency and smuggled jewelry burning a hole in their pockets, had their style occasionally cramped by the inconveniences of war. Restrictions on travel and leisure were not uncommon on the homefront, of course. As well, the government had taken over many of the wealthy's favorite haunts for defense purposes. The Kirkwood Hotel in Camden, South Carolina, for example, a favored spot in pre-Depression days for the rich to spend the winter playing polo, had become by 1941 a training camp for the Army, its "quarters" now filled with officers and visiting dignitaries (300 enlisted men camped out in tents in the back). The resort's polo fields were now used for maneuvers; the lounge became a mock war room, its walls covered with maps indicating troop movements. The grand white hotel seemed to be holding up well in its new role ("no hash has yet been hurled at the gaily colored tropical birds that wallpaper the dining room," a reporter observed), although plaster would occasionally fall from the ceilings and water pipes burst when fourteen-gun salutes honoring the arrival of special guests were fired.[77]

Throughout the war, other fancy hotels usually packed with swells were appropriated by the government and temporarily turned into unusually luxurious military bases. Much of Miami's resort scene became a rehabilitation zone soon after war's end, with no less than eight luxury hotels occupied by 3,000 battle casualties healing from their physical and emotional scars. "In rooms that suckers and show-offs once paid $90 a day for," the *Chicago Daily Tribune* reported in 1945, "the war wounded and sick are finding the road to recovery not at all hard to take." The Biltmore Hotel's three swimming pools were filled not with bathing beauties but convalescing GIs doing exercises, while on the beach, cabanas that usually rented for $35 to $50 a day had been transformed into physical therapy rooms. Wounded vets were also taking advantage of the recreational activities typically reserved for rich sportsmen. Patients who had come straight from European battlefields and prisoner of war camps to "this millionaire's vacation playground," as the newspaper described Miami Beach, suddenly found themselves golfing, playing volleyball, deep-sea fishing, and taking midnight cruises on Biscayne Bay, something not being taken for granted by the war heroes. "This isn't the army, it's paradise," said Private Charles Pinkas, a liberated prisoner, as an orchestra played in the background; another vet declared, "If this is rehabilitation, bring on more of the same."[78]

While most resort hotels would bounce back nicely after the war and be returned to their former glory, many private clubs were not so lucky. New York's Hanger Club, for example, like many others founded in the Roaring Twenties, limped along through the thirties but could not recover from the trials and tribulations of war. In its heyday during Prohibition, men like C. V. Whitney, Marshall Field, and W. A. Harriman kept their private stashes in small lockers that were built into the barroom's paneling—not that it was very likely that New York's finest would choose to bust some of the most powerful people in the world. Members' names were carved into the dining room chairs that were inspired by a couple of mahogany Hepplewhite armchairs in the lounge, just a small portion of the club's collection of eighteenth-century antiques, which rivaled those in some English palaces. In 1941, all the furnishings, including some silverware never removed from its original packaging and inscribed with the club's emblem, the head of Mercury, were auctioned off, the house itself taken over by, of all people, the Missionary Sisters of the Third Order of St. Francis, who planned to use it as a business school. In a little over a decade, the Upper East Side mansion had been transformed from an exclusive club for multimillionaires into a place for nuns to teach the principles of commerce to girls—quite the ironic twist of fate.[79]

Their ranks already depleted by the economic reversals of the thirties, other private clubs were hit hard by the war, as many members left the cushy surroundings for military service. New York's Court House Club had to close its doors in early 1943, its furnishings also to be sold at auction. Founded by seven wealthy men right before the market crash, the Court House was no ordinary club; it was originally intended to be used only by the founding members and their families and friends. Each of the members (again including department store founder Marshall Field) ponied up $100,000 to buy and furnish the Upper East Side mansion, borrowing another $300,000 to create what was popularly called the "$1 Million Club." A few years later, however, the Depression made most of these men look for ways to downsize, and one member, Richard F. Hoyt, bought out the six others. Hoyt, a doctor, used the front half of the house as his private residence and turned the back half into a club for, in current vernacular, his posse.[80]

Hoyt's dream crib was short-lived, however, as was Hoyt himself. Upon his death in 1935, the entire property again became a private club, with a maximum membership of seventy men and, rather surprisingly, women, each paying $300 to $400 in annual dues. With an indoor tennis court, squash court, swimming pool, and other facilities, the place was essentially a country club in the middle of Manhattan, making it truly unique and ultraexclusive. The war, however, threw a monkey wrench into the works as, one by one, members resigned to serve the nation and, no doubt, to disassociate themselves from an organization whose very existence was so contrary to America's democratic ideals. Even the president and vice president of the club, Frank A. Vanderlip and Walter P. Chrysler, each sons of famous business tycoons, were off to become "dollar-a-year-men" for Uncle Sam. Soon the entire contents of the house, including the antique English and French furniture, hand-painted oilcloth wallpaper, hand-tufted carpets, and paneling from a European palace, would be sold off in two hundred lots, although the fate of the tennis court, a replica of the one at Roland Garros in Paris, wasn't clear.[81]

Unlike resort hotels and private clubs, pleasure boating—another staple of the rich—appreciated in value during the war, transformed from a leisure activity for the wealthy into a way home-fronters could do their part. "Yachting, instead of being regarded as a frivolous pastime of millionaires, is hailed this season as a patriotic gesture," observed the *New York Times* in 1942, suggesting the slogan, "Go Boating and Help Win the War." The Navy and Coast Guard were in fact asking yacht clubs to teach navigation and seamanship to civilians who could then enlist as commissioned officers or else patrol coastal areas and harbors. FDR himself urged the Interlake Yachting Association, an organization of forty-nine clubs, three thousand boats, and ten thousand members, to get involved. The former Assistant Secretary of the Navy under Woodrow Wilson knew firsthand that pleasure boating could be an excellent launching dock for naval service.[82]

When it came to wartime propaganda, borrowing the rich

themselves was much better than borrowing the rich's toys. To demonstrate that everyone was backing the war, the government was elated when it had the chance to report that a millionaire had enlisted. When the enlistee was a member of one of America's great families doing menial work in an obscure location, the story proved an especially juicy piece of news. Such was the case with Private First Class George Jay Gould, the twenty-three-year-old great-grandson of railroad mogul Jay Gould, who was spending his valuable time peeling potatoes and driving officers around at an Army camp in Sydney, Australia, in 1942. Gould had married Eileen O'Malley, a New York society woman, just after being drafted, but that didn't stop him from shipping out to the other (albeit quite safe) side of the world when Uncle Sam called. Having "had no time to arrange for this detail after being posted overseas," the *Los Angeles Times* claimed something difficult to believe: Gould was "acutely short of money for the first time in his life." Hearing that the rich were also making sacrifices was welcome news to most American working stiffs and fellow servicemen, however.[83]

Even before Pearl Harbor, instances of millionaires interrupting their charmed lives to become just another soldier were discovered (or created) and turned into patriotic fodder. Everyday military occurrences, such as a promotion, when a person of considerable wealth (and/or fame) was involved were also reason enough for a story to make it into a major newspaper. "T. Suffern (Tommy) Taller, millionaire amateur golfer of Peapack, N.J., who enlisted in the army last January, today was promoted to the rank of sergeant and picked up a $6 month raise," went a classic example, published in the *Chicago Daily Tribune* in May 1941. The message to readers was that if a millionaire golfer was willing to put his clubs down to help win the war, all Americans should somehow jump into the fray.[84] Stories in which GI Joes were somehow living some version of the life of a millionaire also made good copy, a kind of reversal of fortune. "Milne Bay may be exposed to Japanese attack, but it is the only American outpost in the Far East where American soldiers can have millionaires' salad," a sergeant based in Australia told a war correspondent in 1942, millionaires' salad being heart of palm, which was going for a whopping $1.50 a plate in the States, if one was lucky to find it. "Here we eat millionaires' salad three times daily, if we like," the sergeant added, another example of how the war had made the idea of class in America irrelevant or sometimes even turned it upside down.[85]

Instances of millionaires using their money in ways that were less than democratic also popped up during the war, however— proof that the ownership class was alive and well, thank you very much. Not helping the wealthy's public image was their habit of luring nurses away from the armed services by offering them $25 a day and up for their services—quite a bit more than Uncle Sam was shelling out and incentive enough for the nurses to remain civilians. Some war factory executives were hogging nurses by keeping a dozen or more on their staffs, able to pay them very well from their fat military contracts. This poaching of desperately needed nurses from the military did not sit well with government wonks and made those cornering the market on them look bad. "This luxury type of nursing is not only foolishness but pretty poor patriotism when these nurses are needed so badly to care for the wounded who are coming home," said Charles Schlicter of the War Manpower Committee in 1944, who intended to nip such special treatment in the bud, pronto.[86]

Administration officials were also put off when the wealthy used their remaining private railroad cars to get around the country when everyone else, including servicemen and servicewomen, were packed into trains like sardines in a can, especially toward the end of the war. When members of the Weyerhauser lumber family used their private Pullman cars to take a vacation in 1945, for example, Representative Hugh De Lacy, a New Deal Democrat from Washington State, raised a ruckus and demanded that such wastefulness be immediately stopped. "If we are to provide luxury, let us provide it to those who deserve it most, the returning battle-weary GIs," De Lacy told his fellow House members, accusing Great Northern Railway top brass of similar undemocratic behavior.[87]

Even those who were not rich but acted as if they were came under attack for violating the wartime creed of self-sacrifice and restraint. Rosie the Riveters' free-spending ways didn't please more conservative observers of the wartime scene, for example, when it became readily apparent that the women were hardly putting all of their extra cash into war bonds. "We are suffering an alarming oversupply of first-generation new rich these days," believed Alma Whitaker of the *Los Angeles Times*, pinpointing young women as being the most nouveau of the nouveau riche. It was true that thousands of women who had been domestics or shopgirls in the thirties making $30 to $40 a month were now bringing in $60 to $75 a week working in war plants, many of them spending their money like, well, drunken sailors. In addition to going on shopping sprees on the legitimate and black markets for furs, pianos, and very hard-to-find cars, some were actually now hiring maids for themselves and treating them, according to Whitaker, "like a Duchess disciplining a slavey." "Call a halt, sisters!" she urged, pleading with them to not "let these new riches transform you from a nice, normal girl to an arrogant, wasteful hussy."[88]

"Sisters" weren't the only ones feeling and acting like they were rich during the war, however. "The United States is now being swept up by a wave of prosperity that made 1929 look like a ripple," observed Frederick Lewis Allen in 1944, who saw much of the country engaged in an orgy of consumerism. Despite all its wartime economic tricks—higher taxes, bond drives, wage and price ceilings, rationing—the government could not stop Americans from doing what they do best: make and spend money. Hotels and restaurants were filled day and night in big cities and small towns alike; luxury items like jewelry, antiques, and grand pianos were selling like hotcakes; and even racetracks were busy. Alligator handbags at Saks in New York were moving at $49.50, as good an indicator as any that the economy was back on track. Business executives were, not surprisingly, leading the pack, picking up checks again and throwing the kinds of parties in hotels they did in the late twenties. At one company's hotel banquet, all of the women guests received a purple or white orchid at $10 and $25 a respective pop, the tab ultimately picked up by Uncle Sam via lucrative military contracts. Unlike in World War I, when many Americans immediately benefited from the economic boom and spent their newfound riches on things like silk shirts, this boom had taken a couple of years to develop as folks first dug themselves out of their Depression holes. Ironically, it was not the socially progressive maneuvers of the New Deal that were leveling the playing field of wealth but good old capitalism, propelled of course by the winds of war.[89] With the war's end, a new era of the American rich would begin, one that would propel them to unimaginable heights.

CHAPTER 3

IF I WERE A RICH MAN:
1946–1964

"The '400' has been marked down to $3.98."
—ALEXANDER PHILLIPS

O N MAY 11, 1959, SIXTEEN DRIVERS SET OUT TO WIN THE
most prestigious auto race in the world, the Grand Prix de
Monaco. Before the war, the field would have inevitably been filled
with nobility and millionaires, but this year the drivers were remarkable only in their ordinariness. The six finishers were the winner, an Australian garage owner, followed by a British dentist, a
used car dealer, a French wine grower, and two professionals, one
from New Zealand and the other from Santa Monica. The only
member of royalty, Count Wolfgang von Trips of Germany, was
out of the race by the third lap when his Porsche crashed into cars
driven by two different garage owners. The days when princes, mar-
quises, counts, and the extremely wealthy drove fast cars purely for
the thrill appeared to be over, the sport transformed into a more
professional and, most would argue, less glamorous affair.[1]

It could be argued that the 1959 Grand Prix, although just an
auto race, symbolized the tremendous changes that took place

within the affluent class during the postwar years, both abroad and, especially, in the United States. Already reeling from a quarter-century of tremendous social upheaval, Old Money was about to face two new threats: the emergence of an arriviste whose wealth rivaled that of the robber barons in their prime, and the rise of a new professional class of rich. Oil Money made the fortunes of Old Money look puny. Those men and women from the West were more than a little rough around the edges but carried none of the elitist baggage of East Coast WASPs. The second category of nou-veau riche, the proverbial man in the (Brooks Brothers) gray flannel suit, would also put a major crimp in blue blood's style; this first true generation of "mass affluents" were a prototype for "the mil-lionaire next door" who would emerge forty years hence. As a meri-tocracy further displaced the nation's quasiaristocracy, it was "farewell to Fifth Avenue," as a descendant of the Old Guard put it. For some, this ironically made membership in high society all the more important. Now as red-white-and-blue as mom, apple pie, and Chevrolet (actually Cadillac or Lincoln), the rich had been fully redeemed as the most visible symbols of the American Dream.

Big Rich

If New York, the financial capital of the world, represented the locus of American wealth culture in the twenties and thirties, the Southwest best defined the new kind of rich after the war or, at least, presented the most interesting challenge to Old Money. With the demand for oil, cotton, wheat, and meat skyrocketing pretty much everywhere, millionaires were popping up like daisies across the Great Plains and Panhandle, shifting the cultural geogra-phy of American wealth away from the Northeast. As the Carnegies and Fricks had been to steel and the Vanderbilts to transportation, men like H. L. Hunt, Sid Richardson, Clint Murchison, and Hugh Roy Cullen were to oil, blazing a new trail of wealth in their own inimitable ways. With the site of the Dust Bowl of the 1930s now the land of milk and honey (actually wheat), the mild, wet weather there literally turning the area into the breadbasket of the world, ranchers and farmers in this part of the country were also reaping the fruits of their horn of plenty.[2] Bank deposits in Texas, Oklahoma, Colorado, and Kansas tripled between 1941 and 1948, while income tax payments in those states increased more than tenfold. Oilmen, ranchers, and farmers in larger cities like Houston and Dallas were the biggest beneficiaries of this commodity bonanza, but quite a few folks in smaller towns like Midland and Odessa, Texas, were also making a killing.[3]

There was so much money in Texas and Oklahoma in the late 1940s that, rather famously, in these parts it took $30 million to be considered "Big Rich," while those with just $5 million were stuck with being called "Little Rich" (or the even more humiliating "Flash Boy"). "Nowhere in the United States is today's general prosperity more clearly discernible than in Texas," believed Stanley Walker in 1953; the legends associated with the Big Rich from that state were becoming an even bigger part of American folklore. Best of all, this latest mother lode of Texan wealth was what natives called, rather proudly, "clean money," their millions earned reputably and ethically.[4] Some of the real-life stories of fortunes being made and spent rivaled those of future television character Jed Clampett and spawned jokes, such as the one about the Texas millionaire who, called before an IRS agent, interrupted him with, "Don't bother me with all those figures, son, just tell me how much you need to make ends meet."[5] In 1948, for example, Colonel Henry Russell of Dallas bought a new Rolls-Royce for his wife (for $19,500, the cost of a Hyundai today) simply because, as she put it, "it goes with my blue hat." The Russells were also planning to build a new, much bigger house for themselves, having decided to give their current one to their servants.[6] One key member of the postwar Big Rich club was D. Harold ("Dry-hole") Byrd, who would invite the Texas and Oklahoma football teams over to his estate every fall, along with hundreds of other guests. One year, an entire tribe of Indians from Oklahoma was hired to dance around a fountain.[7]

It was readily apparent, especially to East Coast sticks-in-the-mud, that this brand of rich was quite unlike anything seen before. Regional "distinctiveness" and the origins of Big Rich wealth separated them from the Old Money crowd like oil and water. Marketers to the wealthy often found themselves having to adapt to the rather unorthodox lifestyles of Big Rich. Clothing and jewelry salesmen and models from Neiman Marcus, for example, regularly made trips to outlying ranches and oil fields, thinking that if Mohammed couldn't come to the mountain, the mountain would come to Mohammed (or Tex, in this case).[8] Many, if not most, Texan millionaires, however, didn't care a whit about what they wore between their head and feet, but they were more than happy to pay top dollar for a well-made ten-gallon hat and pair of boots. Three- and four-carat diamond rings were also popular among the oil and cattle set, as were solid gold belt buckles with diamond and ruby studs. Ranchers and wildcatters in Odessa and Midland often lived in trailer camps, shacks, and even open tents, but the woman of the house not unusually insisted on using sterling silver for the table, on which she served the family's favorite vittles—salt meat and black Mexican beans.[9]

Dust Bowl refugees who settled in California's southern San Joaquin valley represented the West Coast branch of Big Rich. Jess Goforth, for example, who left Oklahoma in 1931 with his wife and infant son and made it to California with just $1.50 left in his pocket, was growing cotton, wheat, barley, and cantaloupes on his own 6,400-acre ranch twenty years later, his grapes of wrath now quite sweet from the fertile soil. Although a millionaire many times over should he cash out, the aptly named Goforth worked as hard as ever and saw no need to get a telephone for his home on the edge of the prairie.[10]

"Big Rich" was all relative, however. In 1957, only one American, H. L. Hunt, was among the top five richest people in the world, he lagging behind four men who could be considered "giant rich":

King Saud of Saudi Arabia; the Sheik of Kuwait; the Sheik of Qatar; and the Nizam of Hyderabad (who, unlike the others, was not rich from oil money). King Saud, who earned $300 million a year, perhaps lived more lavishly than anyone in history, even the Pharaohs, who weren't exactly cheapskates. Included in his personal household of 10,000 were three wives, eighty to ninety concubines, and "about" twenty-five sons (daughters weren't considered full-fledged children), each of whom received his own Cadillac and chauffeur at age 12. It was known that his own cars were gold-plated, but few people, probably including the King himself, knew exactly how many were in the fleet. And despite owning twenty-four palaces, the King was building a new one at a cost of $50 million, almost certainly the most expensive home in the world.[11]

Although over a million barrels of oil gushed from Kuwait's wells every day, compared to King Saud, the Sheik lived like a monk. For one thing he had only one wife, despite Muslim law allowing four, and he owned only one house and one car (albeit a Caddy). Unlike his partner in oil, the Sheik was in the process of creating what was arguably the world's first true welfare state, investing much of his country's fortune in education, housing, health care, and utilities. Little was known about the Sheik of Qatar except that he raked in at least $50 million from oil, spending a good chunk of it on his four hundred relatives (which did not include his immediate family of wives, concubines, and children). The Sheik also enjoyed giving handouts to the needy from the front steps of his palace, which, with its red neon lights, looked "very much like something in Coney Island," reported the New York Times. The Nizam of Hyderabad had a much different story, having fallen on rather hard times when the Indian government stripped him of his sovereignty. His annual income reduced from about $50 million to $2 million, the Nizam felt the need to put himself on a $20 a month budget, sleeping on a hospital cot in a 10- by 12-foot room. Fortunately for the Nizam, a descendant of Mongol rulers, the Indian government had at least for the moment not seized the $2 billion he had socked away for a rainy day nor his fleet of thirty-plus luxury automobiles. Rather than drive one of these, however, the Nizam preferred to cruise around Hyderabad in a 1934 Ford, and he spent a good deal of his time planning the daily menu for his household, which consisted of three wives, forty-two concubines, thirty-three children, dozens of grandchildren, and hundreds of servants.[12]

Hunt, sixty-eight years old in 1957, had fewer wives, concubines, children, and cars than the other richest men in the world, but with his $2- to $3-billion nest egg and $40- to $50-million annual income, he was not exactly scraping by. His only extravagance appeared to be his home, a five-times-the-original-size copy of George Washington's Mount Vernon. Hunt walked the streets of Dallas largely unrecognized, preferring to stay out of the spotlight and, quite literally, laugh all the way to the bank.[13] By the end of the fifties, however, the inescapable forces of Ben Franklin's only two constants took a heavy toll on independent oil millionaires. The deaths of Cullen and Richardson left only the other half of the industry's Fantastic Four—Hunt and Murchison—alive and kicking, but high taxes and changes in the oil business itself would signal the end of the decade-and-change run for Big Rich. Technical skills in geology and engineering and business skills in management and marketing were surpassing the roll-the-dice approach of the wildcatter and, with college graduates with majors in finance entering the business, oil now wasn't that much different than banking.[14]

The Big Rich fortunes remained, however, and at least some of them were eagerly spent. The very nature of oil money—staggeringly large and instantly made if one could beat the long odds of drilling (1 to 9, experts said)—made for some curious investments. Texas and Oklahoma millionaires were strangely attracted to Broadway in the postwar years, a fair share of them investing thousands of dollars in shows they produced themselves with very little or no knowledge of the theater. *Happy Town*, for example, described by the *New York Times* as "an unhappy musical comedy venture," closed after just five performances on the Great

FIGURE 3-1. Formal portrait of H. L. Hunt in 1965, when the oil tycoon was 76. Although he lived rather modestly. Hunt was known to introduce himself to strangers by saying, "Hello, I am H. L. Hunt, the world's richest man," something that was darn close to being true. *(Hulton Archive/Getty Images)*

White Way in 1959, not too surprising since the oil money investors hired a team with no Broadway experience whatsoever and had never actually taken the time to read the script. Another such group backed *God and Kate Murphy* the previous year, which was staged a relatively impressive twelve times before the plug was pulled. *The Ladder*, a work commissioned by the late gazillionaire Edgar B. Davis, however, perhaps best illustrated the sheer wackiness of oil money. The show, written by an old friend of Davis's who was down on his luck, continued to run on Broadway exclusively and painfully to what the newspaper called "pathetically small houses of curiosity seekers." The common wisdom was that oil money's odd attraction to Broadway was part of a bigger desire to be associated with high culture, a desire felt even more strongly by the wives. "The Southwest is crawling with culture-crazed squaws," explained Richard S. Maney, a theatrical publicist, noting that it was the wives of oil tycoons who were leading the Broadway parade.[15]

One's home offered the best opportunity for Southwestern squaws to show they rightfully belonged to high society, however. Most suburban millionaires in Texas and Kansas, who the *New Yorker* dubbed "Super-Americans," lived rather modestly as their fortunes increased through the postwar years, yet another eccentricity of the Southwestern nouveau riche. Most millionaires in the United States spent an average of $250,000 to build a new home in the early sixties, but the Texas chapter typically spent just $100,000 on standard, contractor-built homes—what the magazine called "de-luxe row houses." After building a new home, it was de rigueur for suburban Dallas and Houston wives to hire the same professional decorators, making the houses look, one reporter thought, "as if they had been furnished a la Conrad Hilton to suit well-heeled interchangeable tenants." Still, these women were eager to display their modern-day palaces to friends and neighbors and hosted highly ritualized "house-showings," which typically included inspections of the closets and tours of the basement.[16]

Jim and Sally Hershberger's house-showing in 1964 was a classic example of oil money's determination to demonstrate their good taste in order to climb up the social ladder. In their invitation to the press, the Hershbergers of Wichita listed the dimensions of their new house (192' by 50'); its 14,000 square feet of living space made it the biggest private residence built in the country since the end of the war. Fourteen hundred people showed up to tour the home's twenty-six rooms and nine baths; the closet doors were conveniently left ajar so guests could sneak a peak at the couple's rather astounding amount of clothing, including Jim's 110 pairs of pants. Following a very long tradition of the nouveau riche, the Hershbergers looked to Europe to lend their house a sense of instant patina. A carved wood headboard with gold leaf copied from a seventeenth-century Roman church door and a sword from the Crusades, for example, were each intended to locate the couple's fortune far beyond that of twentieth-century Kansas. Jim was especially proud of a table in the front hall that he claimed had come from the Hearst estate in California, a prime symbol of well-established, even legendary, wealth. "You can tell it's an antique because of the cracks in the bottom," the thirty-two-year-old oilman confidently told a reporter, eager to show off his newly acquired sophistication.[17]

THE RIGHT PEOPLE

Building the biggest house in the country in almost a quarter-century showed not only the extent some would go to make their wealth publicly known but also the enduring pull of society upon the newly rich. By the end of the 1950s, "society" had split into three different but overlapping segments: Café Society, American Society, and International Society. The poor man's kind was without a doubt Café Society, which relied on publicity and public relations for its social currency. Mentions in a newspaper's society column were considered by many to be not an achievement but, as one anonymous critic put it, "an indictment." Interestingly, half a century later, Café Society is arguably the only kind of society that really matters, with publicity (good or bad) the truest measure of one's fame quotient and, in turn, earning power.[18]

For many wealthy Americans in the postwar years, however,

formal recognition as a member of local society was an integral part of maintaining the right kind of relationships, both personal and professional, with the right kind of people. Because it instantly confirmed one had the desired kind of background and/or requisite amount of money, being listed in the *Social Register*, the Bible of Old Money, was key to membership in American Society. First published by Louis Keller in 1887 (soon after Ward McAllister, Mrs. William Astor's social operative, published his famous list of "The Four Hundred"), by 1959 the *Register* listed over 75,000 people in eleven different cities. Keller was succeeded in 1922 by his secretary, Bertha Eastmond Barry, who almost four decades later still had final say over who was in and who was out. Getting into the book was hardly easy. First, a current listee had to recommend a new applicant, who would then submit information about his or her family and social activities. If the applicant was approved by an advisory board, he or she then had to get recommendations from four or five other listees. Only then, with the board's second blessing, could the happy society-member-to-be be listed in the *Register*.[19]

The *Social Register* board's decision-making process was without question more art than science. Evidence that one was loaded certainly helped, but it didn't guarantee acceptance. Like getting into an exclusive condominium today, any and all ties to show biz were definite strikes against. Elliot Roosevelt, the fourth of Franklin and Eleanor's six children, was dropped from the *Register* when he married the actress Faye Emerson, and the same happened to heiress Ellin Mackay (the daughter of Clarence Mackay, whose father had laid the first cable across the Atlantic) when she got hitched to Irving Berlin. Common sense suggested that marrying the biggest opera star in the world, Enrico Caruso, would be a feather in one's society cap, but Dorothy Benjamin's decision to do just that got her, the daughter of Park Benjamin Jr., a wealthy patent lawyer, dropped from the *Register* like a hot potato. ("It must be love," said an anonymous member of Philadelphia's Old Guard upon learning of Grace Kelly's intent to marry Prince Rainier, showing the extent of anti-celebrity sentiment among society.) Criticizing society was also cause for excommunication, the fate bestowed upon none other than Cornelius Vanderbilt Jr. after he made some disparaging remarks about New York's crème de la crème in his book *Farewell to Fifth Avenue*.[20]

Not surprisingly, getting onto the New York society list was more difficult than those of the other ten cities; if one could make it there, as one definite nonmember later sang, one could make it anywhere.[21] Texas society, on the other hand, was about "as hard to get into as the telephone directory," as popular lore went. (All Texas cities were conspicuously absent from the *Social Register* into the 1960s.) Part of the social snubbing of rich Texans—besides the fact that almost all of them were New Money and that some of them were apt to do gauche things, like spontaneously buy the entire contents of a department store window as a gift for one's wife—had to do with the perception that people from the state were less than erudite. The late, extremely wealthy Everette De Golyer, a geophysicist, was known as "the Texan who could read," a backhand compliment made even further puzzling by the fact that the man was actually an Oklahoman.[22] The belief that in Texas, "crude oil produced a crude society," was even harsher, the basis for that being the state's apathy when it came to the lineage of the wealthy. "Texas aristocracy," wrote Robert Rourk, "is not based on how long you lived there . . . and the thin blue blood-lines of some long-dead ancestor . . . [but rather] what you are . . . or might yet be," not exactly the stuff that would impress a board member of the *Register*.[23]

While membership in International Society required jumping through far fewer hoops—actually none; all that was required was a title, great beauty or fame, political clout, a terrific sense of humor or ability to make witty banter, or, of course, ridiculous amounts of money—belonging to this club was, many believed, more prestigious than being part of American Society. Bigger-than-life personalities such as Elsa Maxwell, Noel Coward, and the Greek tag team of Aristotle Onassis and his brother-in-law Stavros Niarchos were the poster children of International Society in the fifties, making America's *Social Register* members look like a bunch of Puritans. One of the closest observers of the postwar wealthy elite, Cleveland Amory, believed 2,400 global gadabouts belonged to International Society in 1959, publishing that list of lists (with photos, rather shockingly) that year.[24]

In the postwar years International Society was the last real vestige of traditional wealth, which was rapidly being turned into somewhat of an anachronism in those days that were heavily defined by John Kenneth Galbraith's "affluent society" and largely ruled by William Whyte's "organization man." Still, these folks remembered how to throw a party, their joie de vivre hearkening back to a different era, often consciously so. One party in Venice in 1951, hosted by a "mystery man," was the kind of bash that one could perhaps have attended at Versailles a couple of centuries back, before the masses decided to take issue with how the upper crust was spending their taxes. The rich and famous from three continents gathered at Carlos de Bestegui's palace on the Grand Canal in eighteenth-century-style dress, the host fittingly decked out in a governor's costume complete with jewels. "The international ermine and coronet set began arriving at the lantern-lit gondola landing at 10 p.m., an hour earlier than the 3,000 invitations had specified," as the *Chicago Daily Tribune* reported. A thousand police and carabineers guarded the gates should the large crowd outside—some cheering, some hissing—cause trouble. The Aga Khan and his wife, in period Oriental costume, were among the first to arrive, soon followed by American actress Gene Tierney (in a $16 peasant dress), Barbara Hutton (in a $15,000 black lace and sequin knight's outfit), and Christian Dior (disguised somehow as a giant). A gaggle of ladies, dukes, viscounts, and baronesses from across Europe were also in attendance, although invitees Winston Churchill and the Duke and Duchess of Windsor were party poopers, perhaps too . . . well, *British* for the festivities. Ballet dancers from France and Spain, a thirty-piece orchestra, and a troupe of tumblers completed the courtly scene, made all the more intriguing because virtually nothing was known about the mysterious, monocled host except that he was originally from Mexico and seemed to be equally obsessed with the eighteenth century and royalty.[25]

When not attending masquerade balls like the ones Louis XIV threw, many members of International Society in the fifties considered the Waldorf Towers, the most exclusive apartment hotel in the United States, their official home base. The Towers, as it was called by those in the know, was home sweet home to such personalities as Cole Porter, Maurice Chevalier, Gina Lollobrigida, the Duke and Duchess of Windsor, Xavier Cugat, Abbe Lane, and Maria Callas, at least when they were in New York. (Many of the International Set also had places in Palm Beach, Palm Springs, Beverly Hills, Paris, or Cannes.) Ex-presidents, reigning kings and queens, and captains of industry also took apartments in the Towers (for $8,000 to $36,000 a year), as did the occasional Texas millionaire wanting to show the world he wasn't just an ole cowhand from the Rio Grande. And while the Queen Mum and Middle East potentates like Crown Prince Al Faisal of Saudi Arabia and Crown Prince Abdul Ilah of Iran (not to mention the slaves they brought with them) caught people's attention when they dropped in, it was Elsa Maxwell who held court at the Towers. Maxwell attracted desirable members of International Society to the hotel like moths to a flame, her status as a social arbiter unsurpassed by any and all others on the circuit. Maxwell threw the occasional party but spent most of her day in bed, chatting on the phone to other Very Important People, presumably about other Very Important People. For this, Maxwell's rent at the Towers was half the regular rate ("How else could I afford to live here?" she asked), a bargain for the hotel's management, given that her mere presence made the joint *the* place for some of the wealthiest people in the world to want to call home.[26]

The debutante ball, a staple of society, naturally remained an important ritual, designed to perpetuate the species and fill the elite ranks of the next generation with the right people. The energy

FIGURE 3-2. Elsa Maxwell, socialite extraordinaire, at the peak of her considerable powers in 1957. *(Ray Fisher/Time Life Pictures/Getty Images)*

and expense devoted to these parties, opportunities to both to display one's royal plumage and to begin the mating dance, was sometimes truly astonishing. In 1960, for example, Henrietta Tiarks, daughter of an international banker, was presented to society in no less than six cities (London, Paris, Madrid, New York, Washington, and Baltimore) and, for good measure, less formally circulated around Boston and Philadelphia as well. This Debupalooza paid off, however; Miss Tiarks snagged the Marquess of Tavistock, the eldest son of the Duke of Bedford (and a Harvard man to boot), bringing not just another fortune into the partnership but a title as well.[27]

Society in off-the-beaten-path cities, including those in Texas, also relied heavily on debutante balls to expose the cream of the crop to each other. The 1960 Dallas–Ft. Worth debutante season consisted of no less than six dozen balls, luncheons, dinners, and receptions, each one an opportunity to announce society's children's arrival on the local stage. None compared to one held the

FIGURE 3-3. The Waldorf Towers in New York circa 1940, ground central for International Society for decades. *(Popperfoto/Getty Images)*

previous season, however, when Mr. and Mrs. Robert Windfohr threw a bash for their daughter Anne that impressed even been-there, seen-that Texans. The event, orchestrated by a New Yorker, was held at Ft. Worth's Ridglea Country Club, its Olympic-size swimming pool covered by a parquet dance floor custom-built for the occasion and illuminated by 80,000 blinking lights. Three bands, including none other than Louis Armstrong's, played past dawn (the guests were given sunglasses), interrupted at 3 A.M. by a huge fireworks display. Hopefully the $100,000 party produced a suitable beau for young Anne.[28] In the pecking order of the rich, however, even the Windfohrs were trumped, so to speak, when Henry Ford II reportedly spent $250,000 on a coming-out party for his daughter Anne in 1961.[29]

Given the increasingly higher stakes required to make a dent in society as more and more people became wealthy in the prosperous postwar years, desperate measures were occasionally in order. Many of the nouveau riche, having yet to reach "Fifth Avenue," much less say farewell to it, were eager to welcome society with open arms (and wallets). A small cottage industry had sprung up by the early sixties to do just that by helping New Money convert their windfalls into social currency, something that did not gush out of the ground like the oil that made many of them rich. One such wealth liaison was Marianne "Mimi" Strong, who, with her staff of seven, helped New York society wannabees scale its imposing and often impenetrable walls. Strong turned away the especially vulgar and those with a prison record but was happy to take on pretty much anyone else who wanted to get into the city's social swim, assuming he or she was comfortable plus, as it were. Strong's primary M.O. was to get the name of the client (or "newcomer," as she referred to her or him) in newspapers' society pages, ideally alongside the names of "the right people." Such name-dropping could lead, in the case of the daughter of a newly wealthy but "socially unestablished" family, for instance, to an invitation to an important debutante ball, a huge step up the ladder for the lucky lass and her aspiring kin.[30]

Strong's credentials for working such miracles were impeccable. The debutantes of debutantes, having herself come out at the Junior Assemblies, with fourteen years of newspaper experience, including a stint as society editor, Strong could not only talk the talk but walk the walk as a sort of uberpublicist. Before newcomers could come out, or be "launched" in the parlance of deb trade, however, Strong made sure they were ready. This part of the process demanded something she called a "Pygmalion Job." "You can't take people with hayseed sticking out all over them and call them socialites," she made clear. "You have to hone them down." While Strong's kind of professional services had taken the care and feeding of the nouveau riche to a different level ("Social climbing is no longer a pastime—it's an occupation," she insisted), there was a long history of prominent family members taking a newbie under his or her wing for a fee on the down low. Social secretaries even more subtly helped propel New Money into the social scene, typically when the client hosted a cocktail party to which a few A-listers could be persuaded to attend. Whether undertaken by an amateur, semiprofessional, or professional, it was usually wise to start bumpkins on the B-list before trying the A-list, a sort of wading in the shallower end of the pool before diving into the deep end headfirst.[31]

As well, delicacy of the first order was required if mentions in the society pages were part of the campaign. The worst-case scenario was that the launchee get mistaken for a publicity hound or, heaven forbid, someone in the entertainment industry. The father of society public relations, at least in postwar New York, was one Count Lanfranco Rasponi, who had been plugging both individuals and businesses since the late forties. The Count explained the need for his kind of services: "Society is no longer a '400,' it's more like 20,000 or 30,000." With its fast pace, constant reinvention, and ruthless competition, New York society demanded a publicity component, the Count believed, in stark contrast to Paris or London, where a five-year absence would not affect one's social standing. Despite this (and the Count's name), the historically unique American phenomenon of society public relations was gradually spreading to Europe as gossip columns sprang up in newspapers there.

Interestingly, it was more difficult for a native New Yorker of newish money to enter Big Apple society than someone from a small town in another part of the country. The latter's obscure background presented an advantage over the former's well-known nouveau status. As well, when an arriviste couple used their teenage daughter as a wedge into society, the scheme could backfire if the girl had, as Strong tactfully put it, "nothing to recommend her." Strong felt that given eight or ten years to work with she could do something with a young lemon, but by, say, age 16, such a girl was a lost cause. Strong was powerless when it came to getting people into the *Social Register*, and not even an act of God could get a young outsider into the Junior Assemblies or her parents onto certain Upper East Side charity committees.[32] There were the right people, after all, and then there were the really right people.

THE STATUS SEEKERS

Most agreed that the flattening of the wealth curve in the 1950s (oil money being the notable exception) was a good thing; it allowed more Americans to share a piece of the prosperity pie and moved us closer to the national mythology of equality. There were, however, exceptions to this rosy picture, particularly when it came to patronage of cultural activities, which, as the richest of the rich got less rich, seemed to be suffering. The very tip of the wealth pyramid had indeed shrunk (276 individuals made $1 million or more in 1955 versus 513 in 1929), these very wealthy the ones most likely to support the arts with the kind of contributions that could make a huge impact. "The magnificent angels who used to sponsor the opera and the theatre, build college dormitories and municipal auditoriums, support orchestras, back promising writers, painters, sculptors, dancers are gone," bemoaned Helen Hill Miller in 1958, "their feathers plucked by time and the income tax." Miller and others feared that with the rise of the middle class at the expense of the super-rich, the days of there being another Morgan Collection, Mellon Galleries, (Rockefeller-endowed) Colonial Williamsburg, Duke University, Hayden Planetarium, or Huntingdon or Carnegie Library were over, victim at least in part of the federal government's conscious effort to stack the deck in favor of the "average" American.[33] "The genuinely rich can do great things, in building, in founding educational and charitable institutions, in patronage of the arts," echoed Russell Kirk in 1963, "while modest fortunes allow their possessors only the indulgence of consumer appetites."[34]

Other institutions were not exactly happy either as Old Money slipped off the marble pedestal of the American rich in the postwar years. Many private clubs in big cities, for example, were in quite a quandary as the dynamics of wealth churned in the 1950s, unsure if they should try to stay aboard what appeared to be a sinking ship or rather reinvent themselves to meet the interests of a new, different kind of wealthy individual. There was little doubt that the fraternity of the wealthy elite that existed before the war had by all measures broken down by the late 1950s. In more fluid, mobile, and class-averse postwar America, "old boys" (and "old girls") were still around, of course, but hardly the tight community they used to be.[35] Some clubs were trying to hang on to their tight membership policies even as old-line members were heading off to the Big Bridge Game, while others were pursuing rising stars in business, recognizing that these men represented their future. The former, the Wall Street Journal reported, "fail to see that the so-called social aristocracy is in the ascendancy," the newspaper knowing firsthand that Corporate America had changed the rules of the game with the perks it happily and freely handed out to its executives. Expense accounts were in fact responsible for as much as 90 percent of revenues at some clubs, paid by members who, as one manager put it with no complaints at all, "will spread his damned papers all over the luncheon table."[36]

The pressure traditional clubs were feeling from "below" was just one sign of the blurring lines between the wealthy and the new upper-middle class of the late fifties. "Increasingly," wrote Richard Schickel for The Nation in 1959, "you can't tell the rich without a tax return," as an increasingly prosperous middle class, often equipped with credit cards and expense accounts, brought democracy to the marketplace.[37] Emulating the rich had in fact become a popular pastime for many middle-class Americans, which was made more possible by the ability to rent luxury if one couldn't afford to actually buy it. Many museums and galleries across the country (even MOMA) had gone into the business of renting original paintings, for example, and fine antiques were also available on a part-time basis at a fraction of the cost of owning them. Hosts wishing to impress their friends could have cooks, bartenders, and butlers along with silver, china, and linen delivered to their house with just a phone call, turning an ordinary dinner party into quite the fancy affair. Formal gowns and minks could be had for a special night on the town and a chauffer-driven Cadillac rented for just $7 an hour. In a few cities, even a yacht complete with captain could be temporarily had, an experience guaranteed to make anyone with $100 (mini-orchestra or catered meal extra) feel and look like a king or queen for a day.[38]

As the bourgeoisie took on the trappings of the affluent in the 1950s, a wide variety of voices were quick to point out that the American upper class had, thankfully, not disappeared, but rather had been made over into something new and, nearly everyone agreed, far less exciting. "The power of money has not vanished," wrote David Cushman Coyle for the New York Times in 1951, "but it has taken a more corporate and less personal form."[39] Fortune, the following year, saw it similarly, stating, "Since 1945 a brand-new crop of rich men has risen in the U.S.," describing this new crop as "studiously democratic and almost instinctively labor minded."[40] Vance Packard, whose landmark 1959 The Status Seekers was just about to be published, likewise claimed in Ladies' Home Journal that, "Our new fortune builders are perhaps less colorful than the glamorous millionaires of more reckless eras . . . [but] prove that [America] is still a land of opportunity for the individualistic adventurer."[41] That same year, Cleveland Amory astutely assessed the less-than-meteoric ascent of the not-very-colorful rich, noting that "the combination of borrowing, going to bed with tax books, and amalgamating and merging tax loss situations has hardly caught the fancy of the American public in the same way the old Horatio Algering, empire-building buccaneers did a century ago." Had "real" millionaires gone totally extinct, some wondered? One woman from Pittsburgh felt strongly that Eugene Grace, the recently retired chairman of Bethlehem Steel, was the last real millionaire at the end of the decade, the proof in the plum pudding being that she always felt "like standing up when he comes into the room, as if he were the Pope or something."[42]

The wholesale enlistment in the postwar military-industrial complex was largely responsible for the narrowing of the gulf between the upper and middle classes. "All sorts of inducements to zeal and productivity have been proffered to an ever-enlarging group of qualified people," *Look* pointed out in 1961, naming credit cards, stock options, profit sharing, expense accounts, club memberships, and the personal use of company-owned cars as perks that were "help[ing] commoners to live like kings." A look at the lifestyles of Packard's "status seekers" confirmed that the peasants were beginning to look a lot like the folks in the big house on the hill. Home ownership had jumped about 50 percent in the 1950s, and second homes were increasingly popular among the upper-middle class. More amazingly, there were just 3,600 swimming pools in the whole country in 1951, but 77,000 were constructed in 1961 alone. Traveling internationally for recreation, a fairly ridiculous idea for the middle class before the war, was approaching the ordinary. Skilled workers, housewives, students, teachers, clerks, and secretaries received the majority of passports in 1960, according to State Department data, a rather remarkable shift in who was going where.[43]

The blurring of lines between the wealthy and the upper-middle class—as clear as day just a generation earlier—was for the former well worth the cost of appearing less fascinating. Disliked or distrusted in the thirties and early forties by the average American, who felt the rich had not had to undergo the hard times and sacrifices they themselves had, the wealthy had been, rather suddenly, redeemed. "It is not only easier to get rich," observed *Look* in 1961, "it is also more acceptable." A less onerous tax rate, more entrepreneurial business climate, and easier access to Wall Street had made rich people, in a word, more likable, no longer akin to Ebenezer Scrooge or *It's A Wonderful Life*'s evil banker, Mr. Potter. The magazine explained the cultural shift: "The ways in which wealth is now being achieved are useful and creative"—not exactly how you would describe the robber baron's scorch-the-earth methods for acquiring their fortunes.[44] "The classic doctrine that great fortunes are always ill-gotten is losing force," agreed William Letwin the following year, "and the image of the Robber Baron is being superceded by that of the Efficient Manager." Much of the romance of the wealthy elite may very well have disappeared, but at least the rich had been transformed into decent, if boring, people.[45]

After the war, the shifting dynamics of the American rich could also be felt at the nation's most elite universities. A study in 1964 discovered that fewer and fewer sons of socially prominent families were attending the "Big Three": Harvard, Yale, and Princeton; they were displaced by less wealthy, more academically qualified students. Meritocracy was replacing aristocracy as these universities gradually and somewhat reluctantly prioritized intellect over social status and inheritance in their admission process, a decision with huge implications in terms of the makeup of the next generation of the upper class. Interestingly, a similar thing had occurred after the Civil War, when the sons of a reshuffled upper class began to attend distant colleges made more accessible by train.

While choosing talent over wealth was perhaps democracy at its best, some administrators were concerned that rejecting less qualified but rich students would hurt their university's bottom line. The sons of the British well-to-do, however, were still following in the footsteps of their fathers' exclusive alma maters, Oxford and Cambridge; the heads of these universities were apparently more interested in where their scones were buttered than in egalitarian ideals.[46]

INCONSPICUOUS CONSUMERS

The implications of the collision of Old and New Money and of the upper and upper-middle classes in postwar America were, of course, many and far-reaching. Most important, perhaps, was the encroachment of middle-class values among the rich, especially as consumers. Anticipating "the millionaire next door" of some forty years later, in 1952 *Fortune* saw these new rich as much different than the variety that Veblen had famously described in his 1899 *Theory of the Leisure Class* and which had served as the primary archetype of the wealthy American through the first and, to some extent, second world war. "These individuals, the inconspicuous consumers, live no fancier than does the $12,000-a-year neighbor down the street," the magazine reported, quite a remarkable thing given that up to that point, the American rich had indeed acted, well, rich. Although this under-the-radar affluent likely had a new house and a big car—who didn't in 1950s America, one can ask at least half-seriously—he and his wife typically sent their kids to public school and had no servants or cook, both breaks from the traditions of the prewar upper class.[47]

Others chirped in about what they saw as a sea change in the ways of the rich. "The old habits of smoking cigars wrapped in hundred-dollar bills, throwing banquets for dogs, or giving $50,000 parties with automobiles as door prizes are out," *Science Digest* had already observed in 1948, while *Coronet* in 1955 succinctly exclaimed, "Today's Millionaires are Pikers!" in its look back to when big money spent real money. "America still has wealthy people, but they don't live with the lavish prodigality of the older breed," the magazine observed, comparing the lifestyles of the Astors, Vanderbilts, and Schwabs to those of contemporary society. Ensconced in Park Avenue apartments instead of Fifth Avenue palaces, their parties held in nightclubs and restaurants rather than their own ballrooms, the mid-century rich paled in comparison to those of the turn of the century when it came to showing off their wealth. Sure, the New York, Washington, and Hollywood A-list didn't flinch at spending $10,000 on a party, but their predecessors had spent that on *flowers* for a party. "The old titans not only had money but were proud of it, want[ing] to advertise their bank balances to the world," *Coronet* reminded readers, this peacock-like behavior now as dated as a Victorian corset.[48] Keeping up with or staying one step ahead of the Joneses was one thing, it seemed, but looking like the Vanderbilts was quite something else; it simply did not fit within the everyone-is-middle-class ethos of the postwar years.

Even the two most beloved havens for the rich, Newport and Palm Beach, had lost much of their luster by the early fifties, invaded by the nouveau riche and, even worse, the not-so-rich. In Palm Beach, in fact, the president of the once ultra-prestigious Everglades Club resigned in frustration in 1952, a clear indication that the town was going to hell in a handbasket. "You have to be psychic to know who's who these days," declared Hugh Dillman, and "I'm not." Other members of society across the country, aware of the club's fall from grace, were sad to see one of their own go south. "Belonging to the Everglades Club today is like belonging to Grand Central Station," stated Harvey Ladew, Maryland's Master of Foxhounds. Newport was experiencing a similar fate as the formality and traditions of the grand social resort fell by the wayside, another victim of the more democratic, less elitist kind of plutocrat on the rise. "Frankly, I can't remember when I had a white tie on last," observed Schuyler Livingston Parsons, one of the Old Guard whose name alone suggested he'd worn quite a few in his time. Mrs. "Kitty Mouse" Cook, one of Newport's notable women-around-town, was more concerned about the trickle-down effect and specifically the local unemployment rate, thinking Newport's slide wasn't "so bad for us" but was "terrible for the servants."[49]

All was not lost, however, for either "us" or their servants. Fleeing Newport and Palm Beach like they were the *Titanic*, blue bloods washed ashore on two nearby resort communities, Fishers Island (off New London, Connecticut) and Hobe Sound (also called Jupiter Island, twenty-five miles north of Palm Beach). Ironically, these

sanctuaries for the rich were even more informal than the places
the who's who had left, but, more importantly, they were their own.
"We don't mind it getting crowded, if it's only our crowd," said
one resident of Fishers at the time, seconded by Mrs. "Bud"
Adams, wife of a real estate agent who worked both islands. Adams
maintained that, "Everyone knows that Fishers is the last stand in
the North and Hobe the last stand in the South"; her apparent view
was that barbarians were not only at the gate but ready to jump
over it. Henry L. Ferguson, whose family once owned all of Fishers,
likewise felt that the island was one of the few places left in the
United States for those he called "the right people," saying, "We
don't even have what you might call the wrong element of the
rich." A number of Du Ponts from Wilmington lived on Fishers,
in fact, while Hobe's tiny community of two hundred included
Whitneys from Long Island, Fords from Detroit, and Armours from
Chicago. Less than impressed with celebrities (Katherine Hepburn,
along with her sister Peggy, had been familiar faces there before
the war and, yes, each wore slacks), Hobeans once let Gary Cooper
drink his martini on the front steps of their beach club, there being
no open seats inside. (Cooper reportedly loved the inattention.)[50]

Happily for its residents, Hobe Sound and Fishers appeared to
be avoiding the fate of what had for its residents been the most
renowned of social islands, Jekyll. With its "one hundred millionaires," the island off Georgia's coast was said to account for one-
sixth of the world's wealth; this rather amazing claim seemed con-
ceivably accurate, given that its residents included the families of
J. P. Morgan (the younger), the Rockefellers, the Vanderbilts, the
Goodyears, the Goulds, and the Pulitzers. The resort closed in
1941, however, a victim of various economic factors, and was seized
by the state in 1947. A candidate running for governor that year,
eager to win votes, announced that if elected, he'd make it possible
for every man in the state to sleep in J. P. Morgan's bed, a rather
dated declaration of war on the super-rich if there ever was one.
Five years later, preparations were being made for "every man" to
actually enjoy this experience, as the cottages once occupied by the

richest people on the planet were in the process of being converted into a 4-H club.[51]

The rise of the inconspicuous consumer at the expense of Old Money in resorts like Newport and Palm Beach in the 1950s could be backed up with real numbers. In its 1957 survey of the very rich ($50 million or more), *Fortune* found that some of the iconic families of Old Money, notably the Morgans, Goulds, and Guggenheims, were no longer at the top of the heap. Other great American fortunes—those of the Rockefellers, Mellons, Du Ponts, Whitneys, Astors, and Harrimans—were as enormous as ever, however, their heirs having adjusted well to the new ways of preserving and multiplying wealth. Although all those on *Fortune*'s list of 155 "Fifty-Million-Dollar" men and women were pursuing their own particular paths when it came to how to spend their money, one thing was quite clear—there wasn't a ne'er-do-well in the bunch. "It is hard to find an out-and-out hedonist, dedicated solely to self-enjoyment, among the fifty millionaires," the magazine reported a little disappointedly, concluding, "The weight of $50 million seems to have a sobering effect on its possessors." Whether it was the Rockefellers' and Pews' philanthropy, the Harrimans' and Kennedys' politics, or the vast majority's determination to simply make more money, the work ethic of the extremely wealthy in the 1950s confirmed that, as *Fortune* neatly put it, "The sport of spending money has lost much of its dash."[52]

Boston, not too surprisingly, seemed to be the model of restraint when it came to millionaires' spending money or, more likely, not spending it, in the 1950s. Few private homes remained on the north side of Commonwealth Avenue—the address of choice through the 1920s—but it was on clothing where rich Bostonians really saved their pennies. "It is better to be a frump in Boston," said one observer of the wealthy scene, noting "they've all got a hat and they've all got a fur coat and they don't want any more." And while new shoes not that long ago had meant their owner was likely not on intimate terms with physical labor, the city's most affluent were wearing cracked and regularly repaired shoes around town without an iota of embarrassment. Their standing assured after a few generations of huge wealth, Boston's Brahmins had apparently embraced the trappings of Bohemian chic.[53]

The new conservatism of the wealthy after the war also affected how parents went about leaving money to their heirs. In fact, *Fortune* found that "the most nagging problem confronting today's Very Rich is their legacy," a problem many were solving by doling out their estates in small chunks over an extended period of time. Sometimes this sensible idea went to extremes, as in the case of a Chicago millionaire who decided to pass on his money only when his children reached the ripe age of fifty. Oil millionaires, fully aware of the here-today, gone-tomorrow nature of money made sometimes literally overnight, were especially careful not to give too much too soon to their children. (Regarding the sheer luck associated with the fortune of a certain Louisianan, another one explained that, "he made it on a herd of cattle—found an oil well under every cow.") The late Houston real estate and banking titan Jesse Jones, for example, left only $300,000 to his principal heir, a nephew, publisher of the *Houston Chronicle*, who was hardly likely to blow millions on racehorses and women. Another Big Rich from the Lone Star State was having his daughters learn typing, his fear being that they "may even be waiting tables before this deal is over."[54]

The "egghead millionaire" was a subset of the inconspicuous consumer of postwar America, a brand-new kind of rich archetype. Invariably men in their thirties whose science- or technology-based companies (almost always with the word "data," "instruments," "systems," or "research" in its name) had gone public, egghead millionaires, destined for $10,000-a-year jobs as researchers or professors, were in the right place at the right time as the Cold War made brainy types a hot property. Like dot-commers who hit it big with software or the Internet a few decades later, these guys had little interest in the trappings of wealth that others were so obsessed with. "They disdain keeping up with the Joneses," *Fortune* said of them in 1960. "In fact, they do not *know* the Joneses, and don't want to." Clustered in southern California (aerospace), northern Florida

(Cape Canaveral), Washington (the Pentagon), Boston (MIT), and San Francisco (Stanford, Berkeley), this group of affluents looked and acted like no others before them, completely oblivious to the usual codes of American wealth. Not only did these proto-nerds forgo the gray flannel suit for sports coats and chinos, but, when they weren't working (forty-eight plus hours a week), they preferred to ski rather than play golf or tennis or sail, a choice your typical well-off businessman didn't quite know what to make of.[55]

The rise of rich eggheads and the fact that there were about 100,000 millionaires in the United States in 1961 (versus 27,000 in 1953) were definite signs that the wealthy were now a legitimately diverse group, quite a different story than between the wars.[56] This diversity, ironically, pushed some to try to figure out if there was a common defining trait among the tremendously wealthy and, if so, what it was. In his 1961 study of six multimillionaires (American oilman J. Paul Getty; British retailer Simon Marks; Greek shipping magnate Aristotle Onassis; German industrialist Alfred Krupp; British takeover artist Charles Clore; and French textile tycoon Marcel Boussac), Welsh journalist Goronwy Rees discovered only one strong common link: an inclination to roll the dice and, after winning a hand or two, the guts to let it all ride. "It is the willingness to accept . . . huge risk," Rees wrote in *Multimillionaires: Six Studies in Wealth*, "that psychologically distinguishes the multimillionaire."[57] Another book published that same year, *The New Millionaires and How They Made Their Fortunes*, by the editors of the *Wall Street Journal*, identified a somewhat different but related common denominator among the super-rich: extreme self-confidence. Other factors one would think mattered quite a bit when it came to making a fortune—place of birth, how much money one's father had made, even education level—were of little or no importance, the authors of this study found.[58] Whether the secret to getting rich was a large capacity for risk-taking or a profound faith in oneself, one thing seemed clear—the wealthiest of the wealthy did it on their own, more so than your run-of-the-mill millionaire.

MASS LUXURY

Alongside the rise of inconspicuous consumption in the 1950s was
the phenomenon of mass luxury, another idea that would have
been considered largely oxymoronic before the war. We tend to
think of the democratization of luxury as a relatively recent thing,
brought to us by the likes of Target and IKEA, but the middleclass-
ing of fine living has been around for more than half a century.
"Luxury has reached the masses in the U.S.," proclaimed *Fortune*
in 1953, reporting the concept to be "more spectacular, pervasive,
[and] significant" than any other change in the American marketplace. Luxury, historically the province of the few in both the
United States and Europe, had become, according to the business
magazine, "unexceptional, habitual, functional," no longer the exclusive domain of the wealthy elite. With Americans' income
steadily rising as the postwar economy chugged along (J. Walter
Thompson estimated that U.S. households had $138 billion in dis-
cretionary spending power in 1953 versus $27 billion in 1940), the
previously distinct markers between what was a "necessity" and
what was a "luxury" were blurring, making the marketplace much
more complex and confusing. High-end furs, haute couture, rare
gems, and customized cars—the latter the tricked-out or pimped-
up wheels of their day—remained unaffordable for all but the most
affluent, but most other goods were firmly within the grasp of the
new upper-middle class. Whether business executive or tradesman,
"$20,000-a-year-men" were buying the heart and soul of the Ameri-
can Dream—a suburban house with state-of-the-art appliances and
a two-car garage filled with Chrysler Imperials and Buick hard-
tops—lock, stock, and barrel, something well beyond the reach of
most citizens before the war.[59]

The early 1950s were the years in which the concept of "mass
luxury" was officially born, offering millions of Americans what *Fortune* referred to as "few precious rarities but many non-necessities."
Some things that only the wealthy could afford a generation earlier,
say a well-appointed bathroom or a good lightweight summer suit,

had become almost standard equipment for the middle class, while true luxuries, e.g., electrically heated socks and a coffeemaker with gold plating ($19.95 a pair and $50, respectively) were popular holiday gifts in 1953. Activities once exclusively reserved for the smart set had become the stuff of weekend recreation for the average Joe. There were far fewer yachts but many more boats cruising around in the 1950s, for example, a clear sign that the middle class was co-opting the wealthy in the postwar years. Some staples of the upper class—custom tailoring, for instance—had all but gone extinct in the United States, its cachet no longer what it used to be, while the quality of an off-the-rack suit had significantly improved. Two principal social themes of the fifties—conformity and what Alain Bottum would later term "status anxiety"—seemed to drive the spread of mass luxury, the contradictory desires to both fit in and stand out from the crowd proving to be powerful incentives to surround oneself with the symbols of the good life.[60]

As mass luxury became business as usual for affluents in the 1950s, it was natural that true luxury return to the wealth scene as the postwar economy continued to chug along. In particular, the renaissance of the newly built mansion was a sign that the American economy had fully revived and that being wealthy was no longer something to be ashamed or embarrassed about as was often the case during the Depression and war. "Rich Americans have begun to build big expensive houses again," reported *Fortune* in 1955, noting that precious few had been constructed over the last quarter-century and that many older mansions had been torn down or sold to corporations and institutions. High taxes, a lack of servants, and public scorn toward those living in one of these white elephants had pushed many of the wealthy to rid themselves of the "big house" and, often, take up much more modest digs somewhere on or near the grounds, such as the gardener's cottage.[61]

Even some of the richest people in the country had to endure this ignominy, as practicality took precedent over their absurdly lavish lifestyles of a previous era. In 1957, for example, Mrs. Horace Dodge, the widow of the automotive tycoon, gave up Playa Riente, considered by many to be the grandest house in Palm Beach, which she had bought for $2 million thirty years earlier (when she and the Fords were considered by local society to be "just rich mechanics," as one socialite later put it). Unable to find and manage the requisite number of servants to keep up the 100-room house, Dodge tried to sell it to a private school, but the town's zoning board nixed the idea. Forced to tear it down and auction off the furnishings, Dodge decided to go out in style with a party like those in the good old days, when the rich behaved as if they were rich. More than two hundred members of New York and Palm Beach society danced to two orchestras, sipped from a champagne fountain, and snacked on Beluga caviar served from, of course, a carved-ice swan, much like the previous generation of the wealthy would have done in the Roaring Twenties. Now homeless (her other mansion in Gross Pointe was also too difficult to keep up, and her yacht required a seventy-eight-person crew), Dodge moved into a two-story apartment at the (no longer chic) Everglades Club. Fortunately, the octogenarian was able to take along her Empress Catherine of Russia string of pearls, said to be the finest in the world, which her husband had bought for her after winning his $40 million suit against Henry Ford.[62]

By the mid-fifties, however, the rash of new $250,000 houses springing up around the country—quite an exorbitant sum of money at the time—signaled the comeback of the most obvious symbol of wealth. Unlike the grand mansions of the late nineteenth and early twentieth centuries, however, these new versions were designed primarily for informal living and family comfort, with features like rumpus rooms, outdoor grills, and five-car garages. "It seems to be the spirit of the Fifties to spend a lot of money on a new house (often pretending you haven't spent so much) and try to live more or less as you would in a suburban split-level," concluded *Fortune*, aptly capturing the new, more populist brand of wealth coursing through postwar America.[63] More importantly, the return of the big house was a harbinger that, after almost three decades of keeping a low profile, the American rich were crawling out from under their collective rock.

"The Rich Come Out of Hiding," *BusinessWeek* happily proclaimed in 1958, the magazine's "scouts" seeing definite signs that
"the old inhibitions, the taboos on spending, are fading," especially
in New York. "The rich . . . are coming out of their holes, and
they're having a ball," agreed one top interior designer; another
said, "The wealthy no longer have anything to be defensive about."
Spencer Samuels, president of French & Co., a posh art and antiques dealer, also believed that "being rich has lost its stigma"; he
and his competitors were delighted that affluents were once again
dropping thousands on a single painting. The Draconian income
and inheritance taxes levied on the rich appeared to be instilling a
use-it-or-lose-it philosophy, and a falling dollar was sufficient cause
to convert extra cash into valuable objets d'art and jewelry.[64]

The renaissance in high-end consumerism was also due to the
more sophisticated breed of nouveau riche, who knew what they
wanted and were prepared to pay for it (while typically driving a
hard bargain). Unlike those of the recent and not-so-recent past,
New Money of the late fifties knew their way around a Tiffany store,
quite aware of which china and silver were a good value and which
were for suckers with Ben Franklins burning holes in their pockets.
For marketers of luxury goods, New Money was much more important than Old, the former more likely to be in full acquisitional
mode, to have more liberal tastes, and rather bluntly, to still be
alive and kicking. The loosening of affluents' wallets and pocket-
books was not yet a national phenomenon, however; those in more
conservative, older-line cities like Boston, Milwaukee, and New Or-
leans were still saving for the proverbial rainy day.[65]

And like in the good old days, the wealthy were buying art in
bulk, building world-class collections in the process. As the robber
barons or their wives did a half century or so earlier, postwar barons
like Chicago's Nathan Cummings (Consolidated Foods), L.A.'s Edward Carter (Broadway-Hale Stores), and Norton Simon (Hunt
Foods) were making regular buying trips to Europe, gobbling up
Old Masters with New Money. "Having a Renoir or a Picasso in
your living room today is more important than owning two Cadil-

lacs," said one wealthy St. Louisan, fully aware that anything mass
produced and mass consumed carried little real social currency in
the big leagues. (That apparently wasn't stopping Lincoln from introducing two new models, each designed to be driven by a chauffeur.) Tastes in art seemed to reflect the cities in which collectors
lived, an ideal breeding ground for a healthy, competitive market.
Seventeenth-century Dutch was particularly hot in Philadelphia;
Atlantans preferred American paintings; and Seattleites collected
contemporary and Asian works. As well, collectors were loaning
their works to museums in return for full acknowledgment, something many would have avoided just a few years back.

Besides the renewed interest in art collecting, more cases of
extreme extravagance, recalling those of the Gilded Age, seemed
to be popping up. Detroit auto kings were on an island-buying
spree; travel to Russia, the Far East, and Africa was up; and sales at
Harry Winston and Van Cleef & Arpels were booming. In L.A., a
few gourmet societies had recently formed; one in Beverly Hills
flew in two chefs from Maxim's, along with the Parisians' special
pans, silverware, and Baccarat wine glasses, for a $300-a-plate din-
ner. Reports of the death of the American rich were, it seemed,
greatly exaggerated.[66]

NINE MILLIONAIRES AND A PLUMBER

The American rich were certainly alive and well in politics, of
course, with the entire string of postwar presidents getting wealthy
or significantly adding to their portfolios while in or as a result of
being in office. The best example of someone becoming wealthy as
a result of being president in the twentieth century had to be Harry
Truman who, before being elected, was not just broke but reportedly $50,000 in debt (he even had to put Bess on the payroll when
he became vice president in 1945). When he left the White House
in 1953, however, Truman had about half a million dollars in the

bank, much of it from scrimping on his $90,000 annual travel and entertainment allowance. (Apparently the buck really did stop at the man's desk.) Even Margaret, his daughter, had made hundreds of thousands of dollars from her singing career while her dad was in office, her fame as the first daddy's little girl no doubt a bigger factor in her success than her chalk-on-a-blackboard voice. While Truman's salary was not that of your typical rich man ($75,000 to $100,000 during his eight-year run), the perks definitely resembled those of a free-spending millionaire. The thrifty man from Independence, Missouri, lived in a mansion rent-free, had a twelve-room vacation retreat in Key West, a yacht with a 164-man crew that cost $500,000 to keep up, a plane, a private railroad car, and a fleet of limousines, including one that was bulletproof and had gold-plated fixtures. Truman also had a staff at his disposal—three military aides, five personal assistants, a pool of secretaries, a personal physician, a private lawyer, and nine chauffeurs—that probably rivaled that of the richest man in America, except maybe that of higher-than-high-maintenance Howard Hughes.[67]

Despite these posh perks and the fact that Truman had clearly benefited financially from being president, politics and wealth were, where the public was concerned, uncomfortable bedfellows. President Eisenhower came under particular criticism for stacking his first administration with rich men; his "millionaire Cabinet" was considered by some as a symbol of the cultural divide between Republicans and Democrats. People joked that his first cabinet consisted of "nine millionaires and a plumber," and when the ex-plumber (Secretary of Labor Martin P. Durkin, who had been the head of the United Association of Plumbers and Pipe Fitters union) resigned, just the millionaires were left. Among the cabinet appointees and three secretaries of the armed forces were a total of seven millionaires and seven nonmillionaires, giving Eisenhower a .500 batting average when it came to rich men on his staff. A look back on FDR's New Deal and Truman's "Fair Deal" administrations revealed that while each of these former presidents included rich men on their own staffs, the Republicans were indeed running ahead of the Democrats on the millionaire-as-appointee quotient. Only seven of FDR's twenty-five cabinet officers were millionaires, while only six of Truman's thirty-two appointees were wealthy (the richest was clearly W. Averill Harriman, who served under both presidents), a far lower percentage than Eisenhower's even money, so to speak. Still, Eisenhower's "millionaire Cabinet" followed a long tradition in politics of direct involvement of the wealthy, particularly in diplomatic service as ambassadors. Rockefellers, Whitneys, Guggenheims, and Mellons had all served as public servants, their success in private life (and connections, of course) making them much sought after by sitting presidents, who were no doubt also eager to rub shoulders with them in hopes some of their good fortune might rub off.[68]

Lesser political offices, not only the presidency, attracted the media and public's attention when one or both candidates were undeniably filthy rich. The increasing likelihood that Nelson Rockefeller would challenge incumbent W. Averill Harriman for governor of New York in 1958 was too much of an embarrassment of riches, one might say, to not recall the often more than platonic relationship between wealth and politics. That Harriman, heir to a huge railroad fortune, and Rockefeller, inheritor of a vast oil empire, would each be in such a position was obviously more than coincidence, which challenged one of the fundamental American mythologies: That we were a nation in which self-made men, not aristocrats, ruled. The truth was something different, of course; the line of presidents, from Washington to FDR (the two loudest voices of the common man, ironically), was peppered with men of considerable wealth. Even Andrew Jackson, the populist frontiersman, was part of the landed gentry, truth be told, another blow to the idea that most American politicians grew up in log cabins.

The rich man's desire to be king of America really kicked in during the reign of the robber barons, however, when businessmen realized that political clout was the path of least resistance toward reaping monopoly-style profits, turning the federal government into what E. Digby Baltzell called "a profit-sharing annex of Wall

Street." A generation later, FDR and his crew of noblesse oblige entered politics for a much different cause—to help bail the nation out of the Depression; they were succeeded by a group of wealthy Republicans determined to run government their way. Underlying all these changes of the guard was of course the most seductive elixir of all, power. "Power is ancient wealth," goes an old Chinese proverb, with many a rich man understanding that Washington was the place they'd have to go to get it.[69]

As Election Day 1958 approached, it was clear that two of the richest men in America would spend whatever was necessary to win New York's State's "battle of the millionaires." By mid-October, the Republicans had spent almost $1 million on Rockefeller's bid for governor, quite a bit of money at a time when television was still a relatively young medium. A good chunk of this money came from Rockefeller's family and some close family friends, namely the Astors, Du Ponts, Whitneys, Firestones, Guggenheims, and Aldriches. The Democrats countered with almost as much money to keep Governor Harriman in office. Like Rockefeller, his own family kicked in thousands of dollars, and support came from those nice people down the block, the Morgenthaus and Lehmans.[70] Rockefeller won the race by a wide margin; talk was in the air that he would make a run for the presidency in 1960 even before he got to Albany.[71]

Although Rockefeller did not make a bid for president that term, another rich man did, again raising scrutiny about the intersection between politics and wealth. In his campaign to become the Democratic candidate for president in 1960, Hubert Humphrey positioned himself against John F. Kennedy, whose family money was famously, or perhaps infamously, well known. "I don't think elections should be bought," Humphrey told a crowd in West Virginia, pointing out to the mostly economically disadvantaged audience that he was the only party candidate who was not a millionaire and who had grown up poor. While some of his rivals "had been born with silver spoons in their mouths," Humphrey went on, he as a child had watched his mother "crying when our family home had to be sold," something a fair share of his listeners could easily relate to.[72]

In his own attempt to appeal to the common man and preempt such kinds of attacks while running for president against Barry Goldwater the following election, LBJ took the bull by the horns by releasing his financial statement to the public in 1964. The document, issued by the White House, showed that the Johnsons were worth about $3.5 million, but this figure, based on the original cost of Lady Bird's broadcasting stock and the president's ranchland versus its current market value, was obviously low. What was clear was that LBJ had made his fortune—estimated by some fellow Austinites as actually around $20 million—while in public office, something that the Goldwater camp readily described as "peculiar."[73] Although certainly not as rich as LBJ, Goldwater himself was reportedly loaded from his family's retail stores, described by his own banker as "a modest millionaire." The Republican candidate for president denied this, however, yet another attempt by a politician to minimize his economic standing in order to maximize his appeal to the average voter.[74]

Politicians' desires to keep their net worth on the QT captured the democratic spirit of the postwar years, when most wealthy Americans, even some of the richest people in the world, looked and acted like they were middle class. The upper end of the middle class, meanwhile, increasingly looked and acted like they were wealthy; these two forces smashed together to further erode Old Money elitism and exclusivity, already much weakened between the wars. The changes that took place in the postwar years, as vast as they were, were pocket change compared to those about to happen in the late 1960s and 1970s, however, as a new generation brought revolution to the streets of the American rich.

CHAPTER 4

LORD, WON'T YOU BUY ME A MERCEDES-BENZ? 1965–1979

"Lucre used to be filthy, but now it's lovely."
—KENNETH LAMOTT, 1977

I N NOVEMBER 1977, FORTY-EIGHT PEOPLE GATHERED IN A SAN Francisco hotel ballroom for a four-day therapy session, during which both food and bathroom breaks would be in short supply. This wasn't an est session, although it did share much in common with Werner Erhard's group awareness training seminars, which had also been born in San Francisco and were now sweeping across the country (and, in the process, making Erhard more than $13 million that year). As with est training, these participants sought to solve personal problems by directly and emotionally confronting them, a classic example of the pursuit of "self-improvement" that was all the rage during the decade. The kind of problems these attendees wanted to solve, however, were exclusively about money—specifically how to get more of it or feel better about it if you already had a lot of it.

This was Prosperity Training, a therapy steeped in the novel idea that wealth was a virtuous thing or, in self-help speak, "I'm-ok-if-I'm-rich, you're-ok-if-you're-rich." Through a variety of intensive games and exercises (including chewing $1 bills), the guilty rich and puzzled poor would develop positive feelings about money, the twenty-eight-year-old founder of Prosperity Training, Leo Sunshine, promised, as his students came to the big realization that, as he put it, "abundance is a natural state." "I want to bring the fundamentals of prosperity to those who want to clear out their self-limiting attitudes and conditioning," said Sunshine, a.k.a. Brian Murphy, who often used a hand puppet named "El Protecto" to get his points across. Although his methods were perhaps a mite unorthodox, Sunshine seemed to have mastered his own teachings, earning about $360,000 a year from his seminars and additional revenue from $5,000-a-pop private training sessions.[1]

The popularity of Sunshine's course was just one of many signs that a major shift had occurred in the nation's psyche when it came to money. Between the mid-1960s and late 1970s, Americans of all stripes embraced the idea of wealth as never before, believing that they had just as much right to be rich as anyone else. Wealth had somehow become not the exclusive province of an elite class but a normal, desirable state that anyone and everyone had claim to, completely devoid of the nefarious qualities associated with it at various times in the past. The focus on the self and the splintering of American society would have much to do with this trend, of course, as the postwar consensus crumbled into an ideology of every man for himself and—for perhaps the first time in history— every woman for herself.

Although the rich had long been a source of fascination for intellectuals and laypeople alike, during the counterculture years the wealthy emerged as a distinct subculture worthy of study. Like other slices of the American pie, wealth culture has its own social dynamics, academics and journalists discovered; they also found they had a receptive audience for any information at all relating to the rich. Palm Beach was undoubtedly the winter home of the remaining Old Money, but it was the international jet set, or "Beautiful People," who really commanded people's attention, their (often cosmetically enhanced) good looks and glamorous lifestyles a source of considerable envy for the rest of us. Rich would get hip in the late sixties, the party at the Old Boys' Club crashed by the likes of movie stars, fashion designers, professional athletes, rock stars, and the occasional radical. Others historically barred from entry—gays, African Americans, and women—would also get in the door in the seventies, ensuring American wealth culture would from now on be a much more diverse affair.

THE SELF-MADE MAN

Millionaire mania didn't change a bit in the mid-sixties, however, as the postwar American Dream reached its zenith. The Horatio Alger mythology, the idea that anyone could become not just successful but rich, was at its peak, now a central theme in American society. And because of a host of factors—including rapidly changing technology, the shift to a service economy, and Americans' proven desire for pretty much anything either new or improved— wealth was now, more than ever, a realizable goal. Easier credit at modest annual interest rates (5 percent, on average, in 1965) and more consumers with more money than ever before also created a perfect climate for risk-takers to beat the odds. It was, in fact, the "self-made man" who best symbolized the American rich in the mid-sixties: the ambitious, energetic (often workaholic), and confident entrepreneur who, in classic fashion, came up with an idea and made it happen, conquering the myriad of obstacles that typically stood in the way.[2]

The ways these men, and the occasional woman, made their money were all over the map, with no particular recipe for success except perhaps an overwhelming faith in oneself and in the merit of one's pursuit. Mobile-home builders, publishers of trade journals, and makers of convenience foods were all seizing the day, contributing to the booming postwar economy and, in return, getting their piece of the pie. Developing or manufacturing new technologies, from transistors to microwave ovens to computer parts, was a common path to wealth, as was involvement in all aspects of the real estate business, from construction to mortgages. Banking and life insurance also remained staples of the how-to-get-rich scheme, of course, but more creative enterprises better illustrated the entrepreneurial spirit that was flourishing and, quite often, rewarded. Joseph McVicker, for example, a thirty-four-year-old Cincinnatian, was enjoying the fruits of his labor, which he literally cooked up in his kitchen when he transformed a doughlike wallpaper cleaner into a nonsticking modeling compound for children. "Play-Doh," as he called the stuff, would never sell, said the toy industry experts he showed it to, but McVicker knew better. By 1965, he was selling $4 million a year of the goop. Meanwhile, across the state, another relatively young man, Art Modell, had recently come up with the notion of installing TV sets in supermarkets and selling advertising on them, an idea that proved to be in the right place at the right time. The forty-one-year-old former shipyard worker made so much money from his idea that he went out and bought the local football team, the Cleveland Browns, something that turned out to be another wise business decision as professional sports franchises evolved into big moneymaking operations.[3]

In some ways, entrepreneurs like McVicker and Modell were following in the giant footsteps of a century past: Men like Rockefeller, Carnegie, and Harriman who had started out poor and had taken full advantage of their own era's version of free enterprise. Rather than railroads or oil, things like textured stockings, electric carving knives, skateboards, and diet cola were now the stuff of fortune building, marking the cultural shift from industry to consumption. Also like their nineteenth-century predecessors, the new rich of the mid-1960s were working ten- to twelve-hour days as well as nights and weekends, driven to succeed and thriving on the competition (their marriages often a casualty). Self-made men were not only bypassing corporate life, which allowed only a few to squeeze through the layers of bureaucracy, but traditional roads to wealth like medicine, law, and architecture, not at all cut out for the kind of discipline these professions required.

While usually not the brightest guys in the room, these entre- preneurs were highly focused, able to keep their eyes on the prize. And men like Howard Prince were bringing sound management principles to their businesses, knowing that it was the less than glamorous aspects, like good accounting practices, that often meant the difference between success and failure. In 1965, the thirty-seven-year-old New Yorker had made his first million on Broadway by producing an amazing run of ten hit musicals, includ- ing *Damn Yankees*, *West Side Story*, and *Fiddler on the Roof*; his skills at keeping costs down were as important as his keen instinct for a hit show. "In no other country of the world, at no other time in history, have the chances to make a fortune been better than right now," claimed *Time* that year, something that the American rich of a generation earlier, thinking their days were numbered, would have found very difficult to believe.[4]

Indeed, the postwar flood of American millionaires seemed to be showing no signs of receding. There were seven times as many millionaires in 1965 than 1948, with 90,000 American families— one in every 625—now able to consider themselves part of this select breed. And with most of these millionaires' net worth in stock holdings, not in the bank, there were bound to be many more if the market continued on its bullish path.[5] The federal govern- ment's controversial income and inheritance tax policies designed to soak the rich had, apparently, hardly made a splash; millionaires increased at a faster rate than the population. Finding ways to avoid paying heavy taxes had in fact become one of the primary occupations of the rich. They simply put more of their money in increasingly popular Treasury bonds or hired an accountant or law- yer who could find a quasi-legal loophole with his eyes closed.

On paper at least, 40 percent of these millionaires were women, a remarkable statistic given how male-centric the earning of money remained. "The men may make the money in the first place, but somehow or other the women manage to get their hands on it," observed Herman M. Miller in the *New York Times*. Truer words were rarely uttered when it came to the accumulation of wealth.[6]

Rather than reduce the number of American rich through taxes targeted directly at them, in fact, Uncle Sam was doing virtually everything it could to help create more of them. The dime-a-dozening of millionaires in the mid-sixties had much to do with LBJ's "Great Society" programs, which pumped money into local economies and, by creating new jobs for the middle and lower classes, gave consumers more to spend in the marketplace. Federal funds devoted to health, education, and welfare were helping upper income groups as much as those with lower incomes; corporate executives and small-business owners alike benefited from the greater number of people able to afford houses and take vacations.[7] More than five hundred Americans made $1 million or more in 1966, this notable because the nation had finally produced as many millionaires as in 1929, when 513 achieved the feat. The American rich were, after a generation and a half, back in force.[8]

THE RICH AND THE SUPER-RICH

By the late sixties, so were the group now being called "the super-rich." More than 100,000 Americans were worth a cool million or more in 1968, a number big enough to nominate certain members to an even more exclusive club, the centamillionaires. One hundred and fifty-three Americans were worth at least $100 million, according to *Fortune*. J. Paul Getty, the seventy-five-year-old founder of his titular oil company, and Howard Hughes, the sixty-two-year-old aircraft and tool recluse, were the richest of the super-rich (with nary a Rockefeller, Ford, or Carnegie to be found nipping at their heels).[9]

While the president and vice president of this most exclusive of clubs took privacy to new extremes, they were not alone in their quest to distance themselves from public view. Mere millionaires were, as usual, interested in showing off their wealth to anyone and everyone who might notice, but the super-rich were becoming virtually obsessed with concealing theirs, often driving Buicks and hiding their big houses from view. Behind their hedges and privets, however, it was a different story, with pools and tennis courts galore on the outside (John D. Rockefeller's 3,500-acre compound in Tarrytown had its own 18-hole golf course) and, increasingly, high-tech features like projection rooms and closed-circuit TVs on the inside. Besides proving to oneself and others what good taste one had, collecting art was an ideal way to keep people from knowing how much one was worth. Paul Mellon, whose family's fortune remained intact, was an especially avid art collector, with masterpieces scattered around his houses like tchotchkes. Wandering around one of the banker's homes one day, in fact, Mellon's daughter and a classmate from Foxcroft, the Virginia boarding school, came across a Van Gogh. "Who paints in the family?" asked her friend, to which Mellon's daughter sensibly replied, "Nobody, Dad gets them at a store."[10]

The surge of millionaires in the late sixties was cause for a flurry of books about the American rich, each one in some way echoing Fitzgerald's observation that this particular group of people appeared to be somehow different. In his 1968 *The Rich and the Super-Rich*, Ferdinand Lundberg argued that a few hundred thousand families effectively controlled the fate of the nation, those elite Americans comprising a kind of "oligarchy of wealth." Lundberg claimed that just 2 percent of the country's households possessed 22 percent of its wealth, giving these large stockholders sway over corporations and, through their big political contributions, over lawmakers as well. Lundberg's view went against the grain of one of the most influential books of the fifties, C. Wright Mills's 1956 *The Power Elite*, which made the case that the rich were losing their exclusive grip on power.[11] Mills, backed by other leading intellectuals like Adolph Berle and John Kenneth Galbraith, saw the ranks of the military-industrial complex as rulers of the

game, while Lundberg considered them simple pawns. Because
their power was "appointed," Lundberg believed, even top corporate executives, politicians, and military brass were subservient to
those who held "true" power, i.e., the rich and, even more so, the
super-rich.[12]

Other authors took notice of the ascending power of the
wealthy in America and what appeared to be a growing divide between the rich and very rich. In his 1968 book, *The Rich: Are They
Different?*, George G. Kirstein observed that the rich and especially
the very rich were generally happy, although Old Money felt a sense
of guilt about the wicked ways of their nineteenth-century ancestors. Mingling with "the right people" to write his own book about
the wealthy, *The Right People: The Social Establishment in America*,
Stephen Birmingham discovered, among many other things, that
sports were "out" at the Ivy League schools, and not because organized and competitive activities were symbols of the establishment.
Golf, a mainstay of the prep crowd, had recently lost its cachet
because it had become popular among the upper-middle class, who
had learned the game at the country clubs their parents belonged
to. Another book of that year, Roy Perrott's *The Aristocrats*, took
another tack, arguing that British nobility were decidedly poorer
but much happier than the American rich, the former having mastered the fine art of living very well while having little or no money.
Whatever the thesis or approach of these books, it was clear that
the upper class had reached a new, higher plateau in the late 1960s,
as more millionaires with more millions distanced themselves from
the middle-class pack.[13]

If one were looking for the super-rich to observe if and how
they were different from both ordinary folks and the mere rich,
Palm Beach would be a good place to find them in the late sixties.
Although invaded by riffraff after the war, the place still had more
than its share of multimillionaires and, more importantly from a
sociological point of view, the increasingly rare Old Money. Three
billion dollars' worth of millionaires were said to flock down to
Palm Beach between November and April, including people with

last names like Vanderbilt, Du Pont, Phipps, Hearst, Drexel, Pillsbury, Pulitzer, Kellogg, and Kimberly. Just as had been true for the past century, those putting a guest list together for any kind of party placed those snowbirds of snowbirds at the top, acknowledging that the dwindling numbers of Old Money still commanded a kind of status that the multiplying-like-rabbits arriviste simply did not. Next on the list would be a gaggle of assorted nobility— princesses, countesses, ladies, and dames—followed by a nice mix of military officers—generals, commodores, and colonels—if only to add some color. Following them would be a few celebrities— Morton Downey, Dina Merrill, and Cliff Robertson were usually available—and after them, the plain rich. "The difficulty of hostesses here is that Palm Beach is facing its worst urban crisis in years: weeding out the new monied from the old monied," said one observer of the social scene, as one of the few remaining havens for "the best families" continued its downward slide.[14]

There were, however, definite clues as to who had had money for generations and who had not. New money paid for things with credit cards while Old used a check or cash, for example, and New were apt to put their initials on their license plates (and pretty much anywhere else). New sat in the backseat of their chauffer-driven cars alone, while Old sat up front and chatted with the driver as if he were a chum, which he usually was. New called their butlers by their last names in the traditional manner, while, ironically, Old were now using first names. New Money holed out all putts on the golf course—there was no such thing as a gimme in the ever-competitive world of nouveaus—while Old picked up any and all balls less than five feet away from the cup. If these signs failed to distinguish the two groups, one might simply take a look at a rich person's hairpiece, should he or she have one. New Money wore natural-looking toupees or wigs, trying to disguise the fact they were bald, balding, or otherwise hair-challenged; Old Money wore versions that could never be mistaken for their own hair, as if there were a certain status to be gained by wearing something on your head that resembled the working side of a mop. If only discernable by their hair, or lack thereof, it seemed there was a definite difference between those whose families had been wintering in Palm Beach for years and years and those who had just arrived.[15]

Although Palm Beachers disagreed about which particular event signaled that it was the height of the season—the sporting set said it was when Jack Nicklaus gave his annual exhibition at the Breakers for rich duffers, while the artsy set claimed it was St. Mary's Hospital's black-tie auction, while the fashion set was sure it was when Courrèges presented his spring collection—there was no doubt it was the place where, for half the year, one could rub patched elbows with the extremely rich. Not only was one still unable to find a cemetery, garbage dump, or hospital there (St. Mary's was across the tracks in West Palm Beach), but many of the town's grand estates had weathered the many storms of the last half century (both meteorological and financial).[16] Mrs. Anita Young, sister of Georgia O'Keeffe and widow of Robert Young, of New York Central money, retained thirty servants (twelve of them live-in) at her Palm Beach house; the joint was so big that the distance between the main salon and the dining room was, in the words of a friend, a "five iron." Eugene Howard's house, a trinket resulting from the Georgia Pacific Lumber fortune, had seventeen bedrooms and eighteen baths, so enormous that a housemaid once actually got lost there. "Somebody come get me! I don't know where I am!" the poor woman screamed, unable to find her way out of the maze-like mansion.[17]

The Howard's maid trap was hardly the most impressive quarters on the block, so to speak. The Dodge's Palm Beach spread had an amazing one hundred rooms, while Loeb Guinness of stout fame owned two adjacent homes that were connected by an underground music room. Besides this twin set (his and hers, perhaps?), Guinness and the Mrs. had four other houses scattered around the world; Jack and Dru Heinz had eight including their Palm Beach digs, and Sonny (Cornelius Vanderbilt) and Mary Lou Whitney six. It was Mrs. Marjorie Merriweather Post Close Hutton Davies May's Mar-A-Lago that reigned supreme among Palm Beach dwellings, however. The woman maintained a staff working in three eight-hour shifts to ensure anytime-you-want-whatever service for her guests. Mrs. Post, as she was (thankfully) better known, kept on hand not only three secretaries but three chefs (meat, pastry, and candy, naturally); her living expenses tallied up to a tidy $2 million a year. Noticing that a fair number of Palm Beachers were perfectly willing to spend whatever it took for top service, Eastern Airlines added "all-first-class" flights between New York and West Palm Beach (a forerunner of today's EOS service between New York and London), with porters lifting customers' bags right out of their cars and the ticketing done in the VIP lounge. To steal a competitor's ad slogan, this was "the only way to fly!"[18]

While the Palm Beach super-rich were living high on the hog (or in Mrs. Post's case, the candy) as the postwar economic boom further deflated in the late 1960s, ordinary millionaires were living more modestly and more informally. Most servants used to live on-site, for example, but now the wealthy were keeping few live-ins and bringing in "come-ins" on an as-needed basis (and shedding the antiquated term "servant" for the more professional "staff"). Guests making the party rounds were seeing staff more often than their friends, in fact, with the same local caterers, butlers, and maids hired for all the better events. Servants' rooms were fast disappearing from large estates, with just a handful of old-school rich—William Paley, Jock Whitney, and Charles Payson, to name a few New Yorkers—retaining large numbers of live-ins around the house. For those who could afford to keep live-ins, the rule was "the older the better." Because they'd been around the block a few times and then some, older butlers remembered when service was service and provided such, unlike young staff, who hardly knew from which side the turtle soup should be ladled. As in the old days, British butlers ranked number one, but black old-timers were also considered status symbols among a certain ilk of the American rich. In Hollywood, many of the Old Guard were selling their big houses because staffs were too expensive and difficult to maintain but, thankfully, the Beverly Wilshire Hotel was coming to their

FIGURE 4-1. Marjorie Merriweather Post at her Mar-a-Lago home in Palm Beach in 1965, a few decades before Donald Trump took over the mortgage. *(Morgan Collection/Getty Images)*

rescue, building new apartments for the displaced ex-moguls and stars.[19]

Childcare for the wealthy elite was also undergoing a major shift as the sixties wound down. With kids starting school earlier than they used to, governesses were usually no longer responsible for teaching children. "Governesses," in fact, were now often called "companions," younger and decidedly less dowdy than their predecessors, whose Victorian archetype had somehow survived until around Woodstock. Some companions, like that of recently remarried Jackie Kennedy Onassis, even wore miniskirts, an indication that the American rich had perhaps finally burst from its self-contained cocoon. Jackie O's brand of child rearing was in fact considered the model for the American rich: A British nanny was hired for the first five or six years, followed by a "mademoiselle" who could teach the children French. The Radziwills employed a French tutor for raising their kids, although the Sargent Shrivers hired no less than three governesses. The frugal Ted Kennedys retained just one nanny to help raise their kids, while his sister-in-law Ethel opted for a nurse to help bring up hers. Over in California, young English nannies were all the rage, like their East Coast sisters not required to wear uniforms. The notable exception was the Otto Premingers, whose governess looked straight out of *Mary Poppins*. The man, after all, was in the pictures.[20]

Ted Kennedy wasn't the only person of wealth not throwing money around like it grew on trees. His mother Rose famously carried her own clubs on the golf course, and Marlene Dietrich not only cooked for herself but scrubbed her own floors. David Rockefeller, Jock Whitney, and Averill Harriman rode around in a Chrysler, Buick, and Mercury respectively, not so much to save pennies but in British-style restraint, or "reverse snobbery." Wealthy Los Angelenos were hiring valet services for their parties rather than keeping staff around for such things, even on Holmby Hills, the short street in Bel Air known as "Millionaire's Row." Those in "the industry" had fallen head over heels with the whole idea of "come-in" services and were having both shoe repairmen and beauticians make house calls to cut down on staff and save time driving around the increasingly congested city.[21]

For each instance of scrimping or fiscal prudence among the American rich in the late sixties, however, there were many more cases of classic extravagance. Walter Annenberg kept a live-in golf coach on staff, for example, while Paul Mellon had his own art consultant ensconced in his home (presumably to help him pick out Van Goghs at "the store"). Private jets were becoming ever more popular among the wealthy elite (even while their moniker as the "Jet Set" became rather shopworn), with some owners flying the things themselves. Loeb Guinness kept one around (furnished with Louis XVI antiques) to get to and from his brewery in Ireland and various homes, and Joan Payson regularly used hers to make her appointed rounds. Richard Burton gave a one-million-dollar De Havilland jet to his wife Elizabeth Taylor, upon which Liz promptly gave Dick a half-million-dollar French Alouette helicopter. Helicopters, in fact, were becoming a prized possession of the more adventurous rich, with Lilly and Herbert Pulitzer and Ogden Phipps also investing in a chopper to make the short hop between their city town houses and their country places.

In both New York and L.A., company limos were fast replacing private, chauffeured cars; some drivers were former Pinkerton guards doubling as discreet bodyguards. Security at private parties had been on the rise following the 1965 kidnapping of the society couple John and Sheila Mosler and some big jewel heists, with guards (sometimes women in fancy gowns to keep even further under the radar) working undercover. For better or worse, the wealthy elite had come a long way from the relative intimacy and innocence of Mrs. Astor's ballroom.[22]

The cultural divide between New and Old Money was readily apparent well beyond the city limits of Palm Beach. The nouveau riche could be found engaged in a variety of folie de grandeur, all of them intended to bring attention to themselves and their hot-off-the-press cash. Circa 1969, things like a technology-loaded Rolls set a rich man apart from his older brethren, the finest car in the world apparently incomplete without a television, stereo, telephone, and Dictaphone. If hosting a party, the same man was apt to show every guest not only how large his new stereo was but how loud it would go (trumping Spinal Tap's volume of "11" by a decade or two). His wife, meanwhile, might very well have dyed the flowers at their party to match her gown or had the champagne served in silver goblets bearing the family's initials on their sides, inevitably in Roman italics. (Invitations to the party likely bore their initials, as well as a crown or crest lifted from a real blue-blood family or perhaps conjured out of thin air.) A tour of the bathroom was also in order, to show off the gold faucets shaped like dolphins and the toilet specially designed to look like a throne. The lady of the house could also be found wearing her fur on a summer day despite the heat, as could her little dog, having been outfitted with a matching mini-pelt. Finally, when planning their family vacation this happy couple might rank, of all places, Miami at the top of their list, failing to recognize that the town was considered quite possibly the world capital of nouveau-ness.[23]

"Vieux rich" or "rich d'habitude," on the other hand, wouldn't be caught dead wearing their minks in August or anything at all in Miami. Any day of the week, men of older money could be found in Sunday trousers of equivalent age, once upon a time made by the best tailors in London or Stockholm but now, after a dozen or two too many wearings, literally falling apart at the seams. Also unlike their fresh-off-the-boat neighbors, state-of-the-art technology was hardly a priority for remaining Old Money. A TV could perhaps be found in their dinosauresque houses, probably sitting dormant in the ex-servants' quarters, and priceless paintings were typically under-lit to underplay the fact that they had something on their wall that the Met or Louvre would do backflips to own. Croquet, backgammon, bridge, or mah-jongg would be played at their get-togethers, not gin rummy or, for God's sake, badminton, with red *or* white wine served at dinner (never both, like Mr. and Mrs. No-Class-Whatsoever did at their dos). Port, however, was a must, regardless of which kind of wine had been poured earlier; the stuff was considered the liquid extract of good taste, in more ways than one.[24]

Whether old or new or somewhere in the middle, there were 200,000 millionaires by the end of the decade—three times the number in 1962, a spike much like that of the latter half of the Roaring Twenties. One out of every thousand Americans was now a millionaire, or one out of every three hundred families, odds good enough for *U.S. News & World Report* to remark, "It's getting easier all the time to become [one]." More than ever, millionaires were typically not making their money from jobs (salaries and wages accounted for just 4 percent of their income) but rather from stock holdings, often in companies they owned themselves. Some stocks had doubled or tripled in a single year during the sixties, with capital gains and dividends accounting for an amazing 90 percent of income among the rich. The increasing value of real estate was also helping turn ordinary folks into millionaires, the high inflation rate of the late sixties a cloud's silver lining when it came to net worth. It was, all in all, a beautiful time for the American rich.[25]

THE BEAUTIFUL PEOPLE

Few people knew this better than Stephen Birmingham, author of *Our Crowd* and the just published *The Right People*. As a reporter for *Holiday* magazine, Birmingham regularly mixed it up with the "Beautiful People" in an array of beautiful places, building on Fitzgerald's remark to Hemingway decades earlier by claiming in 1968 that the rich "not only dress differently [but] walk and talk differently, look different, smell different." The writer's latest beat was investigating how the Beautiful People ("BP," for short) got to be or remained so beautiful, especially rich and famous women over fifty. Movie stars of the past like Marlene Dietrich, Norma Shearer, Irene Dunne, Joan Crawford, and Gloria Swanson seemed to be especially well preserved, as were other notable women of a certain age, such as the Duchess of Windsor and Mrs. William S. Paley. "Staying young takes work, work, *work!*" insisted seventy-two-year-old Jolie Gabor, literally the mother of all the Gabors; she was echoed by a New York society woman who felt that, "Looking young and attractive is now practically *the whole point* of being rich."[26]

When it came to what the Beautiful People would do to stay young and look attractive, work, work, and *work* was hardly an exaggeration. Gloria Swanson was reportedly spending $1,200 a week for "cell therapy," for example, while Jackie O. and Mrs. Louis Arpels, wife of the famous jeweler, were devout followers of Kounovsky, the New York exercise guru (the latter wearing diamonds with her leotard). Less famous but equally rich women were regulars at Elizabeth Arden's New York salon in the late sixties, coughing up $100 or more for her "Day of Beauty," designed to doll up everything between head and toes. Arden's Maine Chance on Long Pond, Maine, and the Greenhouse in Arlington, Texas, the Canyon Ranches of their day, were exclusive resorts and health spas where women and some men would go for hard-core beautifying (for $1,000 a week plus tips). The seaweed baths on the Mediterranean and the waters at Montecatini were also popular destinations for Beautiful People, each believed to be a fountain of youth offering healing and restoration powers or, at the very least, an opportunity to impress one's friends with where one got that great tan.[27]

More drastic measures, however, were sometimes called for. Cosmetic surgery, long discouraged by American doctors, became increasingly accepted and popular in the 1960s as techniques gradually improved and as more wealthy women demanded it. The practice was believed to be five times more common in 1968 than ten years earlier, in fact, as women forked out $1,500 for face-lifts and similar amounts to get rid of varicose veins, have some extra weight removed, or reduce the size of their breasts. (Enlarged breasts had yet to become as common as a pair of Manolo Blahniks among rich American women, in part because of the tendency of silicon injections, then illegal, to "travel.") Cosmetic or plastic surgeons often worked in tandem with experts in the fine art of facial peeling, which was very popular among ladies trying to maintain a youthful appearance. Dr. Michael Gurdin of Los Angeles, for example, tag-teamed with Venner Kelsen, a top skin peeler ("he handles the structural problems," she explained, "then I go to work on the skin"). Kelsen, herself a "doctor," charged anywhere from $750 to $1,500 for three peeling sessions, claiming that she could make a forty-five-year-old face look thirty (and that almost every Holly-

wood movie starlet past the age of forty had used her services).
While Tinseltown may have been (and still be) the world capital
of facial peeling, it wasn't the only place where rich women were
literally itching to have the top layer of their mugs removed. (This
despite the process sometimes going badly, leading to some major
discomfort for peelee and a major lawsuit for peeler.) Dr. Thomas
Rees and Dr. John Converse were each doing quite the business
scalping the faces of New York City women not wanting to be left
out in the wrinkled crowd (even with the late sixties feminist movement in full swing). Mrs. Post famously invited her doctor and
three close friends to her 115-room Palm Beach villa, Mar-a-Lago,
for an annual group peel, the foursome playing bridge for a few
days while sequestered, waiting to heal.[28]

More exotic treatments were the order of the day for the
wealthy women and a few men who were determined to look as
young as they felt. Gloria Vanderbilt, Doris Duke, and the Duchess
of Windsor all stopped in to see Erno Laszlo in New York once a
month or so, the ex-Transylvanian go-to guy in that city for all
things epidermal. Laszlo, who had medical degrees "from all the
best universities in Europe," would use his Frankensteinesque electric instruments to "vacuum the pores" and "calm down the capil-
laries," after which various potions and lotions would be applied.
Patients were also urged to wash their faces with his special sea-
mud soap as often as possible, even though the stuff cost $10 a
cake.

For those requiring more hard-core health and beauty therapies, traveling to Europe was necessary, where laws regulating such
things were more relaxed and where doctors had more original
ideas. The Clinique Generale "La Prairie" in Vevey, Switzerland,
run by Dr. Paul Niehans, focused on the inside of the body rather
than the outside, its mission to make internal organs as good as
new. By injecting live cells from animal embryos into the body,
Niehans believed, damage to human organs could be repaired and
restored, including cirrhosis of the liver (the most common ailment
among patients, not surprisingly, given how much they drank). Not

just past-their-prime celebrities like Gloria Swanson were heading to Switzerland to pay Niehans $1,300 a week for his unorthodox treatment but also erudite men such as Somerset Maugham, Bernard Baruch, and, rather shockingly, Pope Pius XII. As with the trend in Los Angeles and Paris for rich men and women with bad hangovers to breathe pure oxygen for fifteen or thirty minutes (many drugstores had it at the ready for such purposes), overindulgence with alcohol seemed to be the primary reason to make the trip to "La Prairie."[29]

For those for whom live cell injections from animal embryos might be a bit too extreme, there was always a really good haircut. Eddie's was just one of a few new high-end salons springing up on Madison Avenue, offering pricey hairstyles (versus haircuts) to its wealthy male clientele. Gay men were the first customers of proprietor Eddie Pulaski, but well-to-do doctors, lawyers, and stockbrokers soon followed, blazing the trail for future metrosexuals. Headhunters had taken to sending their clients to Eddie's before interviews for a trim (or one of his $350 to $500 hairpieces), knowing that in the new youth-oriented America, style mattered. Soon wealthy moms were bringing their sons to Eddie's or to Revlon's or Norbert's for a $12 style, and prep boys were stopping by before heading up to Andover and Groton. Beauty had become "cool" for privileged men and boys, no longer the exclusive domain of the other sex.[30]

THE ALPINE SET

The most beautiful of the Beautiful People, however, could be found only in the most beautiful of places. Aristotle Onassis's yacht, the *Christina* (named after his daughter), was one such place; the world's most luxurious boat was a prime gathering spot for the international jet set in the late sixties. His new wife Jackie, as well as Greta Garbo, Grace Kelly, Cary Grant, and Dick and Liz, were just a few of the beautiful people to rendezvous on the "Golden Greek's" yacht, along with his ex-lover Maria Callas (and her miniature poodles, Pixie and Jeddah, in tow). The *Christina*, which required a crew of fifty, had many notable features, including eight speedboats, a Fiat 500, and an El Greco, but it was the bathroom, a Sienna marble temple, that really impressed people who had seen it all before. The bathroom was an exact replica of King Minos's lost Palace of Knossos in ancient Crete—not a bad room to knock off when designing one's loo. When not occupied in what was probably the finest W.C. on the planet, Onassis and his guests could sometimes be found on Scorpios, the 500-acre island the shipping tycoon picked up as a retreat from his many business ventures, worth an estimated half-billion dollars. Onassis had other homes in Paris, Buenos Aires, Monte Carlo, and Athens (as well as his own DC-6) but he called the *Christina* home—quite understandably, if the rest of the boat was half as nice as its lavatory.[31]

Because of its technicolor scenery, stress-free lifestyle, and, most important, very low taxes, Switzerland was ground zero for most of the Beautiful People of the late sixties and early seventies. "Life here really is terribly sweet," said Noel Coward, who had been spending much of his time in this Shangri-la since 1951, with Mont Blanc the perfect backdrop for his pink-and-white villa. He, along with other rich and famous expatriates including David Niven, James Mason, Deborah Kerr, Orson Welles, Petula Clark, and Joan Sutherland, were part of what they called the "Alpine Set," each of them attracted to Switzerland as a refuge from all the problems of the outside world. With no crime, no racial tension, no violence, no student unrest, no smog, no unemployment, no poverty, and no strikes, Switzerland was perhaps the perfect place for those who could afford to live there. The high prices were offset by the more or less optional taxes (the precise amount actually negotiated with the government), especially for Brits, who could avoid paying their native country's taxes if they spent nine months outside of England. BPs from other countries with high taxes—Baron Edmund de Rothschild, the Aga Khan, Sophia Loren, and Coco Chanel, to

FIGURE 4-2. Shipping magnate Aristotle Onassis and his wife Jacqueline Kennedy Onassis on board their yacht *Christina* in 1969. *(Staff/AFP Getty Images)*

name just a few—also established residences in Switzerland, adjunct but very welcome members of the Alpine Set.[32]

Rich Americans, however, were not so lucky, President Kennedy having put the kibosh on expats escaping the long arm of the IRS by establishing residences in tax-friendly places like Switzerland back in 1962. Liz Taylor was the most famous American to ship out of Switzerland when its tax advantages disappeared, but others, most notably William Holden, stuck around. Holden, who was the straw that broke the camel's back (JFK's new tax policy was nicknamed the "William Holden Law"), arrived in Switzerland in 1959, just a few years before Uncle Sam put the squeeze on those living overseas. Holden remained, however, his big villa outside

Geneva, after a major remodeling, looking remarkably like his house on Stone Canyon Drive in Bel Air. Holden headed there or to his suite at the Sherry-Netherland in New York or to his big-game retreat in Kenya when things in Switzerland got a bit dull, which wasn't too unusual given the utter predictability and famous neutrality of the place. Other Alpiners like Audrey Hepburn also made it a point to get away occasionally, leaving her rather isolated chalet above Rolle for (presumably Gregory Peck–free) Roman holidays. James Mason went to his house in London for a few months a year, while Noel Coward headed to his flat in Manhattan or to Jamaica, where he owned two houses.[33] While Coward, who could often be found wearing the bright purple lounging jacket that matched his sofa, commanded a sort of professorial status among the Alpine Set, Charlie Chaplin served as the group's "dean." Chaplin, who was eighty years old in 1970, lived with wife Oona, his secretary, and the servants in a château above Vevey, very content to be out of the limelight.

With its snow-capped mountains, verdant valleys, and azure lakes ("Walt Disney could have done no better," quipped Stephen Birmingham after his visit), tax-friendly Switzerland was home sweet home not just to celebrities but the occasional rich businessman. Bernie Cornfield, a young New Yorker running a $2 billion mutual fund with more than $100 million in his own account, made quite the reputation for himself there in the early 1970s. More Ugly American than Beautiful People, Cornfield was the proverbial bull in the china shop, shaking things up in this Never-Never Land. A bachelor living in a huge stone castle outside Geneva, Cornfield was fond of wearing silk jumpsuits with wide lapels, sort of like a Swiss Hugh Hefner. Cornfield could be persuaded to leave his castle filled with Euro-bunnies and hippies once in a while, heading to Griffin's, the popular Geneva discothèque, for an evening of dancing or to a formal dinner party, to which he would inevitably arrive hours late and, more interestingly, barefoot. (The centamillionaire also chose to sit on the floor to eat.) Despite his eccentricities, Cornfield was at heart just a nice Jewish boy, moving his mother from Brooklyn into an apartment in his châ-teau, as any successful son could and should have done. Some things, even in the wacky world of the wealthy, never change.[34]

While older BP were comfortably nestled in the Alps, the younger generation was globe-trotting as never before. A week or two excursion to Gstaad for some schussing might be in order and, of course, some sunbathing in the Côte d'Azur and Riviera, but it was the Rome-to-Paris-to-London-to-New York-to-Los Angeles circuit where anyone who was anyone could be found in the early seventies. Nicknamed "Visible People" in the United States, "Roma d'Oro" in Italy, and both "Le tout Paris" or "Les Copians" in France, the international rich and famous had become, with the flourishing of celebrity culture, a branch of society at least as pow-erful as that of their parents' or grandparents' generation. Not that long ago, anyone connected to entertainment, even opera stars, were considered the bottom of the social barrel, but now fame, ideally linked to some artistic or creative profession, was considered the cultural currency of the crème de la crème. As in the late 1920s, a petit noblesse was reinventing the American rich, rejecting the traditional model they inherited and forging a new one that offered much more independence and, as important, lots more fun.[35]

In short, the three F's—film, fashion, and fortune—made up the DNA of this generation of rich and famous, with working, at least a little bit, a vital part of their identity and status. "These days we all relate to our work," said Paloma Picasso in 1973, she leveraging her dad's fame by designing chunky gold jewelry. David Niven Jr. was running a chic restaurant in London; David de Roth-schild was busy being the son of the "bank of Europe"; and Roberto Rossellini Jr. was learning the film biz from his dad. Liza Minnelli, fresh off her success in *Cabaret*, was also part of the scene, as was George Hamilton, trying to live down his Hollywood image as super-playboy (while still working on his tan). The first ladies of rock, Angela Bowie and Bianca Jagger, were major pres-ences, of course, but it was Prince (Egon) and Princess (Diane) von Furstenberg who ruled the Visible People roost. The couple of the moment flitted to and from their places in New York and Paris, their family chalet in Cortina, and a rented villa in Porto Santo Stefano in Italy, taking time out to pose nude for a *Town & Country* cover.[36]

For this crowd, in which image was well on the way to being everything, nightclubs and restaurants were the places to see and be seen (with paparazzi increasingly tracking their every move). Visible People arriving in New York would sometimes go to Elaine's straight from the airport, the Upper East Side restaurant's coatroom overflowing with checked luggage. Then it was off to El Morocco or Hippopotamus, again without stopping at Go to beat the jet lag. In Paris it was Maxim's, Laurent, or Orangerie followed by Castels, Le Prive, or New Jimmy's; in London it was San Lorenzo, Mr. Chow, or Drones (Niven's joint) and then drinks and dancing at Annabel's or Tramps. Le Restaurant, the Green Café, or Le Bistro were where to eat in L.A. before cruising over to Pips or The Candy Store; in Rome it was Bolognese, Taverna Flavia, or Toula and then Treetops for some partying Italian-style. Side trips to St. Tropez meant clubbing at Yeti, which was women-only, or Pigeonnier, which was men-only, although transvestites were welcomed at both.[37]

The coming-out of gay and bisexual culture in the early seventies became entwined with the lives of the rich well beyond preferential treatment for cross-dressers in French resort nightlife. "AC-DC sexuality has jumped out of the closet and into the dinner party," pronounced *Newsweek* in 1973, with bisexual and gay lifestyles altering the social and romantic trajectory of many a bon vivant. More and more wealthy men were preferring to be in the company of their own kind, much to the dismay of wealthy bachelorettes; the fact that these "untouchables," as they were called, tended to be the best-looking guys they knew only added salt to the wound. As compensation, perhaps, single women had taken to becoming "fag molls," choosing to hang out with gay men because they were, more often than not, talented, sensitive, refined, loyal, and, best of all, a barrel of laughs.[38]

How to Become a Millionaire

The inflation and recession of the mid-1970s were much less amusing. The double whammy of "stagflation" signaled the end of the decades-long postwar economic boom. One million 1976 dollars was equivalent to $426,000 in 1948, meaning many millionaires were half as rich as millionaires of the previous generation.[39] For those who could remember, it was a little too close to the dark days of the Depression for comfort, with belt-tightening a must as prices rose and incomes shrank. Wealthy Americans were hardly immune to this economic bummer, doing the same things the non-rich were doing—turning the lights off in empty rooms, lowering the heat to 68 degrees, skimping on holiday gifts—to save a buck or two. The rich were also cutting back on luxuries and their lavish lifestyles to stay afloat, at least until the good times rolled again: giving up their weekly massage, canceling their annual skiing trip, and forgoing the '62 Moet for sparking wine or even Gallo buy-'em-by-the jugs (still served in Waterford crystal, however). Like in the 1930s, an armada of slightly used yachts was for sale, and eight-miles-per-gallon-on-a-good-day Cadillacs traded in for thirty-two-miles-a-gallon Mercedes 220 diesels. Others were leaving their Rollses in the garage, borrowing their kids' VW Bugs to get around town to save on gas. Still others were letting their gardeners go, hiring a service instead, or having their chauffeurs mow the lawn when they weren't driving. Where would the madness stop?[40]

Not at dinner parties, that's for sure. Plastic flowers in place of real ones, chicken or chili instead of filet mignon, and crudités rather than caviar were de rigueur at some of the best parties in town in the mid-1970s, as was hiring just two waiters versus four (the servants had long disappeared). Even more shocking, the word "budget" crept into rich Americans' vocabulary. "I'm learning budgetary disciplines I should have acquired ten years ago," said one Boston society woman, now passing on her older kids' clothing to her younger ones. Susan Frankfurt, a New York City Beautiful Person, did something almost unspeakable in 1974 and held a rummage sale, not for charity or to clean the closets but to make money. Three thousand friends and friends of friends showed up at her fabulous Manhattan apartment, with Ms. Frankfurt turning a tidy $15,000 profit to, well, stay beautiful.[41] As in the 1930s, when frugality took on a certain cachet among the rich, thrifty was now chic, and even the idea of working commanded a certain kind of status. "The rich are looking for jobs now," *Newsweek* reported in 1975, not because they necessarily needed them but because "they sense how very now job hunting has become."[42]

With the dollar falling fast and the yen on the rise in the 1970s, however, there was, rather suddenly, a new rich in town. Flush from their own economic boom, the Japanese were going on a buying spree that could have had Veblen rolling in his grave, pursuing a kind of conspicuous consumption that would have given any Ugly American a run for his or her money. The binge started in 1971, when the Japanese government loosened its import restrictions, and within just a couple of years, "Japan Inc." had become the biggest shoppers in the world. Incredibly, the Japanese were out-spending American tourists, gobbling up luxury items like Cartier watches as if they were penny candy. On the Avenue de l'Opera in Paris, perfume, cognac, and Limoges and Sèvres china were heading to Japan faster than you could say, "tout suite," while in Rome it was all things leather. The area around Trevi Fountain was now being called "Little Tokyo" because of all the Japanese shoppers, their custom there to enter a store, bow, and say two words: "Gucci shoe." In New York, Tiffany had begun to hire Japanese salesclerks and had them wear kimonos to make those dream consumers feel right at home. One of the most popular items was their "Diamonds by the Yard," a jeweled gold chain priced at $333 a foot. Universally, shopkeepers were stunned by Japanese shoppers refusal to haggle, routinely paying the asking price once their questions were answered. For many Japanese in the early seventies, money was quite literally no object.[43]

This was even more apparent in the ways that Japanese businessmen were spreading yen around the world. In 1973, a group of

Japanese investors had recently bought $150 million worth of hotels, condos, and golf courses in Hawaii; another group put their money in South African gold. A whiskey company decided to spend a few million dollars on a seventeenth-century château in Bordeaux with a 100-acre vineyard in the backyard. Japanese horsemen with $15 million in their pockets were roaming around Europe and the United States, snapping up hundreds of thoroughbred mares to mate with their stallions back home to improve their racing stock. One of them, Junzo Kashiyama, a clothing tycoon, spent a million dollars of his money on a single colt in France; the three-year-old Hard-to-Beat lived up to his name by winning the French Derby. Other Japanese businessmen, buyers for high-end clothing stores, had started to appear at Paris fashion shows en masse, scooping up couture and designer garb for their customers back home. Japanese were also sitting in front-row barreras at bullfights in Madrid, replacing the rich Americans who had previously occupied the most expensive seats in the house. Some Japanese were buying ranches in Nevada sight unseen, positively thrilled that they would have real-life American cowboys as their next-door neighbors.[44]

The world of art, however, was most affected by the impact of the new Japanese rich. "Wealthy Japanese businessmen and corporations collect art with all the energy they once put into making transistors," observed *Newsweek*, reporting that patrons from the country had poured $50 to $75 million into the market in 1972, quite a bit of money at the time. Because they were willing to pay top dollar for what they wanted, Japanese collectors were determining the prices for Impressionist and early twentieth-century works and raising the value of certain artists' paintings. "They seem to like the sort of round bottoms and bosoms of the Renoir school," sniffed one London art dealer. One reason for this was that nudes were not part of the Japanese artistic tradition, making them all the more sought after by those wanting Western works on their walls. A Japanese dealer, however, had another explanation for the popularity of nineteenth-century pictures of bathing women. "Japanese woman, though delightful in every way, just does not have a body that should be painted in the nude," the man proposed to account for the escalating prices for century-old paintings of naked French ladies.[45]

A shake-up in the demographic makeup of the rich was not only taking place globally but within the good old USA. Of the 210,000 American millionaires in 1974, 5 percent were under age thirty-five—a relatively small number but enough to be recognized as a new and, with their blue jeans and beards, odd species of rich. Although they looked different and often had more of a social conscience than the fat cats of the past, young businessmen who worked in real estate, owned one of the new franchise operations, or provided financial advice were as success-driven as much less groovy millionaires. "Despite their occasional long hair and casual clothes, the capitalists of the '70s resemble the Henry Fords and George Eastmans of previous generations in their ambitions," noted *U.S. News & World Report*.[46]

Other businesspeople with longish hair—women—were also entering Millionaireville in the mid-1970s; the equal rights movement provided the backdrop for them to succeed by really trying. Advertising big shot Mary Wells Lawrence and Weight Watchers founder Jean Nidetch were perhaps the most famous success stories, demonstrating that it was now okay for women to not just make their own fortunes but to be "aggressive" in the business world, just like men. Only eleven of the 6,500 top executives in the biggest 1,220 American companies were women, however, a *Fortune* survey had recently revealed, a reflection of the still very stacked deck and obvious disadvantages that businesswomen faced. Even Lawrence, who told Fortune 500 company CEOs how they should spend millions of dollars, couldn't yet have lunch or play squash at the Harvard Club like her male competitors could and did, talking business in between bites and games. Almost as important, businesswomen didn't have a wife to manage their homes and families as most of their male counterparts did, making it even more difficult for women to find the time required to get to the top.[47]

More African Americans were also in the money in the 1970s,

their success stories sometimes featured in the media to show others that it could be done. In a multipart series in *Ebony* on "how to become a millionaire," a few wealthy black men shared their secrets of how they made their money; the real message was that the American Dream wasn't out of reach of anyone with a good idea and relentless drive. J. Bruce Llewellyn, a forty-eight-year-old New Yorker, for example, was the head of two of the nation's largest African-American enterprises: Fedco Foods and Freedom National Bank. His personal journey was rooted in the seeds of late 1960s capitalism" that bore some big fruit.[48] Al Johnson was running a $14-million-a-year Cadillac dealership in Chicago, also lending his business expertise to a dozen or so boards. Johnson had become the first black new-car dealer for General Motors in 1967, when the company decided it might be a good idea to have minority-owned showrooms when inner cities burned during the riots. By 1975, Johnson was selling a hundred cars a month, most of them new Caddys, and was living it up in an elegant Lake Shore condominium.[49] Dempsey Travis, a Chicago realtor, was meanwhile flipping buildings in the Windy City, rehabilitating and renovating dilapidated properties and making gads of dough in the process.[50]

An even newer kind of millionaire—the instant one—emerged in the seventies, when a number of states launched lotteries to make up for budget shortfalls. By 1974, thirteen states had started lotteries, most of them offering a top prize of $1 million, not coincidentally still the amount most Americans equated with being rich. Although the prize was never awarded in a lump sum (usually $50,000 annually for twenty years), winners typically experienced all the classic signs of sudden wealth. After the initial shock (fainting wasn't unusual in the early lottery days), hiring a lawyer was often the first order of business, a wise decision given the completely foreign territory most winners were about to enter. Despite their attorney's advice, many winners promptly blew their first $50,000 installment, knowing there were nineteen more to come. Telling one's boss to take this job and shove it was often next on the agenda, after which winners would promptly find themselves bored to tears. Then they would look for something to do part-time just to keep busy. Dealing with the flood of letters asking for money and offering one-of-a-kind "investment opportunities" was a constant aggravation, not to mention all the friends, neighbors, and relatives who seriously expected to get a little taste of the action. Winners also found themselves picking up an inordinate share of checks, the rest of the dinner party sure that "the millionaire" would treat, just as they naturally would if such good fortune had smiled upon them. Losing one's previous identity to become "the millionaire" was in fact a common problem among lottery winners. Waking up to discover they were, to others at least, no longer the person they were when they went to sleep was a truly troubling experience.[51]

Even before they received dollar one, lottery winners found (and, of course, probably still find) that becoming a millionaire overnight was a decidedly mixed bag. Having to deal with all the financial decisions that came with wealth—investing, tax dodging, estate planning—was the least of one's worries. Some winners felt guilty about the sudden wealth or became depressed about having it and consciously or unconsciously found creative ways to rid themselves of the money. Others thought they could repeat the feat over and over again, that they were blessed in some way or had magical powers over the lottery gods. Still others chose not to pay taxes on their income, feeling they deserved to keep every cent of the million dollars. Those who had moved from their neighborhood to buy a big house in a wealthier one sometimes found that you can take a boy or girl out of a Regular Joe neighborhood but you can't take the Regular Joe out of the boy or girl. Not fitting in with one's new neighborhood was, in other words, a common experience, as was losing one's current friends when winners moved to the ritzy part of town. Like the Clampetts, the most nouveau riche family ever conceived, instant millionaires could find themselves living lives disturbingly like those hillbillies who had moved to Beverly Hills, strangers in a strange land.[52]

Interestingly, sudden wealth resulting from a lottery win was often more difficult on the middle class than the working class, something that state officials and sociologists found surprising. Because they were aspirational and wanted to use their money to move into higher social circles, the middle class typically encountered more friction than the working-class winners, who were perfectly content in their own social circle but excited as all get out to be able to buy a fancy car, a color TV, or some of that awesome wall-to-wall shag carpeting. Almost all winners, regardless of class, found that becoming an instant millionaire solved problems but could not buy happiness, something true of wealth in general.[53]

Dozens of millionaires were also popping up in the mid-1970s in one of the most unlikely places in America—coal-mining towns in Appalachia. Like the Texan and Oklahoman oilmen a generation earlier who had ridden the nation's love affair with the automobile to fortunes, coal mine operators in Kentucky and West Virginia were striking it rich as the energy crisis made the fossil fuel a hot property. As many electric power plants converted from oil and natural gas to coal, prices for a ton of the black stuff rose from $7 to a high of $70, a windfall for far-from-rich folks getting it out of the ground. Anyone heading to the hills in the mid-seventies would have had a tough time telling there was a full-blown recession going on in the rest of the country. Real Hatfields and McCoys were driving new Cadillacs, Porches, and Rollses, even flying to the local roadhouse for lunch in their private helicopter. Mine operators' wives were sporting big diamond rings and mink coats and building mansions that would have made any Texan wildcatter who had hit it big proud. People who left the area years ago to work in Detroit auto plants were returning home to become miners again, an ironic twist as the nation looked to coal to satisfy its insatiable thirst for energy.[54]

THE SIX MILLION DOLLAR MAN

If there was any doubt that the Old Boy network still had a virtual lock on power and privilege in the mid-1970s despite the trickle of women, denim-clad men, African Americans, lottery winners, and coal men who were getting rich, all one had to do was head to Bohemian Grove in northern California during the summer. Called "the greatest man's party on Earth" by John van der Zee, this invitation-only retreat sponsored by the Bohemian Club of San Francisco was the boys' club of boys' clubs, the get-together of the year for America's ruling class. For two weeks in the redwood forest, men (whites only, please) with last names like Kaiser and Firestone frolicked with the secretary of defense, governors, and perhaps even the president: the very essence of Mills's "power elite." While eating sumptuous food, drinking thirty-year-old Scotch, listening to big-name stars like Bing Crosby croon, and smoking cigars that would have put a big smile on Freud's face, the powers-to-be affirmed and reaffirmed the business-as-usual rule of scratch-my-back-and-I'll-scratch-yours. Much like wonkish policy-setting groups and metro-politan clubs like Link's, Knickerbocker, and Century in New York; the Somerset and the Philadelphia in Boston; the Pacific Union in San Francisco; and the California in Los Angeles, Bohemian Grove served as a vehicle for some of the richest of the American rich to consolidate their power and, in turn, their personal wealth.[55] Most members of the Bohemian Club in 1976 were among the 240,000 American millionaires who accounted for just one percent of the population but 12 percent of the nation's total net worth, and all were taking full advantage of their influence and connections.[56]

While the institutions of the power elite remained largely in-tact in the mid-1970s, a different set of characters had risen to the very top of the nation's totem pole of wealth. With the first genera-tion of old boys (Rockefeller, Vanderbilt, Gould, Mellon, Frick, and Ford) and, recently, the second generation (H. L. Hunt, J. Paul Getty, and Howard Hughes) having moved on to the happy fortune-hunting grounds, a new generation was now claiming title as America's richest men. Unlike most of their predecessors, this group of plutocrats was largely unknown and ordinary in every way except for their Midas touch. Daniel Keith Ludwig, for example, the richest person in the country in 1976, might have been just

FIGURE 4-3. Inside the rarified air of San Francisco's Bohemian Club, the boy's club of boy's clubs, in 1945. *(Eliot Elisofon/Time Life Pictures/Getty Images)*

another anonymous millionaire, except he was good friends with Ronald Reagan and happened to be worth $3 billion. The seventy-nine-year-old shipping and real estate tycoon had none of the usual accoutrements—yacht, private plane, mistress—that many rich men relied heavily on to signify their wealth, and he was more than happy to stay under the radar of the increasingly inquisitive Fourth Estate (especially that new magazine, *People*). Next on the pole was John Donald MacArthur, also seventy-nine, and an Average Joe in every way (he drove a battered 1972 Cadillac) save for the cool billion made in insurance, banking, and real estate. MacArthur used a lunch counter as his office, a much different approach than the gilded sanctuaries of the Rockefellers and Vanderbilts and the secret enclaves of Getty and Hughes.[57]

The third-richest American in the mid-1970s was Ray Kroc, the seventy-three-year-old hamburger king. He still checked his stores' parking lots for litter despite being worth more than $600 million. "I have no interest in money," Kroc had recently said; his only real extravagance was the San Diego Padres, the baseball team he bought as a toy when Phil Wrigley wouldn't sell him the Cubs. Although he could have hung up his apron long ago, Kroc's passion remained selling burgers (nineteen billion and counting) and literally dwelling in the McEmpire he had created (the doorbell in his Ft. Lauderdale house chimed the "You deserve a break today" jingle each time it rang). Sixty-nine-year-old Paul Mellon, the fourth richest, was the only aristocrat in the bunch, living a life of noblesse oblige with the half billion or maybe billion his dad, Andrew, had left him. After Choate, Yale, and Cambridge, followed by three years at the bank, Paul became a benefactor deluxe and followed in his father's footsteps by heading up the National Gallery of Art, which his old man had founded in 1937. Last in the quintet was, rather improbably, Max Stern, who had parlayed the 2,100 canaries he had brought with him when he emigrated from Germany in the 1920s into Hartz Mountain and more than half a billion dollars. Somewhere along the line, a main road to great wealth—modes of transportation and the fuel they ran on—had crossed over to bird food.[58]

The explosion of consumer and popular culture in the seventies was in fact fast transforming the larger cast of players within the American rich. Wally "Famous" Amos, who had been the first black talent agent hired by William Morris, was selling six tons of cookies in 1977, the forty-year-old having borrowed $11,000 from Marvin Gaye and Helen Reddy to prove that chips could be chic. Nolan Bushnell, a thirty-four-year-old former Mormon, had just sold his company Atari to Warner Communications for a not-too-shabby $28 million, a small bit of which went toward a new sailboat named, not too surprisingly, Pong. Television and movies were also proving to be a gold mine for stars; the emerging concept of "media synergy" allowed not just talent but producers, managers, agents, and even writers to get a piece of the pie. Johnny Carson was making more than $3 million a year as host of NBC's *Tonight Show*, and Barbara Walters earned $1 million from her ABC contract, astronomical sums compared to those of stars during the golden age of TV. Even one-hit wonders like Farrah Fawcett-Majors, the thirty-year-old star of *Charlie's Angels*, were raking it in. The actress and her husband, the Six-Million-Dollar Man, were so overexposed that they had to check into hotels in remote locations as "Mr. and Mrs. John Doe." Even dry-as-a-bone, less than telegenic Henry Kissinger was getting rich from the new media universe, picking up $1.5 million over five years with NBC after his memoirs turned into a bestseller (and $5 million in advance and royalties).[59]

Other authors were showing that it was a brand-new day in entertainment, their books serving as a "platform" for other cross-promoted and even more lucrative products. Colleen McCullough, the thirty-nine-year-old author of *The Thorn Birds*, made $5 million in 1977, the bestseller leading to many foreign editions and magazine serializations, as well as a television "maxi-series." McCullough was admittedly freaked out by her windfall; she owned no house at the time or a single stick of furniture. Stephen King had by age 29 already proved himself to be a writing machine and cash cow, his three bestsellers (*Carrie*, *Salem's Lot*, and *The Shining*) in as many years earning him $2 million in advances. "Somebody ought to give a correspondence course on what to do with sudden wealth," King said, that kind of money unfamiliar and rather scary territory for the crowned prince of horror. King wanted to take tennis lessons but was "afraid of looking nouveau riche," refreshing words given most rich newbies' eagerness to plunge right in and soon find themselves the proud owner of things like gold faucets shaped like dolphins. Alex Haley, who had made $5 million from his *Roots* juggernaut, was glad to be out of debt but exhausted from his marathon of speaking gigs and honorary degree acceptances, a prime example that there were fortunes to be made in the new world of entertainment but no free lunch.[60]

Through endless touring, Peter Frampton was showing that similar mother lodes could be tapped in pop music. His monster album *Frampton Comes Alive!* sold eleven million copies over an eighteen-month period. With his freshly minted $10 million ($6.4 million from album sales and $3.5 from concert revenues), the former get-on-the-bus-to-the-next-gig musician had embraced every stereotype of the rich rock 'n' roller lifestyle. "I guess I'm just a capitalist at heart," said twenty-six-year-old Frampton, now traveling in a private jet and limos, groupies hanging onto every syllable of his $10 million question, "Do you feel like we do?"

Professional sports had also entered a new, more media-driven orbit, with the best athletes catching up to the earning power of stars in other fields of entertainment. Muhammad Ali was making $5 million a fight, win, lose, or draw. Far less charismatic athletes, like Steve Cauthen, the seventeen-year-old jockey sensation, were quickly becoming millionaires from product endorsements. "Sports figures are the Humphrey Bogarts and Clark Gables of today," said Cauthen's agent, Michael Hostead of the International Management Group, although his un-Frampton-like client had so far only sprung for a red Mercury and a new couch for his parents. Without a doubt, however, it was the reclusive actor Marlon Brando who took the rich cake (in more ways than one), earning $2.25 million for just twelve days of work on Francis Ford Coppola's *Apocalypse Now*. The horror indeed.[61]

THE MONEY REVOLUTION

The Brando-sized financial rewards being bestowed upon America's greatest talents were just the most visible signs of the nation's new celebration of money. The late 1970s were, not coincidentally, a fecund time for how-to-get-rich books, all of them at least as interested in the morality and ethics associated with wealth as the ways in which readers could acquire it. With its eight-point manifesto,

Michael Korda's *Success* told readers it was okay not just to be ambitious but to be downright greedy (preempting Gordon Gekko's cinematic claim that "greed is good" by a couple of years). That Korda was not just another financial whiz making a case for the workings of capitalism but the editor-in-chief of Simon & Schuster itself suggested that, as many observed at the time, there was a full-blown "money revolution" taking place. Robert J. Ringer's *Looking Out for Number One*, a bestseller that posited that selfishness was perfectly natural, and William Davis's self-explanatory *It's No Sin to be Rich* also advised readers to rid themselves of any negative feelings they might have about both the pursuit and realization of wealth. "Money has become cleaner than ever before," echoed Kenneth Lamott, author of *The Moneymakers: The Great Big New Rich in America*, reporting the green stuff to be "a good and desirable entity in its own right." Even college students, many of whom not that long ago considered wealth to be exclusively within the realm of "The Man," were now trying their darnedest to get into med, law, or business school, their dreams of a coming Age of Aquarius replaced by ones filled with things like Calvin Klein jeans and Datsun 240Zs.[62]

For those requiring full immersion in the righteousness of abundance, there was, still, Leo Sunshine's forty-hour Prosperity Training course spread over four days. By 1978, another guru, Leonard Orr, was also offering training in prosperity (his a measly six-hour course), as was the king of personal awareness, Werner Erhard. Perhaps miffed that newcomers like Sunshine and Orr were raining on his self-improvement parade, Erhard now offered a six-week course on the tao of prosperity, but only to graduates of his est course. "Money is in this year," noted Nancy Shiffrin, a journalist who attended Sunshine's course to write about her experience in *Human Behavior* (and maybe learn how to get rich along the way). She came to the conclusion that "prosperity is the latest consciousness trip."[63] And with inflation still chugging along, that kind of consciousness trip was getting more expensive. Some New Yorkers were having a tough time getting along on $100K a year in 1978, the high cost of living making even millionaires feel like they were in the poorhouse.[64]

Some young people who were already on intimate terms with prosperity were actually choosing to be in the poorhouse, seeking a consciousness of an entirely different kind. George Pillsbury, Obie Benz, and David Crocker, all heirs to family fortunes, were busily and happily committing "class suicide" in the late seventies, their socialist politics turning them into modern-day Robin Hoods. Largely through two "alternative" foundations these "limousine liberals" had started up, the San Francisco–based Vanguard Public Foundation and Boston-based Haymarket People's Fund, the trio pursued a philosophy of "change, not charity." The "radical philanthropy" movement had actually started a decade earlier, when Abby Rockefeller, daughter of David Jr., decided to go into the same business as her dad but dedicate her own giving program to Marxist and feminist causes. Although the counterculture was now more style than substance, Pillsbury, Benz, and Crocker remained committed to what Tom Wolfe called "Radical Chic," choosing social responsibility over family loyalty by challenging their parents' big-fish-eat-little-fish view of the world. Despite being at the forefront of something that seemed entirely new and maybe even a bit dangerous, Rockefeller and the other three scions were, in a way, merely following in the left footsteps of Lenin, Trotsky, Mao, and Castro, all of whom came from privileged backgrounds.[65]

Comparing George Pillsbury's designated causes to his own dad's offered a perfect snapshot of the generational divide in philanthropy in perhaps its most extreme form. George Sr., a Republican state senator from Minnesota, supported the Minneapolis Symphony, Minneapolis Opera, and the United Fund, a classic mix of high culture and structured giving to the needy. George Jr.'s favorites were, instead, the Mental Patients' Liberation Front, the Prisoners' Legal Education Association, and the Cambridge Women's Center, all aimed at groups "marginalized" and "disenfranchised" from the mainstream. The Haymarket Fund, which George had since moved on from, also targeted causes that even the

United Fund would consider fringe, if not radical, like the Abused Women's Advocacy Project, the Cambridge Tenants' Organization, and the African Heritage Institute.

Benz and Crocker, meanwhile, were venting their existential pain and white liberal guilt by backing neo-Capraesque films like *Harlan County* and *Union Maids* and supporting antinuclear causes with a little help from friends like Jackson Browne, Linda Ronstadt, and the Eagles. The pair had left the Vanguard Foundation in the trusty hands of other trust-babies of the Levi-Strauss, Sears Roebuck, Union Carbide, and JC Penney fortunes; the organization helped out offbeat groups like the Bay Area Black Nursing Mothers, the San Francisco Mime Troupe, and Coyote (the local prostitutes' union). Vanguard had even published a book, *Robin Hood Was Right*, urging other children of privilege to join their noble cause of robbing the rich to give to the poor.[66]

According to a growing number of experts, however, many children of privilege were hardly in a position to help themselves, much less others. The first "poor little rich kid" syndrome was diagnosed in the late 1970s, its proponents, like Burton Wixen, author of *Children of the Rich*, arguing that a "golden ghetto" dwelled within the upper class. Narcissistic, self-centered, and shallow, these waifs, labeled "emotional zombies" by super-shrink Roy Grinker, Jr., were just as deprived as kids growing up in utter poverty, the psychologists treating them maintained. Whether the cause was absentee fathers, alcoholic mothers, or just too-high expectations, a fair number of rich kids were spending much of their time taking drugs, having sex, and getting acquainted with the judicial system, precisely like many disadvantaged inner-city teens.[67] One didn't have to be an expert to take note of a growing number of casualties as the "money revolution" swept across America; the complexities of being born rich pushed some to live lives never imagined by the fortune builders of a century past. As the 1980s loomed, the lives of the American rich were about to become even more complicated, taking the nation's love-hate relationship with them to new extremes.

CHAPTER 5

LIFESTYLES OF THE RICH AND FAMOUS: 1980–1994

"What I want to see above all is that
this remains a country where someone can
always get rich."
—PRESIDENT REAGAN

I N 1986, HISTORY OF A SORT WAS MADE WHEN IT WAS REVEALED
that Americans were thinking more about money than sex.
The average red-blooded citizen had dollars on his or her mind
exactly 13 percent more often than "doing it," a survey had found,
a seminal changing of the guard in the nation's consciousness. It
was long believed that there was a direct and causal relationship
between a dip in the stock market and a bout of impotence in the
suburbs, but this was different. It was indeed, just as the president
had promised, a new morning in America.[1]

As the country in the 1980s turned out to be very much the
kind of "opportunity society" that President Reagan envisioned,
the poll's findings actually weren't too surprising. Despite its own
impressive excesses, the 1970s had not been a particularly good
decade for the American rich. Inflation and an erratic stock market
created a play-it-safe climate in investing in businesses—a terrible
formula for generating new or substantial wealth. The energy crisis

also put a damper on some of the classic habits of the rich (a chauffer-driven limo was not the most sensible option, with gas lines running around the block). The near bellying-up of the world capital of wealth, New York City, was a troubling indicator for any kind of plutocrat.[2] But with a host of economic factors—low inflation, falling interest rates, lower taxes, easy credit—about to start working in capitalists' favor, getting rich or richer would soon be more possible than it had been since the 1950s or even 1920s. Other trends, especially the rise of two-income households and the unmistakable presence of the most populous generation in history, many of whom were now starting to make real money, guaranteed a market of consumers like none ever seen.[3]

The 1980s would become one of the most conspicuous decades for American wealth culture, a period in which it was never easier to quickly make a fortune and then lose it just as fast. With blowing some of that fortune on any number of things—houses, toys, art, or blow itself—now a major pastime for the wealthy, watching the lifestyles of the rich and famous became a popular sport for those on the sidelines. Society was also back in style, with a fat check to the right cause virtually guaranteeing entry to the inner circle. The spectacle was a lot less entertaining for certain social critics concerned about how all this money was being made and being spent, however, the emergence of a new kind of robber baron was something a lot more serious than champagne wishes and caviar dreams.

FLAUNT IT IF YOU HAVE IT

As soon as Ron and Nancy stepped foot in DC, in fact, it seemed as if the master switch of wealth was turned back on. The Reagan's over-the-top inauguration ball in early 1981 made it vividly clear that the frumpy seventies were over, with a more mature and sophisticated aura seeping into the nation's DNA. "Wealth is back in style," declared *U.S. News & World Report* later that year. Experts and ordinary folk alike shared the palpable sensation that the country had turned a sharp corner. "The old less-is-more, down-with-materialism atmosphere that achieved a high-art patina during the Carter years has been brushed aside by the new ruling class," the magazine continued, reporting "A flaunt-it-if-you-have-it style is rippling in concentric circles across the land." With conspicuous consumption the order of the day, more was now definitely more.[4]

Not coincidentally, interest in the Ewings—the only wealthy family more famous than the Reagans—was peaking, with one question on a quarter-billion viewers' minds: Who shot J. R.? Until the Nevada Gaming Control Board put the kibosh on it because "somebody knows the outcome," a Vegas bookie was even taking

FIGURE 5-1. The Reagans at the brand-new president's inaugural ball in 1981, a party that marked the official beginning of the greed-is-good 1980s. *(Bill Pierce/Time Life Pictures/Getty Images)*

bets on the answer, an indication of the world's fascination with the fictional Texans and the show's celebration of greed. People were also making pilgrimages to Southfork, a real ranch that served as the televisual home of the Ewings and was now as popular with tourists as the top Dallas-area attractions, Dealey Plaza and the Texas School Book Depository. *Dallas* had, in fact, put Dallas back on the map, the hit show magnifying the city's reputation for free enterprise, new money, and big hair. The shooting of the nastiest man on TV only added to the public's obsession with the show, some enjoying watching the surrogate rich suffer and others no doubt admiring them for their wily ways.[5]

Despite the nation still being in a recession in the early eighties, Americans' increasing fascination with wealth and a use-it-or-lose-it attitude among the rich were creating a market for luxury goods reminiscent of the 1920s. In New York, $40,000 Russian sables were making real fur less abhorrent if not quite politically correct again, while, just a couple of miles from the Reagans' new digs, gourmet foods such as Moreau chocolates ($18 for a 7-ounce box), Beluga extra royal caviar ($245 for a 9-ounce tin), and leg of lion ($20 a king-of-the-jungle pound) were hard to keep on store shelves. In Houston, $1,500 Frette silk sheets were all the rage, while in Denver it was $800 crocodile-skin cowboy boots. Stores selling luxury goods, like Hammacher Schlemmer in New York, were doing record business, and high-end car dealers put shoppers on waiting lists. The wait for a $32,000 DeLorean was years long, with a mention of the f-word (financing) instantly disqualifying a shopper from any chance of getting one. The demand for other luxury goods—Lafite-Rothschild Bordeaux wine (some for drinking, some to sell at a profit in a few years), $3,200 flotation tanks (sensory deprivation was, ironically, very in during the early eighties), and designer baby clothes (like a Calvin Klein diaper cover or, for that preppy little one, an Izod shirt-and-diaper set)—was also proving that the lingering stagflation from the 1970s was not an issue for those who could afford such things. Broadway was also seizing the discretionary-spending day; one theater asked and got

$100 a seat for a performance of *Nicholas Nickleby*, the eight-and-a-half hour Dickensathon. At least theatergoers were getting a good return on their entertainment investment.[6]

It was not surprising then when, riffing on the size of Mrs. Astor's ballroom and the number of swells who could fill it a century past, *Forbes* introduced its list of the richest Americans in 1982. "The Forbes Four Hundred [is] . . . a periodic scorecard of who is really rich in this country," wrote project editor Harold Seneker while presenting the debut list to readers; the mission of this admittedly ambitious enterprise was also to "delve into the nature of wealth and the wealthy, into how they got that way as well as who they are, and into how they conduct their lives."[7] A dozen billionaires appeared on the first list (including no less than five members of the Hunt family), along with other notables like Bob Hope ($280 million) and Yoko Ono ($150 million). Interestingly, Malcolm Forbes was conspicuously absent from his own list. Like most other fat cats, he was less than crazy about the size of his fortune being made public. Reporters from *Newsweek*, however, were able to figure out that, including his magazine and various baubles (including a palace in Tangier, a French château, and a world-class art collection), Forbes was worth around $200 million, which would have placed him around 125 on his own scorecard.[8] Forbes had come up with the idea for the Four Hundred in 1980, but then-editor of the magazine John Michaels thought even trying to put together such a list was "pretty dicey at first." After testing the waters and realizing that the project was doable, *Forbes* plunged in, sending staffers across the country to dig up information on who and how much. Editors called each of the Four Hundred selected to fact-check before the list was published; some of them told *Forbes* to "drop dead" and threatened to sue if their name and worth were included. "The whole list was completely unnecessary," said Lawrence Tisch soon after the issue came out. He glanced at the magazine and threw it across the room after seeing that he and his brother Preston Tisch, co-owner of Loews Hotels, were members of the club with $300 million.[9]

As what had to be the most thorough investigation into the wealthy elite up to that point, *Forbes'* bold publication not surprisingly revealed some interesting findings. About one hundred and fifty of the Four Hundred had inherited most of their wealth, while the remainder—almost three-quarters—were either "self-made" or had parlayed a small fortune into an immense one. And while a bunch had struck it rich through real estate and oil (sixty-three and forty-three, respectively), the others had done it through a wide variety of businesses, such as media, manufacturing, farming, retail, shipping, construction, banking, and entertainment. The American Dream seemed to be alive and well, judging by the percentage who had gotten filthy rich without receiving a farthing from Mummy and Daddy and by the number of ways one could get there. While there was a respectable showing of Old Money (thirty Du Ponts, fourteen Rockefellers, and five Mellons), the lion's share of the wealth had been made in the last generation or two, more evidence that the United States remained a land of opportunity. Finally, the total wealth of the Four Hundred added up to $92 billion, hardly chump change, but much less than, say, that year's federal deficit. This fact rebutted social critics like Ferdinand Lundberg, who persistently made the case that a small number of families essentially controlled the country—more good news for fans of Horatio Alger. With people like George Lucas, Steven Jobs, and Phil Knight among the nation's all-stars, the American Dream was apparently still up for grabs.[10]

Also not surprising was the kind of response the Forbes Four Hundred received as soon as it was published. "Reaction to the Forbes four hundred richest Americans has been greater than it's been to anything else that's appeared in the magazine in the past sixty-five years," Seneker wrote a few weeks after the issue (which quickly sold out at newsstands despite an extra-25,000-copy run) came out. Print and broadcast media had a field day with the findings, and the magazine was approached by two major publishers interested in a book on the subject. Comments from those on the list streamed in. Some of them were angry at being outed, some

questioned the magazine's accuracy when it came to their own reported wealth (almost always overstated, of course), and some were
amused at the whole business. Virginia McKnight Binger, wife of
3M chairman William L. McKnight, for example, told *Forbes* that
she was truly surprised she was worth $100 million ("Isn't that ter-
rible?" she asked). Leonard Marx, real estate maven and philanthropist, complained that now that his wife had learned they were
worth $300 million, she "will ask not to take in any more washing!"
Some readers even wrote in to say that the magazine had made
those on the list sitting ducks for money-seekers and, worse, the
IRS.[11] If there was any doubt that the first Forbes Four Hundred
had made a dent in the nation's cultural consciousness, it was
nipped in the bud with this personal ad that soon appeared in the
Village Voice:

> Single, serious black woman seeks one fabulous Forbes Four Hun-
> dred man. Find new and exciting ways to spend money. Write VV
> BoxP5377.[12]

How to Marry Money

That SBG (single black gold digger) was not the only one convinced that Mr. Right would be a certain Mr. Rich. As wealth came
back in style in the early eighties, Joanne Steichen, a New York
City psychotherapist, began offering a three-hour "How to Marry
Money" course through Network for Learning, an adult ed organization. The widow of Edward Steichen, the famous photographer,
Ms. Steichen certainly had the right credentials to teach the course,
having herself married a wealthy man (who also happened to be
fifty years older). Fifteen to twenty students typically enrolled in a
Network for Learning course, but a hundred and forty people
showed up for Steichen's; a second section was added, which attracted more than one hundred and fifty more. For a paltry $21,
students (one-third of them men) learned a variety of ways to first

bump into and then snag a rich Mr. or Ms. Lonelyhearts, including attending art auctions, eating breakfast in expensive hotels, shopping for groceries at Gristedes (versus low-brow Grand Union), and flying first class (or, better yet, just sneaking into the VIP lounge). Steichen soon wrote a whole book on the subject, *Marrying Up: An American Dream & Reality*, the definitive resource for anyone thinking about getting rich with a little help from Cupid and his gold-tipped arrows.[13]

Right along with their continued pursuit of equal rights, in fact, many women in the 1980s had designs on marrying a millionaire or at least fantasized about doing so. Lady Di's fairy-tale wedding and *Evita*-mania—real-life examples of women whisked off to a life of privilege by wealthy (if flawed) men—only provided fuel for the fire. To meet their own Prince Charming, women found themselves suddenly committed to fund-raising efforts, reading *Town & Country*, and boning up on dog raising and skeet-shooting, just as experts like Steichen advised.[14] Judging by the number of articles about the subject in magazines like *Mademoiselle*, *Vogue*, and *Harper's Bazaar*, women were, it seemed, spending a lot of time thinking about whether they too should "date up" to nab a sugar daddy or, at least, a diamond in the rough. "Can you bank on a rich boy?" asked Leslie Dormen in 1984, recalling a date back in college with an Ivy Leaguer with one of those monosyllabic names (Web? Tip? Hap?) who picked her up in a red Austin Healey (even more classically, he wore driving gloves). Equipped with all the accoutrements of real money—an old English sheepdog, worn Shetland sweater, Hepplewhite chairs, a private island in Maine— the young man had that certain confidence and poise that often came with being rich, an effortless attitude or even a glow that oozed entitlement. Dormen wondered, should she and women like her seek out such men with three names followed by a couple of Roman numerals and realize those dreams of ski trips to Vail, birthday presents from Cartier, and dinners at that perfect French restaurant?[15] For many women, perhaps Madonna's 1985 "Material Girl" provided the answer; the hit song and video endorsed the idea that a girl had to do what she had to do now that we were living in a material world.

Ironically, some wealthy singles were at least as keen to get hitched, so much so they were paying $100,000 to a professional matchmaker specializing in the rich-but-lonely market if they met Mr. or Ms. Right. Neal Sheldon founded his Florida-based Execumatch service in 1980 and was so successful he opened a Toronto office four years later, charging his clients $100 large for the painstaking task of finding the perfect match. Both client and potential mates (thousands eager to be picked) had to go through a months-long evaluation process, which included numerous one-on-one consultations and a seventy-five-point psychological screening, all intended to determine compatibility on every issue imaginable. With more clients than they could handle, Execumatch appeared to be delivering the goods, their incredibly steep fee happily paid by people with too much money but too little romance in their lives. And, compared to the cost of a divorce settlement, clients felt $100K was a relative bargain.[16]

Others providing advice on how to marry a millionaire offered the specific bonus information of who the best catches were—a fantasy, of course, but entertaining nonetheless. Writing for *Harper's Bazaar* in 1989, Susan Bidel's top-twenty "millionaire bachelors" included Steven Jobs who, although his house was still unfurnished, remained desirable because "he still loves to work." Bill Gates, meanwhile, was a workaholic, "so you'll have to speak computerese," while Lawrence Ellison's environmental interests meant gold diggers would have to "bone up on soil erosion and acid rain." Snagging Julio Iglesias meant having "to put up with a major groupie problem," while George Lucas had "been known to pal around with Linda Ronstadt, but you never know."

Even the richest man in the world, the Sultan of Brunei, wasn't perfect; he already had two wives, but this too was surmountable "if you can get along with the other ladies."[17] At thirty-nine years old and ruler of one of the world's tiniest but wealthiest nations, the Sultan was indeed quite the catch for that special lady who wouldn't mind sharing him. With the biggest palace in the world—a 1,788-room home spread over fifty acres and costing $400 million—it wasn't likely that three wives would bump into each other in the middle of the night, after all. The palace had its own mosque, a heliport, and, just in case the in-laws wanted to drop by, eight hundred parking spaces, more than compensating for having to be one-third of a harem.[18]

Given the stakes involved, experts should probably have offered more advice on how to divorce a millionaire. "It's no longer how well you wed but how profitably you divorce," said *Money* magazine in 1983, suggesting readers prepare themselves for what might turn out to be another of the increasing number of here-today, gone-tomorrow marriages to a wealthy spouse. One critical factor, top divorce lawyers agreed, was how easy a mark your future ex was likely to be. Corporate executives and entrepreneurs were the best catches, attorneys argued, as business types were typically eager to make a deal quickly, just as with any kind of venture. With Old Money, however, it was like squeezing water from a rock; these folks were trained from birth to preserve capital at all costs. Professionals were stingy too, according to divorce lawyers, especially doctors, who, because they could heal people, considered themselves divinely exempt from other forms of giving. Lawyers were almost as cheap as doctors, not because of their litigious natures, but because they didn't want other lawyers to know how much money they made. Engineers were, rather predictably, unpredictable, known to be entirely reasonable about the money involved but prepared to fight to the bitter end about a particular lamp or table. Jewish husbands, some lawyers thought, were especially giving ("trained to put women on a pedestal," said one), and men who were having an affair were also ready to open their wallets because of the guilt they felt. All in all, then, "the best marital bet for a woman with divorce in mind would be a wealthy Jewish businessman who has been having a mistress on the side," *Money* concluded, sound advice given the current number of high-profile breakups among the American rich.[19]

Besides marrying the right kind of person when preparing to get a fat settlement should that rainy day come, there were a number of strategies for the future divorcée to keep in mind. Getting (and documenting) as many gifts as possible from one's wealthy partner during the marriage was vital, lawyers felt, not only because they were legally for keeps but to establish the lavish lifestyle to which the poor soul was accustomed. The dreaded prenup was a no-no, of course, avoidable, one attorney suggested, by the less well-off mate by saying (with a trembling lip) that such a thing would "undermine the trust and love on which our relationship is built." Joint ownership of big-ticket items—house, car, investments—was always a good idea, naturally, as was running up one's expenses to maximize one's postmarital estimated cost of living. Finally, if a breakup was definitely in the cards, going to a psychiatrist as soon as possible to establish "mental cruelty" was a smart move. (Checking into an expensive sanitarium to show extreme heartbreak and despair earned extra points with judges, divorce lawyers seriously advised.) Interestingly, some rich husbands were more than happy to give their wives a big settlement, looking at it as a status symbol of sorts when the amount was "leaked." Love was one thing, after all, but admiration from one's rich buddies quite another.[20]

THE CONTAGION SPREADS

Based on President Reagan's 1982 budget address, which promised tax cuts for the wealthy, aggressive defense spending, cuts in social programs, and deregulation, rich men would soon have plenty to brag about when it came to the size of their divorce settlements. As Reagan's economic plan kicked in (at the price of record deficits, critics pointed out), signs of recovery appeared in 1983, with unemployment and inflation down and the stock market going into high gear. For the American rich, this perfect economic recipe for building wealth, combined with consumers' (especially baby boomers') growing obsession with anything smacking of luxury, couldn't have been scripted any better by one of the president's Hollywood screenwriters.[21]

Although shows like *Dallas, Dynasty, Knot's Landing,* and *Falcon Crest* certainly got an "A" for effort, it was *Lifestyles of the Rich and Famous* that, when it came to capturing the zeitgeist of 1980s style, took the Godiva chocolate cake. The hottest syndicated show on TV in the early eighties, *Lifestyles* was a shameless celebration of pure, unadulterated materialism, an intentionally over-the-top trifle that viewers couldn't get enough of. "For whatever sociological reasons," wrote *Newsweek* in 1984, explaining the show's popularity, "the ebb and flow of the lumpen's fascination with the rich has hit a historic high." Originally a couple of two-hour specials, *Lifestyles* was promoted to a weekly series, calling itself, rather hilariously, "an open ticket to the 22-karat core of success." Declaring that "fortune is the final frontier" (with no apologies to *Star Trek*), the show was hosted by ubersycophant Robin Leach, who had left *Entertainment Tonight* for bigger and, well, bigger things. Like the prime-time soaps that let viewers into the rarified air of the oil business, a California beach community, and wine country, *Lifestyles* offered fans a peek into the private lives of the actual wealthy elite. "My show is *Dallas* brought to life," Leach admitted—a vicarious, voyeuristic bon-bon that many found simply irresistible.[22]

A few segments in the show's first season explained its popularity as escapist entertainment par excellence. A tour through Cher's $6.4 million Beverly Hills mansion, a thirteen-bedroom, Egyptian-style palace, gave viewers an inkling of what life was like for America's royalty. "She never wears a single pair long enough for any of them to need repair," Leach fawned, speaking of course about the diva's hundreds of pairs of shoes. (Impressive, but peanuts compared to Imelda Marcos's collection of 2,700 pair; if the First Lady of the Philippines had changed her shoes three times a day and never wore the same pair twice, it would have taken her more than two years and five months to walk through her supply.)[23] We next learned that Princess Diana spent $300,000 a year on clothes ("much of it on hats") and that George Harrison's toilet played "Lucy in the Sky With Diamonds" when its seat was lifted. Mark Goodson, the renowned game-show producer, meanwhile, had his wash done by his favorite laundry in New York, this news worthy of the show's high standards only because he happened to live in L.A.

Sensing plenty of room for such displays of conspicuous consumption, no less than three other knockoffs—*The Good Life* ("the most luxurious half-hour on television"), *The Robb Report* (a spin-off of the ultra high-end auto magazine), and *Eye on Hollywood* (the tinselest side of Tinseltown)—were soon on the air, each also a tour de force of hedonism and exhibition. While many critics had a field day with these easy targets, others saw some value to *Lifestyles* and its clones, beyond being mere eye candy. "Examined from a more positive perspective, television's celebration of excess may well turn out to be a wondrous motivational force," concluded *Newsweek*, the shows possibly serving to spark some viewers to, like their heroes, succeed beyond their wildest dreams.[24]

The fascination with the rich among the lumpen would increase through the 1980s. By 1987, *Lifestyles* had become the most watched show in its time slot for households with incomes of $40,000 or more, suggesting that wealthy viewers liked to see even wealthier people on TV. The show was, not surprisingly, Donald Trump's favorite thing on TV, and David Rockefeller reportedly planned cocktail parties around an airing. If that wasn't enough, sales of caviar and champagne were up, perhaps at least in part because of viewers' desire to vicariously enjoy, as the show's introduction went, "champagne wishes, caviar dreams."[25] Even *Teen* magazine jumped on the *Lifestyles* bandwagon, doing its own "Lifestyles of Rich 'n Famous Teens" story the following year. "In the land of fancy-car wishes and lavish-wardrobe dreams," the magazine Robin Leached, "*Teen* takes you for a luxury ride where teens go first class." The story dished out juicy tidbits about teenagers like Andrea Salzman, the fifteen-year-old daughter of David Salzman, president of Lorimar Telepictures, who had recently added a letter written by Helen Keller to her collection (which included one from Beethoven and another from Thomas Edison), and Francine Sinatra, the fifteen-year-old granddaughter of Ol' Blue Eyes, who owned over a hundred Cabbage Patch Kids dolls (but was now into more refined things, like life-sized stuffed animals).[26]

The cultural adoration of not just consumerism but downright excess in the mid-eighties no doubt had Karl Marx rolling in his grave; the gears of capitalism had never before run so smoothly. With stacks of money beginning to pile up, more and more market-ers were, of course, happy to take some of it off the hands of the American rich. At Bijan's men's store on Fifth Avenue, for example, shoppers needed an appointment just to get through the doors, the new New York store even swankier than his original haberdashery on Rodeo Drive. Once inside, however, Bijan (Pakzad) himself was often there to serve up his Italian suits starting at $1,100 ($400 extra for vest), $250 ready-made shirts, and, perhaps for the double-agent off to London, a bulletproof, mink-lined raincoat for $14,000. Robert Wagner, O. J. Simpson, and King Juan Carlos of Spain were all big fans of Bijan, who confessed that the price of his shirts was "the mortgage payment on a home."[27]

Those wanting to go from New York to L.A. in style in the mid-1980s would have traded first class for one of the thirty-five seats on Regent Air's 727–100s, originally designed to accommodate one hundred twenty-five less wealthy passengers. Not only did Regent flyers have lots of elbow room, but secretarial, haircutting, and manicure services were at their beck and call, as well as a stand-up bar, all for a very reasonable $810 including limo to and from air-ports ($2,160 for a stateroom for two, complete with double bed).

Private chefs, such as Pierre Bitterer, were also ready to prove that money, rather than variety, was the spice of life. Bitterer's eight-course dinner parties, priced from $2,000 to $4,000 (wine, waiters, and transportation extra), were just the thing to impress increasingly fussy guests and the most demanding of hosts. None other than Imelda Marcos had once flown Bitterer to the Philip-pines to cook for her, the president, and six other lucky guests, exactly the kind of experience that more and more of the American rich now wanted to share.[28]

The phones of private chefs like Bitterer were no doubt ringing off the hook as, even with a slight dip in the stock market in 1984, the individual and collective wealth of the American rich began to reach a new plateau. Takeovers, mergers, acquisitions, leveraged buyouts, and other big-fish-eat-little-fish deals were now the stuff of getting rich quick, with the conversion of apartments to condos in New York also increasing the fortunes of people like Donald Trump, Harry Helmsley, and Samuel LeFrak.[29] The dubious practices of these corporate deals-for-deals-sake—"greenmail," "golden parachutes," etc.—reminded some of the not-so-good-old-days of a century past, when the robber barons used "the methods of their time" to crush anyone or anything that stood in the way of making a killing. "It seems to me that the sheer love of money—and the gaga admiration of people who have it—has become enormously widespread," wrote Loudon Wainwright in 1984, concluding that, "greed, for the moment, seems to be in a state of ascendancy." The commercialization of the 1984 Olympics, where athletes seemed to be competing less for medals than the chance to get their picture on a box of Wheaties or score another sponsorship deal, sent a message that even the ultimate amateurs really just wanted to get rich. "Richness" seemed to be well on the way of becoming perceived, just as loonies like Leo Sunshine had claimed, as the most normal state of all, with anyone unable to achieve such a state deficient in some way or, in short, a loser. "The contagion spreads," Wainwright fretted, seeing nothing on the horizon to suggest that the worship of money wasn't going to continue to grow.[30]

TOO MUCH MUCH

Expensive clothing certainly was contagious among the American rich, a backlash against the unisex look and denim-mania of the sixties and seventies. Couture, in fact, was doing great in the early 1980s despite the economic doldrums, given a boost by fashionistas Nancy Reagan and Lady Diana. It was no secret that Diana often went on shopping binges in London and spent as much time at the British offices of *Vogue* as she did at Windsor Castle; her clothes were sewn to order by designers after private showings. "The economy does not affect a certain segment of the population," explained Bill Blass. Palm Beach socialite Mrs. F. Warrington Gillet II agreed: "Women dress better than ever when you have a recession." The first lady and Lady Di had nothing on Rick James, however; the King of Funk possessed 100 sport coats, 300 pairs of pants, 400 pairs of shoes, and one traveling valet to keep track of all the stuff.

Arabs, though, were the biggest clothesaholics in the world (*People* called Rodeo Drive "Beverly Hills's Arabian Annex"); their money and what it could buy surpassing anything possible in the West. Saks in Las Vegas stayed open after hours for Nabila Khashoggi and her mother Saroya (who had snagged $100 million in a divorce settlement from her husband, Saudi arms dealer Adnan), for example; the department store's managers were happy to let the women have the place to themselves to shop. Saudi men were more partial to Henry Poole & Co., the former clothier to Napoleon III and Winston Churchill. Sheiks dropped by the London store once every five years to buy twenty suits. King Hassan II of Morocco, who appreciated clothes as much as Rick James, was so appalled at how his press corps dressed that he sent them to a fancy boutique and picked up the tab.[31]

While New York society women were undoubtedly the best dressers, their sisters in Texas were definitely the more adventurous. Phyllis Morrow, the wife of Houston oilman T. C. Morrow, for instance, proudly wore a brown sequined gown adorned with feathers plucked from wild turkeys from their game preserve at one of her parties, a fashion Don't even in anything-goes Texas. Like oilmen of a generation past, Texan men of the 1980s would be considered style-challenged anywhere but the Lone Star State and

Oklahoma. Texan TV personality Marvin Zindler fully lived up to his claim that, "Polyester is the miracle fabric of this century," eschewing any garment constructed with material that occurred in nature. Zindler gave his extra suits to prisoners so they could look snazzy in court but, given his Monsanto tastes, the jailbirds might have been better off wearing their striped uniforms.[32]

Whether it was Chanel and Valentino in New York or turkey feathers and Dacron in Texas, there was no doubt that rich American women were spending a ton of money on clothes in the style-obsessed eighties. Martha Phillips, owner of the Martha boutiques on Park Avenue and in Palm Beach and the nearby exclusive village Bal Harbour, thought that $40,000 to $50,000 a year was "not a lot" for her customers to spend on clothes in 1986. Some rich women, in fact, were spending a lot more. Johnny Carson's ex, Joanna, had included $37,000 a month for clothing and jewelry in her recent divorce petition, and Carolyn Farb, a Houston socialite, reportedly had more than $1 million worth of clothing in her six-room, tennis court–sized closet.[33]

Like in the 1920s, another flush decade, wealthy women were bringing their slightly used designer clothing to resale stores, a way to recoup some of their investment in the expensive rags. Not wanting to be seen in the same suit or gown twice, poor little rich girls, including not just society women but famous actresses like Dyan Cannon and Diahann Carroll, were happily swapping their "gently worn" duds for hard cash, sometimes as much as $1,000 a month. More than a dozen such boutiques had sprung up in Houston alone, with business way up in L.A., Chicago, New York, and Dallas. Sometimes these exchanges were on the down low, the shopaholics having their housekeepers make the drop, without feeling the need to tell their husbands what happened to that slinky black Dior. Women with champagne tastes but Budweiser pocketbooks were naturally delighted to snag an Adolpho suit or Yves Saint Laurent gown for a fraction of its original cost, and clotheshorses were relieved of some of their guilt about being such spendthrifts. A side benefit of thinning out one's closet was, of course, that more room was created for new things, keeping the wheels of commerce spinning in perfect alignment.[34]

Women, of course, weren't the only ones spending big money in the mid-eighties. Lanmark Cars, a dealer of personalized autos, purposely located itself in lower Manhattan, within walking distance of Wall Street, so that rich boys could easily buy their vehicular toys. Customized Mercedes, Jaguars, Porsches, and Ferraris were all there for the asking, each auto unique in some way, so that the moneyman driving from or back to Greenwich or Westchester wouldn't have to see a car just like his. Although yachts had made a giant comeback from the 1970s, luxury cruises were becoming a popular alternative for wealthy couples who didn't want to get stuck with a floating white elephant when the next recession came along. The crème de la crème was the *Sea Goddess I* and *II*, which, because they were less than half the size of your average cruise ship, could port at exclusive yacht clubs and marinas in the Caribbean and Mediterranean. A staff of eighty for just 116 passengers was another plus, the almost one:one service well worth the more than $1,000-per-day cost of a cabin.[35]

Nowhere in the United States was flaunt-it-if-you-have-it more in vogue than in Houston, where hundreds of millionaires and a few billionaires called home. The biggest players in the town that oil built, further glitzed up by the resulting boom in real estate and banking, were the two richest women in America, Margaret Hunt Hill and her sister Caroline Hunt Schoellkopf (each daughters of H. L. Hunt). In the early 1980s, Ms. Schoellkopf built the Remington Hotel, which quickly became the place of choice for Big Rich to spend as much of their fortunes as humanly possible. Every morning, for example, one lady would show up at the hotel for her breakfast of deep-fried potato skins, a glass of milk, and an 8-oz. tin of caviar (bill: $650), while every evening a man would consume two or three bottles of Louis XIII brandy, the stuff going for $50 a shot at the hotel's bar. The most ostentatious displays of wealth could be found in the River Oaks section of town, with River Oaks Boulevard the primary artery of what some locals called *aufgeputz*, or "too much much." Society diva Lynn Wyatt had a home there in the mid-eighties, her Lalique crystal banister quite the sight to see, as did the Di Portanovas, who hung three crystal chandeliers over their two-story, glass-enclosed Olympic-sized swimming pool. Houstonians claimed that too much much had actually peaked there around 1970, but with a recent dinner party involving a three-and-a-half-foot-high wall of malossal caviar, one could reasonably make the case that there was still a heckuva lot of much in town.[36]

Eighties drug culture, however, claimed the ultimate prize in too much much, with a good number of American rich active players on both the buying and selling ends of the trade. Quite a few upper classers got busted in the early eighties for dealing drugs; the most famous was undoubtedly maverick automaker John DeLorean. Despite the lines leading out of showroom doors for his double-winged car of the future, DeLorean was charged in 1982 for conspiring to distribute $24-million worth of cocaine, the proceeds of which were to be used to keep his Northern Ireland factory afloat. "This is better than gold," DeLorean told an undercover agent with a kilo of white powder in his hand; the ex-GM exec's case was not helped by the fact that the attempted transaction was captured on videotape. DeLorean wasn't the only person of means to try to get richer a little too quickly, with a Texan oil millionaire sent up the river for shipping marijuana across state lines, a cadre of Miami professionals nabbed for smuggling dope, and an assortment of other bankers, lawyers, accountants, and doctors caught with their hands in the Dr. Feelgood cookie jar.[37]

For every millionaire drug dealer in the eighties, naturally, there were plenty of millionaire drug users. Pot, hash, Quaaludes, coke, and heroin went hand in hand with the international club scene that the wealthy were so much a part of, especially in New York. At clubs like Danceateria and Xenon, local dealers often worked the crowd, with Wall Street brokers and trust fund kids some of their best customers. Wealthy young Americans were, as usual, imitating their European counterparts, many of whom were heavily into hard-core drugs, especially heroin. Rich American twentysomethings found themselves rubbing shoulders (or swapping needles) with European aristocracy and heirs to industrialists' fortunes in sketchy Lower East Side or Harlem tenements, desperate to score some "boy" (heroin), as well as some "girl" (cocaine) to make a speedball. Just as marijuana and psychedelics matched the anything-is-possible sixties and cocaine the feel-good seventies, a segment of the rich believed heroin was the perfect drug for the boring eighties, the only thing in the world that could, at least for a while, numb the despair they felt.[38]

While extreme times called for extreme drugs like heroin, cocaine was adapting very nicely to the faster and faster pace of the eighties. Called "that special high-octane solvent of America" in 1986 by a society dealer, coke was a (sometimes *the*) main feature of the everyday lives of those rich looking for not-so-cheap thrills. Mad rushes to bathrooms in all sorts of places at all sorts of times were a common sight, the man or woman in a hurry soon returning a few hundred dollars poorer and with what appeared to be a sudden, particularly bad case of hay fever. Even at black-tie benefits for the most conservative of causes, young Republicans were known to disappear with alarming frequency, the pockets of their Paul Stuart tuxes or Hermes bags stuffed with Dristan and $100 bills (the unique scent of which a cokehead could easily pick out of an olfactory lineup). As with heroin, many recreational users soon became addicted, consuming a gram or more per night and losing both their friends and trust funds with astonishing alacrity. Having to scurry through the netherworld of New York's drug culture was one of the costs of business for cocaine aficionados, an ironic clash of classes brought together in the true spirit of 1980s-style laissez-faire capitalism.[39]

Although rich kids were hardly the only ones shooting up, drugs were reason enough for social critics and psychologists to argue that children of privilege often suffered from what one of them cleverly termed "affluenza." This affliction, the dark side of too much much, seemed to follow a fairly predictable path. First was the obligatory summons on their eighteenth or twenty-first birthday to

Morgan Guaranty or another trust fund officer, during which the young man or woman was informed that he or she was, in a word, rich. (Because their worth was often more than they suspected, the young man or woman would sometimes ask to see the actual money, as if the trust fund officer had a few million in cash in his desk drawer.) The next stage was the wild buying spree: clothing at first, but soon escalating to bigger-ticket items like first-class seats to the scene-of-the-moment, purchased at the airport before the next plane to Paradise left. The last and most dangerous phase was a gradual loss of identity and general aimlessness, experts maintained, often associated with the consumption of alcohol and drugs and involvement in sundry other reckless behavior to fill the void. The lack of interest in a career or inability to even hold down a job was considered a primary cause of affluenza, according to the shrinks; a disproportionate number of young rich called themselves "movie producers" despite having precious little to show for it. Sarah Pillsbury, producer of the 1985 film *Desperately Seeking Susan* (featuring the Material Girl herself), was the rare exception, proving that a successful career might very well be the best cure for the disease. With ever more money around in the 1980s for young rich to (literally) blow, however, were the American wealthy a doomed species?[40]

SOCIAL SAINTHOOD

Definitely not, judging by the number of young American rich interested in perpetuating the species via society. Eighties socialites in training were not just plugging into their parents' scene but forming organizations of their own in order to mingle with the Right People, in the process rescuing society from its decidedly square image during the counterculture years. In New York, "a new dashing breed of self-created young swells" was on the prowl in the mid-1980s, according to *Mademoiselle*; the magazine dubbing these rich, precocious twenty- and thirtysomethings "aristobrats." Five hundred such brats belonged to the Junior International Club, a group apparently entirely committed to partying, holding black-tie formals one night, getting together at the Surf Club, an Upper East Side dive bar, the next, and walking past the velvet rope at new clubs like Tunnel or Nell's the next. A mix of career students (often bouncing back and forth between NYU or Columbia and the Sorbonne) and career fast-trackers, Junior International included members like Windi (seriously) Phillips, a deb from Ft. Worth whose most remarkable achievement to date seemed to be that Frank Sinatra sang at her coming-out party. ("The only private party he's done since Henry Ford's," Windi proudly claimed.) Besides resembling the uberpreppy characters featured in Whit Stillman's three comedies of manners about the urban haute bour-geoisie (*Metropolitan, Barcelona,* and *The Last Days of Disco*), aris-tobrats appeared to all have gender-neutral names like Tory, Dylan, Kip, Baird, and Devon, and, for the moment at least, sought no higher calling than having fun. "We're not looking for any inner meaning at black-tie parties," explained one twenty-two-year-old male aristobrat. "We're just looking for hot girls."[41]

Reinvigorated by the nation's more traditional and conserva-tive values, society as a whole came back with a vengeance in the 1980s, with New Money as eager as ever to upgrade their fresh-off-the-boat millionaire image. As always, recognition that one was officially part of society was dependent on some very specific crite-ria that differed by city. In L.A., simply belonging to Hillcrest or another A-list county club went a long way to conferring member-ship in society, as did living in the tony neighborhoods of Holmby Hills or Bel Air. In New York, getting invited to certain dinner par-ties was considered the gold standard, although both Old and New Money used the incestuous art world, specifically relationships with dealers, artists, critics, gallery owners, museum curators, and other collectors, to move up the food chain. Getting in early on a particu-lar artist in the art-crazed 1980s was a shortcut up the social ladder, the savvy collector admired for his or her foresight, willingness to roll the dice, and good taste. More desperate society wannabees resorted to hiring decorators whose clients or friends were in the swim, hoping that he or she would introduce them to the Right People. The net result of this strategy was, more often than not, an apartment or house that looked like those of the Right People but was visited by few or none of them.[42]

In Washington, a one-industry town, invites to state dinners at embassies and, for bonus points, the White House, proved that one truly belonged to DC society. Dian McLellan, the longtime DC gossip, considered an intimate dinner in the Reagans' private quarters to be nothing less than "the absolute, ultimate social event in Western civilization," those lucky enough to be invited to those soirees elevated to "social sainthood." McLellan believed the first Reagan administration raised the bar in how much money was spent on parties to sway people of influence in Washington, which had a trickle-down effect on people in the rest of the country as Americans watched some of the spectacle on TV.[43]

Far more than anything else, however, charity offered wealthy nobodies opportunities to scamper up the social ladder. As the most frequented intersection of the rich and famous, it was the charity gala or fund-raiser where that unknown but ambitious nouveau had the best chance of cracking the society code. The first such event had been staged by Mrs. William K. Vanderbilt in 1893; the bash, thrown in the Waldorf-Astoria ballroom for the benefit of St. Mary's Free Hospital, set the pattern for almost all of those to follow. Combining conspicuous consumption with support for the sick or financially strapped, the charity gala was the perfect way for the rich to rid themselves of some of their guilt while improving their social status, all of course in grand style. (The irony of this was not overlooked; in the eighties, Felix and Elizabeth Rohatyn created a firestorm when they criticized the amount of money spent on parties and which organizations were receiving support.) The formula for a successful benefit was (and remains) no secret: appoint a big name (Jackie O, Nancy Reagan, and Brooke Astor were the unequivocal power trio of the 1980s, with Blaine Trump, wife of Donald's brother Robert, coming on strong in the latter part of the decade) as honorary chair and attract rich people with social aspirations like bees to honey. With Wall Street creating new multimillionaires in the mid-eighties almost as fast as the guy in the FedEx commercials could talk, the charity scene in New York was constantly morphing—a volatile, exhilarating scene that mirrored and helped shape its time and place.[44]

Despite the continual influx of new blood with their new money, philanthropy on the local level was a small, definitely feminine, world, and board members of the top charities knew each other quite well. Women would usually support each others' causes, a friendly competition that socialites, many of them empty nesters, found deeply rewarding. While their husbands made lots of dough in their careers, society women (who went by Mrs., not Ms.) brought home the bacon-wrapped liver through their charities, their own moneymaking skills serving as a real source of pride and symbol of equality. With as many as four parties a week during the fall season in New York, galas became more and more lavish through the eighties in order to attract guests, pushing new causes (notably AIDS, until the end of the decade) to the sidelines. Men were agreeable about attending the galas as long as they didn't start or finish too late, especially if they knew that they might be seated next to a Beautiful Young Thing (BYT) invited specifically to bring in older guys with big bucks. Junior members of a particular organization were often scattered among the old-timers, just one of many tactics that made up the fine art of seating at charity events. Favors, the predecessors to today's swag bags, were a must; giving away the smallest and least expensive items (e.g., a disposable camera) somehow made some of the wealthiest people in the country open up their wallets, if not their hearts, to a worthy cause.[45]

Whether supporting the "arts" or "diseases," as those in the biz rather crudely sorted causes, the New York charity scene in the 1980s presented the ideal opportunity to witness the Reagan era's meteoric rise of New Money. Acceptance into prominent circles was never before so available for sale; a board position on a perfectly respectable charity was in one's Chanel pocket should one have an extra $50,000 or so already in it. There was, however, a clear pecking order within the local charity universe, with the Metropolitan Museum of Art at the top (among diseases, cancer was number one), followed by the New York Public Library (which Brooke Astor essentially ran as her private club), the Central Park Conservancy, and the Boys Club of New York. Interestingly, while Nancy Reagan was a hot property as a gala chair, her antidrug Just Say No Foundation events were an unequivocal bomb (perhaps because a good number of potential patrons were eagerly saying yes). "Adopting" an entire elementary school class in a low-income neighborhood became quite the thing to do among wealthy patrons in the eighties, although there was nothing quite like donating a wing to a museum for pure effect (as Mortimer D. Sackler, the pharmaceuticals poobah, did in 1987, earning him the right to hold his seventieth birthday party there). Even out-of-towners like Ann Getty of San Francisco and Sonia Cole of Phoenix entered New York society though charity; they and others recognized that, for women especially, involvement with a gala was the smoothest way to become part of the scene. While there were alternative routes, such as wangling an invitation to Manhattan real estate broker Alice Mason's famed salons (or buying Mar-a-Lago, which Donald Trump did in 1988, which instantly improved his image despite his diminishing fortune), charity remained the path of least resistance for the socially aspirational throughout the decade.[46]

Old Money may have been falling off the Forbes Four Hundred like overripe fruit off a tree, but their Bible, the *Social Register*, remained very much in print. Despite being around for a whole century, the book retained a mythic sort of status, to be seen by perhaps a select few at one's own risk, like the Kabala. For just $85, however, the 1988 edition (winter or summer) of the *Register*, still as complete a listing of the American rich as any, could be anyone's. Spending some time with the book suggested that the twentieth century almost never happened; the list of 32,500 people was skewed geographically, ethnically, racially, and of course financially toward a ruling class of a different era. The American aristocracy remained heavily Northeastern, for one thing, the top four cities for blue bloods being New York, Philadelphia, Boston, and Washington, DC. Over three-fourths of the surnames in the latest edition were of English origin, with nary a Latino or Asian American (and just a smattering of African Americans and Jews) to be found. "This is essentially a racist organization," argued Stephen Higley, a professor at Oklahoma State, whose dissertation was about the *Register*. Higley saw George Bush as the archetypical *Register* listee, his credentials—born in Greenwich, son of a senator, coastal Maine summer home, captain of the Yale basketball team, member of Skull and Bones, and married to a Wellesley girl—as precisely the right stuff to get and stay in the book. "It's a list of the people whom listees would like to have dinner with," Higley concluded, anyone without an old boy, prep school background unlikely to be invited to the table. The president may have had the perfect profile for the *Social Register* but many active politicians asked to be taken out of it, seeing official membership in such an elitist organization as a liability. And although actors were now some of the richest people around (including ex-President Reagan), very few show biz folk had yet to make the cut, one notable exception being Jane Wyatt. Playing the mom in *Father Knows Best* was, apparently, white bread enough even for the *Register*'s snooty editors.[47]

THE METAPHOR OF THE MOMENT

Although he was probably worth as much as a good chunk of the collective listees in the *Social Register*, it was highly unlikely that Sam Walton was in the good book. In 1985, Walton moved up from number two to top dog on the *Forbes* list, his 750 Wal-Mart stores making him the richest person in America. Even if there was a society in Bentonville, Arkansas, Walton would have had little interest in joining the club. "All I own is a pickup truck and a little

Wal-Mart stock," the modest man said, his fifty-four million shares worth a very immodest $2.8 billion.[48]

The following year was a particularly notable one for the *Forbes* list, something best expressed by the magazine's rather understated news that, "It has been a splendid year for billionaires." Twenty-six Americans were now in the ten digits, in fact, nearly twice the number in 1985. As well, the 1986 list included a number of Wall Streeters, like Michael Milken (the "junk-bond impresario . . . transforming the financial landscape almost single-handedly," the magazine gushed), Irwin "The Liquidator" Jacobs, and the leveraged buyout triumvirate of Jerome Kohlberg, Henry Kravis, and George Roberts. Thirty-year-old Bill Gates also made his debut on the list, his first $300 million resulting from having recently taken Microsoft public.[49] 1986 was also the year that *Forbes* started to track global wealth, putting together an additional list called "The Richest Man in the World and 95 Also-Rans." (The Sultan of Brunei, with his 800 parking spaces, took the blue ribbon.) *Fortune* magazine, apparently peeved that its rival had become the definitive authority on the American rich, finally decided to fight back, issuing its own list of the world's wealthiest people that same month. "It was amateursville," *Forbes* editors said, taking issue with its competitor's methodology and firing the first salvo in the business-magazine-tracking-the-rich wars.[50]

Forbes and *Fortune* were hardly the only ones raising the profile of the extremely wealthy, however. Unlike the American rich of the past, in fact, many of the nouveaus of the 1980s wanted to be in the spotlight. "The pervasive cultural dream is to be both rich *and* famous," stated *Harper's Bazaar* in 1986, arguing that, "the phenomenon of celebrity has democratized the social stage once inhabited strictly by the wealthy." Once scorned by the wealthy elite, "Café Society" was now the premier group to be part of, with a mention or photo in magazines like *Town & Country*, *W*, or *Women's Wear Daily* highly sought after by anyone who was anyone. Due in part to eighties' star worship, the rich were becoming famous simply for being rich, media darlings in their own right.[51]

"We media folk are becoming fascinated with wealth," admitted Robert J. Samuelson that same year, noting that *Money* was now one of the hottest magazines around. (It actually included *Vogue*-style fashion pages for a while, and that brainy periodical the *New Republic* had recently added a column called "The Money Culture.")[52] Indeed, *New York* magazine considered America's greatest new fortune builders—John Gutfreund, Henry Kravis, Saul Steinberg, Alfred Taubman, and Donald Trump—the "rock stars of the 80s," the art of using a company's assets as capital to make gobs of money the ultimate in sexiness and glamour circa 1986. Even Trump's wife Ivana was putting three days a week in as CEO of the Trump Castle Hotel & Casino in Atlantic City, as sure a sign as any that punching the time clock, as long as it paid extremely well, was in style even for jillionaires.[53]

Americans' love affair with wealth showed no signs of letting up as the eighties rolled merrily along. By 1987, money had become, according to Holly Brubach of *Vogue*, "the metaphor of the moment," referring to the decade as the "Gilded eighties." Stephen Drucker, writing for the same magazine, compared the decade not to the robber baron–controlled 1880s but to an even more auspicious era for the making and spending of money, the 1920s. "The eighties are officially roaring," Drucker announced, musing, "So this is what a Jazz Age feels like."[54] (As in the twenties, the eighties had its own automotive folk hero, Lee Iacocca.) And like the Roaring Twenties, the 1980s were turning out to be a time for the nouveau riche to shine, with displays of wealth that would normally be considered vulgar now viewed as perfectly appropriate, proud displays of Reagan's red-white-and-green patriotism. Plastic surgery, for one thing, was more in than ever among the wealthy. It was now very acceptable, even fashionable in these superficial times, to mention to friends that one had or was planning to have a nip or tuck or two. The middle-class-ness of 1950s-style wealth, meanwhile, was gone with the wind, way too pedestrian and egalitarian for the bright and shiny American rich of the 1980s. Although the particulars of flaunting it differed by region—clothes, generally speaking, in New York, cars in L.A. (a new Porsche was now the gift of choice there for a just-turned-sixteen-year-old), and homes in Flyoverland—you were, more than ever, what you consumed.[55]

What more and more Americans of all economic classes wanted to consume, arguably more than at any other time in history, were things that symbolized wealth and the wealthy. The rising popularity of iconic brands—the Louis Vuitton bag, the Gucci loafer, a Cartier Tank or Rolex watch, a Mark Cross or Mont Blanc pen, and, perhaps even more so, their street knockoffs—further reinforced the cultural codes of the American rich and, as a result, their social power.[56] Ralph Lauren's Polo best captured the dynamics of 1980s-style wealth; however, the fact that a New Money Jew was repackaging the look and lifestyle of Old Money was just one of many ironies of the times. Image, as a popular commercial of the time went, was everything.[57]

Not coincidently, polo itself reached a new level of popularity in the United States in the eighties, not just to watch but to play. The sport eclipsed golf, tennis, and sailing as a symbol of old-school wealth. Prince Charles had jump-started interest in the sport of kings, with investment bankers and other yuppies joining British royalty and Argentinean playboys on the club circuit. The Greenwich Polo Club in Connecticut was one of the hotbeds of the sport, with Wall Streeters in jeans and Tony Lama cowboy boots spending $1,500 a week learning how to whack a little white ball with a mallet while riding a pony.[58] Polo, as well as another pursuit of royalty experiencing a revival, fox hunting, were featured in magazines like *Town & Country*, with a bevy of other glossies—*Vanity Fair*, *Vogue*, *Harper's Bazaar*, *W*, *Connoisseur*—celebrating the (very) good life. *Women's Wear Daily* was a primary voice of eighties-style wealth, the magazine chock-full of photos of rich women wearing their designer labels (either at benefits or, more often than not, Mortimer's or Le Cirque). *Spy*, a magazine that could only have been conceived in 1980s Manhattan, was a snarky look at the society scene, shredding scenesters like John F. Kennedy Jr., Martha Stewart, and, especially, Ivana and Donald Trump (famously described as a

"short-fingered vulgarian"). Television about the wealthy, meanwhile, went from the not-so-sublime of *Lifestyles* and *Dallas* to the
downright ridiculous. *The Colbys*, an Aaron Spelling *Dynasty* spin-
off, made the Carringtons of that show look like country bumpkins,
its Bel Air settings, sea of mauve and taffeta and, to boot, God
himself, Charlton Heston, solid gold proof that the medium's pre-
occupation with the American rich had jumped the proverbial
shark.[59]

While nouveau's star shone in the eighties, that of Old Money
further faded, increasingly dwarfed by the sheer immenseness of
Texan (the Hunts, the Basses, Trammell Crow, and Ross Perot) and
new Wall Street fortunes. Hard-to-miss things like ping-pong-ball-
sized diamond rings, crocodile shoes, and Texans' current and
somehow disturbing habit of calling $50 million simply a "unit"
made Old Money seem as antiquated as Confederate currency.
Even more maddening to Old Money, late 1980s nouveaus were a
pretty sophisticated lot, hogging tables at the best restaurants in
town by slipping Francois a fifty. Trying to distance themselves
from all the new and much bigger money, the old moneyed were
doing things like commissioning portraits—not only of themselves,
but of their long dead ancestors. The oil paintings served as a
proud reminder that even for the biggest "takeover artist," some
things simply couldn't be bought.[60]

And while they were able to buy nearly anything else, the
"paper entrepreneurs" of Wall Street were not considered rock
stars by everybody. In his 1987 *Tales of a New America*, Robert
Reich was particularly harsh on investment bankers and security
brokers, arguing that moving money from one place to another
hardly qualified one as a true entrepreneur. Still, many of America's
best and brightest MBAs were heading right to Wall Street, se-
duced by the shocking starting salaries of $80,000. Talented young
lawyers had also started going downtown in the mid-eighties to
become investment bankers, their salaries jumping from under
$80,000 to over $200,000 in the process. Part of these dealmakers'
higher salaries, however, may very well have gone to psychiatrists,

some of whom, like Lanmark Cars, were intentionally setting up shop within spitting distance of Wall Street to serve the paper entrepreneur crowd. For these clients, the usual issues that surfaced in therapy—control over one's life, self-respect, completeness, etc.—all seemed to revolve around how much money they made or didn't make, the heroes of the day apparently having a one-track mind. Some clients showed all the classic symptoms of addiction, with money the substance being abused. And with wealth the most powerful aphrodisiac of the day (Drucker saw money in 1987 as "positively arousing," echoing Tom Wolfe's famous claim that writing and reading about the super-rich was the 1980s' version of pornography), there seemed to be less need for or interest in more traditional pleasures. "There's less sex out there now," reported one Wall Street shrink, additional evidence that Americans had more important things—money and what it could buy—on their minds.[61]

For many American rich, what money could buy was another three-letter word—art. Among the very wealthy, collecting art in the eighties wasn't just a way to negotiate one's way through labyrinthine social circles but a game every bit as competitive as high finance. With heavyweights such as condo king Gerald Guterman, corporate raiders Steinberg and Kravis, publishing magnate S. I. Newhouse, media mogul David Geffen, advertising bigwig Charles Saatchi, and cosmetics' dastardly duo Ronald and Leonard Lauder battling it out for paintings that came on the market, collecting art was, as *New York* magazine described, "the ultimate rich man's sport in the late twentieth century." In early 1987, a Japanese insurance company purchased Van Gogh's "Sunflowers" for $39.9 million, shattering the previous high auction price for a painting and thus raising the stakes for other "players," as serious collectors were known. Even the Met, its acquisition budget spread thin over many departments, couldn't compete with the Japanese (and their strong yen), the Getty Museum (and its $3 billion trust left by J. Paul), and American art lovers with deep pockets (and their deeper egos). American collectors were in fact hiring Met curators as their private advisers; others used Citibank's new Art Advisory Service to help them invest their money wisely. Like the robber barons who tussled with each other over masterpieces (Jay Gould and William K. Vanderbilt went *mano a mano* on more than one occasion), the wealthy elite of the 1980s loved the chase at least as much as the catch and were attracted to the world of art as a therapeutic palliative for all their hard-nosed wheeling and dealing. Unlike their predecessors, who subscribed to the "social gospel" of turning over great art to the public when they were done with it, however, the American rich of the late twentieth century were showing no signs of doing the same. Again, the paper entrepreneurs of the day appeared to be no match for the Fricks, Carnegies, and Morgans of the past who, despite their nefarious ways, redeemed themselves through their tithing and good works.[62]

The less-than-altruistic ways among the real-life Gordon Gekkos were even more abhorrent given the fact that the richest people in America were getting richer in the late 1980s. "Billionaires have been busting out all over," *Forbes* beamed in 1987, its Four Hundred list again including almost twice as many of them as the year before. The latest list reflected the continued ascent of New Money at the cost of Old. Most dramatically, Bill Gates became the world's youngest self-made billionaire, while seven more Du Ponts as well as six Mellons and five Rockefellers dropped off the list. *Forbes's* 1987 list was published just a bit too late to reflect that year's huge stock market drop, however, when Black Monday reduced the fortunes of some its Four Hundred by a hundred million dollars or more. (Sam Walton, who had pulled away from the rest of the pack, lost an incredible $2.6 billion in the October 19 crash.)[63] The following year, *Forbes* reported that a resurging Donald Trump had joined the ranks of billionaires, although they had doubts about his own "conservative" claim of being worth $3.74 billion. "After applying the appropriate discount to a Trump estimate—we threw out Trump's number and started from scratch," the magazine explained, "we found that while he isn't worth what he says he's worth, he is worth plenty."[64]

Indeed, the 20 percent or so drop in the market on Black Monday seemed, in the long run, to have little effect on the lifestyles of the super-rich and super-famous. While Saul Steinberg's birthday party in 1989 wasn't your ordinary picnic (the festivities included a five-tier cake surrounded by human cherubs and a live nude posing as Rembrandt's "Danae"), no other single event symbolized 1980s wealth more than Malcolm Forbes's seventieth birthday party that same year. Forbes had spent $2 million on a seventieth anniversary bash for his magazine at his New Jersey estate just a couple of years before, but for this occasion, New Jersey just wouldn't do. Before you could say "abracadabra," 800 handpicked guests and 110 reporters were off to Palais Mendoub, Forbes's Moroccan palace, previously occupied by a sultan (and his multiple wives). Except for a few guests who flew over in private jets (Lee Iacocca, Calvin and Kelly Klein, and Liz Taylor, who hopped a ride in the host's own plane, the *Capitalist Tool*), three planes—a Concorde, Boeing 747, and DC-8—whisked the "Forbes 800" from JFK to Tangier. Nibbling on their in-flight meal of Cornish hen and brownies direct from Le Cirque (Concorde passengers gulped down salmon, lamb noisettes, potato pancakes, and chestnut mousse during the three-hour-and-eighteen-minute flight), the who's who of who's who (including Barbara Walters, Katherine Graham, Helen Gurley Brown, Diane von Furstenberg, Donald and Blaine Trump, Nan Kempner, and Henry Kissinger) were welcomed by hundreds of locals, who clapped, danced, and blew horns. "Black tie, ball gowns, turbans, and tiaras are all in order for an evening of exotic dancing and fireworks," the invitation read, recalling the famous 1951 party in Venice thrown by the international man of mystery. Overlooking the Straits of Gibraltar, partiers supped on 100 barbecued lambs, 830 chickens, and a desert of couscous, entertained by 200 horsemen and 750 performers personally provided by King Hassan II. As a finale, Beverly Sills sang "Happy Birthday" to Ali-Dada, as Forbes called himself for the evening, followed by sixteen minutes of fireworks accompanied by "Bolero." As guest Rupert Murdoch had put it as a headline in his London tabloid *Sun*, EITHER YOU'RE THERE OR YOU'RE NOWHERE.[65]

BONFIRE OF THE VANITIES

Forbes's epic blowout was a fitting way to send the 1980s era of wealth out in grand style. The October 1987 crash and subsequent recession were the most obvious signs suggesting that "the eight-

FIGURE 5-2. Elizabeth Taylor and Robert Maxwell at Malcolm Forbes's 70th birthday party in Tangier, Morocco, in 1989. The bash to end all bashes was one last hurrah for eighties-style conspicuous consumption. *(Ron Galella/WireImage/Getty Images)*

ies," as we knew them, were over. "Behind every great fortune stands a crime," a well-known aphorism went, and the 1980s were a major crime scene. By decade's end, Ivan Boesky, the model for the film *Wall Street*'s Gordon Gekko, was in the clink for insider trading, and the Hunts were found guilty of trying (unsuccessfully) to corner the world's silver market. The Queen of Mean, Leona Helmsley, was sent up the river in 1992 for fully living up to her creed that "only the little people pay taxes," and banker Charles Keating was also in big trouble with the feds for engaging in some major financial funny business. Michael Milken, whose arrival on Wall Street had been hailed by *Forbes* as something akin to the second coming, had been hit with a laundry list of security law violations (he had made more money in 1987 than McDonald's, suggesting that something was rotten in the state of junk bonds) and was also doing hard time.[66] Other events, particularly Forbes's death in 1990 and the financial meltdown of an overleveraged Donald Trump, added to the sense that an era had ended.

Not only the SEC but pop culture seemed to be turning against the moneygrubbing eighties. The savings and loan collapse was believed to be costing taxpayers an estimated $500 billion; the underlying corruption and climate of greed stopped middle-class Americans' admiration of the wealthy in its tracks. By 1989, *Dynasty* was as dead as doornails, and *Dallas* was defunct two years later, viewers having become weary of having spoiled rich people, even fictitious ones like the Carringtons and the Ewings, in their living rooms. A parade of books, including Tom Wolfe's 1987 scathing satire of New York society *Bonfire of the Vanities*, Dominick Dunne's thinly cloaked 1988 novel *People Like Us*, and Michael Lewis's 1989 *Liar's Poker* all questioned whether greed really was good. As well, the exploits of Henry Kravis were featured in Bryan Burrough's and John Helyar's 1990 *Barbarians at the Gate*, and those of Boesky, Milken, and others appeared in James B. Stewart's 1991 *Den of Thieves*. Only Robin Leach, with his *Lifestyles of the Rich and Famous* franchise, seemed to want to continue celebrating the exploits of the extremely privileged. By 1990, *Lifestyles* was being broadcast to twenty-two markets outside the United States, its almost as popular spin-off *Runaway With the Rich and Famous* (where celebrities captured their exotic experiences with video cameras) in its fifth season. Despite the latest recession and populist backlash against the wealthy, Leach was gung ho about his televisual empire's prospects for the 1990s. "There's more fascination with a Gatsby in a depression, when no one's rich, than in a time when everyone's rich," he explained, although he jokingly proposed a backup if he was proved wrong: *Lifestyles of the Poor and Unknown.*[67]

Social critics and intellectuals also went to town on the evils of the current American rich, not surprisingly. Lewis Lapham's 1988 *Money and Class in America* was a vitriolic attack on the super-rich, chastising the upper class for their obsession with money and firm conviction that they never had enough. "The rich have the temperaments of lizards," Lapham wrote, the *Harper's* editor (and greatgrandson of a founder of Texaco) suggesting that the current wealthy elite were not just cold-blooded but infantile in their relentless pursuit of things. For Lapham, the spiritual vacuum in American society had very much to do with the loss of faith in its core institutions, an idea seconded by, of all people, the sycophantic, sybaritic Liz Smith, who looked to the lack of real heroes as a reason for the worship of false idols like the rich.[68] In his 1992 *The Culture of Contentment*, John Kenneth Galbraith chimed in on who he called "the fortunate and the favored," blaming the "socially contented" for reconfiguring the American economy to their advantage through deficit-inflating tax cuts and outrageous military spending based on "anti-Communist paranoia."[69] The public celebration of money was shrinking faster than had the Dow Jones average, a less extreme but still jarring reminder of the cultural somersault of the early 1930s. Like then, the American rich of the early 1990s now seemed to be taking a duck-and-cover tack, keeping a low profile until the tide once again turned in their favor.

As Americans woke up in the early 1990s with a bad hangover from the party that was the 1980s, there was heated debate over whether the rich had gained at the expense of the non-rich or, conversely, whether everyone had, to some extent, enjoyed the ride. Democrats and Republicans tumbled the numbers every which way to make their cases; a definitive answer is still elusive today. George Bush's call for a "kinder, gentler" America sent a clear message, however, that even those who had thrived most in the eighties recognized the decade's outrageous excesses and hubris and were ready for something different.[70] Although it was hardly clear what "something different" would be, there was no doubt that in the 1980s the American rich had had their best decade since the 1920s—another era of conservative politics, big tax cuts for the wealthy, skyrocketing personal and national debt, and, most important, glorification of capitalism. The 1980s were also reminiscent of the 1880s, when the top one percent of Americans in the late nineteenth century pulled farther away from the remaining 99 percent, the truly wealthy being the biggest beneficiaries of a Republican, pro-business administration.

Like those past decades, the cast of characters within the wealthy elite changed dramatically during the 1980s. The new generation of nouveau riche were able to make their Monopoly money not through industry but by moving and manipulating corporate assets. As the nation wondered what a "post-greed" society might look like, another generation of new American rich waited in the wings out west; the size of their future fortunes would stun even the robber barons of Wall Street.[71]

CHAPTER 6

WHO WANTS TO BE A MILLIONAIRE?

1995–

> "Okay, I'm tired of beating around the
> bush. . . . Are there any guys who make $500K
> or more on this board? . . . $250,000 won't get
> me to Central Park West . . ."
> —EXCERPT FROM A 2007
> Craigslist posting

IN HER 2004 NOVEL *BERGDORF BLONDES*, PLUM SYKES EX-
plored the rarified air of wealthy Upper East Siders, no doubt
drawing from her personal experience with maneuvering through
society circles. One of Sykes's more piquant insights was the keen
interest in rich boyfriends among single women of that particular
hair shade; the code name for such men was "A.T.M.s," as in "Au-
tomated Teller Machines." "M.I.T.s," were not brainy types but
"Moguls in Training"—essentially A.T.M.s with long-term potential. With her blue-blood background topped off with a degree in
modern history from Oxford University, Sykes was ideally qualified
to recognize and report the priorities of American wealth culture
at the beginning of the twenty-first century, most of which, not
surprisingly, had to do with making, spending, and even giving
away gobs of cash.[1]

Bergdorf blondes were hardly the only ones with big bucks on
their brains in New York and the rest of the country, however, as

Americans of all stripes declared their unrequited love for the almighty dollar as never before. Turbocharged by digital technology and an apparently insatiable desire for media and entertainment, the New Economy that emerged in the mid-1990s provided an ideal platform for generating unprecedented levels of wealth. Wealth would arguably be the biggest story of our time and place at the close of the second millennium and start of the third, the economy boom of the last half century climaxing with a McMansion-sized explosion.

Looking more like Bart Simpson than J. P. Morgan, tech millionaires and billionaires would prove to be a much different breed of American rich than previous plutocrats. Initially not sure how to spend their money, software and Internet geeks learned very fast, however, eventually rivaling the robber barons in sheer extravagance. Happily, the beneficiaries of IPOs would do more with their instant fortunes than buy basketball teams and shrines to rock 'n roll, creating a new, more personal model of philanthropy. The dot-com bust threw a major monkey wrench into the technology works, but an even bigger American rich would soon rise as hedge funders raised the bar of what it meant to be really wealthy. With a turbulent economy and the shifting of the global plates of wealth, the near future of the American rich will no doubt be a rocky ride, but history tells us that reports of their collective death are greatly exaggerated.

THE NEW ERA OF CYBERBUCKS

Not coincidently, never before in history—even when exploitation of the world's natural resources was raised to a near art form in the nineteenth century and you could virtually print money if you were in the stock market in the late twenties—had there been a faster way to get rich. "We have entered the new era of cyberbucks," proclaimed *Forbes*, introducing its 1995 list of wealthiest Americans by explaining that, "The computer and all its digital offspring are creating vast fortunes, sometimes almost overnight." Netscape had yet to make a dime on its Web browser, for example, but such details hadn't stopped its chairman, James H. Clark, from making $500 million when the company went public. "Pioneers like Bill Gates begin to look as old money as the Rockefellers once did," the magazine's editors observed in compiling their list, also taking note that more Americans were heading west to strike gold. Ten years earlier, there were about thirty more New Yorkers than Californians in the Four Hundred, but now the tables had been turned—there were about thirty more Californians than New Yorkers.[2]

The cybertrain picked up more steam the following year, and it became apparent that the American rich was undergoing another sea change. "Forget America's fifty families. Forget old money. Forget silver spoons. Great fortunes are being created almost monthly in the U.S. today by young entrepreneurs who hadn't a dime when we created this list fourteen years ago," claimed *Forbes* in its 1996 "Four Hundred" issue; the average net worth of a listee exceeded a billion dollars for the first time. Rather remarkably, physical assets—timber, oil, real estate, manufacturing plants—were no longer the key to amassing great fortunes. "Ideas and organizing principles," as the magazine called them, were now the primary M.O. for getting on the list. The Industrial Revolution, which had ably served as the machinery for getting rich over the last few centuries, was being swept under the rug by the Information Revolution, the new path leading to tremendous wealth.[3]

Even more remarkably, this generation of the new rich seemed to be acquiring their wealth fair and square, unlike the scorch-the-earth robber barons of the Gilded Age, the overleveraged stock traders of the 1920s, or the smoke-and-mirrors Wall Streeters of the 1980s. Also unlike the American rich of the past, one didn't have to be a big cheese to reel in the big dough. Employees at all levels were becoming instant millionaires, on paper at least, because of their stock options; secretaries and mid-level managers were in the right place at the right time when their company decided to go public. Initial Public Offerings, or IPOs, which were kick-started by Netscape in April 1995, were generating millions, sometimes billions, of cyberbucks for a lucky few. The high-tech entrepreneurs of the mid-1990s raised the bar for creating wealth in terms of both speed and volume.[4]

Because of the almost freakish nature of getting rich quick at the close of the twentieth century, software millionaires not surprisingly looked and acted very differently than their older wealthy kin. All the typical trappings of previous generations of American rich—the Newport or Palm Beach "cottage," the jet-set lifestyles, the Armani suits—were almost entirely absent; these folks were fully aware that their newfound wealth was primarily funny money. Net worth was a much different thing than the balance in one's bank account, making it much more likely to discover a techie tycoon in a two-bedroom rented apartment in San Jose than a fifty-room chalet in Lucerne. And even if the money was real, most of the digerati wouldn't think of buying a yacht or collecting art; their real passions—typically work first and family second—took precedence over showing off their good fortune and good taste.[5]

Within a year, however, it appeared that the richest technobarons were starting to enjoy some of their money as they engaged in a my-whatever-is-bigger-or-better-than-yours competition that would have made the tycoons of a century earlier proud. Charles Simonyi, the chief software designer of Microsoft, for example, in 1997 was building a Xanadu right out of *Citizen Kane*, a 21,000-square-foot techno-temple (Villa Simonyi) on Seattle's Gold Coast that had everything from a heliport to an art museum to a video arcade. Paul Allen had recently bought himself an island near Seattle, while Larry Ellison of Oracle was building a $40-plus-million replica of the Japanese Katsura palace in Woodside, California, the garden spot of Silicon Valley, where starter homes began at $800,000. Jim Clark was more partial to airplanes—his yellow German Extra 300L stunt plane rivaled Allen's Boeing 757 for pure effect—while Ellison was doing everything he could to get his hands on a $20-million Russian MiG-29. Rumor was that Ellison intended to use the jet to buzz over Gates's house at supersonic speed to blow out his rival's new, and undoubtedly pricey, windows.[6]

As if there were any doubt, the mid-1990s had clearly been a bonanza for those living and working in Silicon Valley. According to Payment Systems, Inc., the number of millionaires swelled from 45,000 in 1994 to 187,000 in 1996—very likely the biggest increase in rich people in one place in such a short period of time anytime, anywhere.[7] By 1999, Silicon Valley (nicknamed the "Valley of the Dollars") had the twelfth-largest economy in the world; a quarter-million millionaires lived there and sixty-four new ones appeared every day. More software engineers were on that year's Forbes Four Hundred than Hollywood execs, and people like Jerry Yang of Yahoo! were popping up on the covers of laddie magazines, the unlikely sex symbols of the day.[8] *Vanity Fair* had started a "New Establishment" list, a decidedly cooler version of the Forbes Four Hundred, made up of digerati, another sign that it was out with the old and in with the new within the wealthy elite.

"The act of trying to get rich quick by, say, starting an Internet company, has become virtually the sole requirement for entering the ranks of the nation's elite," reported Joseph Nocera of the *New York Times* in 1998. He suggested that the rapid ascent of technology millionaires and billionaires had the peripheral effect of making Old Money not just less influential but "ever so slightly disreputable." (Warren Buffett mused that those who had inherited their money were now considered by the average American to be merely "members of the lucky sperm club.")[9] People like Bill Gates of Microsoft, Jeff Bezos of Amazon, Scott McNeely of Sun Microsystems, and Yang of Yahoo! "have become something akin to national heroes," Nocera argued, the technology tycoon displacing the president as the highest possible aspiration for children in the United States. The tables of the American rich had fully turned, with social status entirely a function of how much money one had versus privilege and birthright.[10]

Uninterested in developing a patina of wealth, something previous generations of the American rich were very committed to in

order to show their peers they were no longer arriviste, these nouveau riche flaunted their youthfulness with reckless abandon. Techies were the most juvenile, but other wealthy men, in the full throes
of boomeritis, also acted like kids in a candy store. Steve Hilbert,
CEO of Conseco, for example, built a full-scale replica of Indiana
University's Assembly Hall basketball arena in which to shoot
hoops (he was too short to make the team when he went to school
there), while horror titan Stephen King bought the local rock 'n
roll radio station in Bangor, Maine, to prevent it from changing
formats. Paul Allen, an even bigger fan of rock 'n roll, was bankroll-
ing the Experience Music Project in Seattle to the tune of $60
million; he was known to strap on a Stratocaster in the hope he
could sound just a tiny bit like his biggest hero, Jimi Hendrix.[11] The
times they were a-changin' when it came to America's richest men.
The ghosts of old coots like Andrew Carnegie, John D. Rockefeller,
and Henry Ford were no doubt rolling in their graves as they
watched their billionaire successors behave like teenagers whose
parents were away.

Some of the living weren't very pleased about the Romper
Rooming of the upper class either. Joe Queenan, a writer for *Forbes*,
in 1997 asked the timely question, "Why can't billionaires grow
up?" obviously peeved by such adolescent behavior from some of
the richest people in the world. Seeing photographs of Allen with
his ax, Oakley Inc. founder Jim Jannard in sunglasses, and Nike's
Phil Knight in sneakers in the "Four Hundred" issue of his magazine, Queenan made a convincing case that, hardly the cool cats
they perhaps thought they looked like, "The billionaires with the
guitars and the shades and the workout gear . . . look like middle-
aged men whose kids—and employees—probably wish they'd get a
clue."[12] Two years later, Queenan was still riled up about super-rich
West Coasters not acting their age. "Deep-six the baseball caps,"
he implored, griping that, "Billionaires who dress like twelve-year-
old boys look like jackasses."[13] Queenan wasn't the only one dis-
cussing this new, younger breed of plutocrat. "The concept of the
scruffy-looking twenty-eight-year-old with a net worth of $100 mil-

lion is a 1990s invention," stated Dinesh D'Souza in 1999, correctly observing that no previous age had produced such a motley batch of boy billionaires.[14]

Softwarers' penchants for wearing Gap chinos and polo shirts to work only magnified the juvenile appearance of the e-rich, but they looked downright dowdy compared to the dot-commers' standard uniform of surf shorts and high-top sneakers. Not merely West Coast casualness, "There's a sort of nose-thumbing at the East Coast Establishment dress code," thought George Bell, CEO of Excite in 1999, the suit and tie a symbol of the Old Economy and Old Money that was being squashed by the New. In the post-grunge Pacific Northwest, appearing to have any fashion sense at all seemed to be at odds with having great technical chops, the latter the primary currency within digital culture.[15] Besides the cultural differences, numbers confirmed the trend that the American rich were, in fact, getting younger. NYU professor Edward Wolff found that in 1998, 16 percent of heads of American households in the top one percent of net worth were forty-five years old or younger, versus 11 percent in 1983 (14 percent versus 6 percent for thirty-five and younger). If the super-rich were acting like nouveau riche, at least part of the reason was that they were, quite literally, more nouveau than their more mature predecessors.[16]

IT'S THE SOFTWARE, STUPID

The youth movement within the affluent class went hand in hand, of course, with the tech-driven "New Economy." Technology stocks were buzzing past bricks-and-mortar and "old media" companies at warp speed; investing in the New Economy was the way for the average Joe to get in on the action. By the summer of 1998, the market capitalization of Yahoo! exceeded that of The New York Times Company; Amazon.com was worth more than Barnes & Noble and Borders combined; and Microsoft snuck past General

Electric as the highest-valued company in the world. "It's the soft-ware, stupid," said Rich Karlgaard, the publisher of *Forbes*, as if there were any question that the digital revolution wasn't rocking Wall Street's world.[17] By 1999, certain pockets of Seattle and the Silicon Valley—Medina, Mercer Island, Menlo Park—had about two hundred millionaires per square mile, leading some to compare these communities with Florence during the Renaissance in terms of the concentration of wealth.[18]

Just as eighties-style wealth had invaded television and the movies, Hollywood bigwigs were soon looking to late-1990s digital culture for inspiration. It was now obvious that an economic and social revolution was taking place. *Pirates of Silicon Valley*, a TV movie celebrating the rise of the ultra-rich computer nerd (with Anthony Michael Hall playing Bill Gates and Noah Wylie in the role of Steve Jobs), aired on TNT in 1999, taking viewers back to the Wild West days of PCs.[19] Also in the works that year was *20 Billion*, a feature comedy from Paramount about a software kingpin whose company's stock plummets when his product goes ker-blooey, and *Killer App*, a Fox sitcom (cooked up by Robert Altman and Garry Trudeau) about the wacky lives of a group of Silicon Valley techies (think *Friends* set in Menlo Park). In each case, stu-dio execs or test audiences apparently found that sufficient hilarity did not ensue—not too surprising given that it is hard to imagine any scenario, real or imaginary, in which a Bill Gates–like character could be funny.[20]

Although their lives may not have translated well to the big or small screens, the late 1990s were, truly, the revenge of the nerds. Stock options, which had appeared in the late 1980s to reward top executives should their company's stock rise, took off in the tech industry as a way to compensate for start-ups' low pay and long hours. Within the next decade, options had become the most likely path to great wealth. Employees who got in on the ground floor became vested and exercised options at a much higher value after their company's IPO.[21] At AOL, custom-support people making $7 an hour in the late 1980s were cashing out big time, their stock options and splits making them rich beyond their wildest dreams. A bookkeeper at that company with only five hundred shares of options in the early 1990s could cash them in for $3.5 million in 1999, not a bad return on investment. No less than 2,000 million-aires were created at AOL alone in the 1990s, many of them having kept the company's stock price constantly posted in the corner of their computer screens in order to have a 24/7 read on their market value.[22]

In historical terms, the tech company IPO made previous means of getting rich quick in the twentieth century—the stock tip of the 1920s, the big contract with Uncle Sam during World War II, the gusher in the 1950s, even the junk bonds of the eighties—seem feeble. The ways of getting rich that had held firm for decades, if not centuries—inheritance, education, membership in the Old Boy network, even, if absolutely necessary, hard work—seemed to have been chucked out the window, replaced by the well-I-could-do-that start-up of an Internet company.[23] And while being a software geek in the mid-1990s required one to know how to write arcane code, have an intimate relationship with semiconductors, or at least possess a degree from Stanford, being a rich dot-commer in the late 1990s seemed to require only a ten-page business plan and a thirty-second elevator pitch. The long, winding road to the American Dream was now a shortcut.[24]

As tech employees began to exercise their options through the late 1990s, it became apparent that an entirely new kind of rich American was being born. RIMs, or Retired Instant Millionaires, the beneficiaries of huge, sudden, and typically unplanned wealth, represented a class that had not existed before in America or any-where else. The few mega-lottery winners every year usually had their windfalls doled out over ten or twenty years, but RIMs got the whole ball of wax in one fell swoop, the psychological impact of which was hard to imagine. Although some cash-outs lived in the DC area—all ex-AOLers—many more were springing up in or near Seattle and Silicon Valley, ex-employees of Microsoft and In-ternet start-ups. The first wave of Microsoft RIMs were referred to as the "Class of Two Thousand," with many thousands more rolling out into the Puget Sound area as they too sold their stock.

Predominantly thirty- and fortysomethings, RIMs with, as it was known, "fuck-you money" kept busy pursuing their particular passions, whether it was trekking in Nepal, opening a boutique, having a spiritual awakening, or devoting their time and money to a particular cause. Others were off and running on another start-up, having fun and seeing if lightning might strike twice. Very few were just lying on a beach or simply improving their golf handicap; their A-type personalities drove them to achieve something else or "make a difference," whatever that might be. Yahoo! alone created 450 new millionaires from the $10 billion it spent on acquisitions between 1998 and 2000, the overwhelming majority of them still working a few years later, not content to just sit on their "purple dollars."[25] Most of the relatively few RIMs in New York, the beneficiaries of Goldman Sachs and Neuberger Berman IPOs, had not yet found their next calling, however, leaving them at sea in a city in which one was defined by work (and how loud one's money could say "fuck you").[26]

A BEASTLY FRENZY OF CONSPICUOUS CONSUMPTION

Even before the tech boom kicked into high gear, it was clear that when it came to spending money, one era was ending and another beginning. After a period of relative austerity between the late 1980s and early 1990s, affluent consumers were again keen on luxury goods, the social taboo of conspicuous consumption fading fast. Despite costing about $6,000 each, for example, Mont Blanc's gem-studded Prince Regent pens could hardly be found on store shelves in 1996, and Chanel had a waiting list for both its $3,000 double-breasted tweed dresses and its $750 khaki pants. Other tony brands like Lalique, Gucci, and Hermes were also back in a big way, helping revive nearly out-for-the-count upscale department stores such as Bergdorf Goodman and Saks. Managers of the Ferragamo store in New York's Trump Tower were even limiting how many pairs of shoes, bags, or jackets one could buy (just ten of each to a customer, please), an unusual but necessary step to ensure that every rich dog could have his or her day in fine leather.[27]

Like the domestic shortage of another flush time, the twenties, the American rich were also finding it hard to find good help these bountiful days. This time it was the retail arena that was cramping their style; there were not enough workers to go around to tend to wealthy consumers' finicky desires. "Several years into the boom," noted *New York* magazine in 1998, "so many consumers are willing to shell out for so many previously obscure services there just aren't enough people to provide them." High-end pet salons in the city, like Doggie-Do and Pussycats, Too!, were having major trouble finding qualified people to coif only-the-best-will-do pooches and kitties, and limousine drivers were also in short supply. Food service workers at upscale restaurants were equally scarce, especially sommeliers, which were now a virtual necessity for any bôite intending to cater to the money crowd. A good masseuse was worth his or her weight in gold, so much so that spas were recruiting them from out of town by offering juicy benefit packages. Like the maids, cooks, and butlers of three-quarters of a century ago, those in "service" in the late 1990s were a hot commodity, and demand far outstripped supply.[28]

Nowhere was the demand for the finer things in life greater than the eastern end of Long Island, which remained a stomping ground for American and European rich during the summer. Spending the summer of 1998 in the Hamptons, Bruce Nussbaum of *BusinessWeek* found the place "so awash in money this season that it makes the Reagan years look downright bourgeois." Nussbaum was in the midst of what he considered "a beastly frenzy of conspicuous consumption"; the East Coast put West Coast tech money to shame when it came to pure excess. Personal jewelers, 20,000-square-foot tear-downs, and a Land Rover and Porsche Boxster in every garage were just a few sights leading the reporter to claim that "a money-to-burn milieu defines the moment." Despite the all-the-rage carrot-tofu birthday cakes, the personal trainers for children, and the 66,000-square-foot houses (bigger than Gates's), Nussbaum sensed a palpable edginess. "When would it all end?" seemed to be the question on everyone's mind there, meaning when would the stock market get as flat as three-day-old champagne. "It's like that other Long Island party that Gatsby threw in the '20s, waiting to end badly," he speculated, the knowledge that everything that goes up must come down a nagging fear as the good times rolled.[29]

A stock market slide in August, climaxing with a 500-point drop the last day of the month, justified East Enders' fears. Gates himself lost $9 billion and Buffett $7 billion in a six-week stretch, but the average American millionaire felt some of the sting.[30] For the holiday season that year, even those with big bucks were looking to save a dollar here or there, shopping at discount retailers like Wal-Mart, Target, or Kmart rather than expensive department stores. Target was showing that design and style could be found on the cheap, and Kmart's Martha Stewart line of housewares looked right at home alongside the Swarovski crystal. If one could bear mingling with the hoi polloi, one could find 230-thread-count sheets at Wal-Mart, every bit as good and a lot cheaper than ones at Neiman Marcus and Saks.[31]

With the market correction of 1998 soon just a bad memory, it was full steam ahead for the making and spending of money in 1999. "Throwing money around is becoming a new sort of performance art," wrote Rene Chun of *New York* magazine; "Wall Street's spending habits have never been so irrationally exuberant." The evidence for what economists were now calling "hyperconsumerism" was pretty clear. Trend-forward brokers and investment bankers had taken to wearing Rolex Daytonas and Bulgari Scuba Chronos, each a steal at around $5,000 (compared to a $25,000 Patek Phillipe) but very hard to find. For the ladies, only a Tod's "Lady D." bag would do, the $1,300 Vachetta leather sack carried by Uma, Gwyneth, and Julia now scoring more points than the legendary Kelly bag. The Boeing Business Jet (BBJ) was the ultimate (and biggest) status symbol, however, the $35 million (add $10 million for a custom interior) modified 737 eclipsing the much smaller Gulfstream V ("The Five" to private jet-setters) as the way to make a grand entrance and departure. Wall Streeters also started adding a Wyoming ranch to their portfolio of residences, now that Montana was so over after the invasion of all those Hollywood types. Anywhere from $4 million to $30 million (a nice bonus for an investment banker who had a good year) bought at least 5,000 acres with postcard views and a "fishable" body of water, the latter just in case Mr. Pinstripe Suit felt like catching his own dinner.[32]

When it came to homes for the wealthy, size definitely mattered; the late 1990s were the golden age of the McMansion (or, more kindly, the mega-house). Bill Gates's $53-million home in Medina, Washington, contained a salmon stream, one-and-a-half-story trampoline room, and miniature golf course, his ID chip for every visitor a way to track who was where.[33] Gates's thirty-car garage was a mere carport compared to financier Ira Leon Rennert's 17,000-square-foot version, however, which could hold a hundred cars. (The latter's Tuscan-like villa house in Southampton covered an additional 52,000 square feet). Some new kitchens had three cooking areas—one for him, one for her, and one for the cook—with a separate breakfast room and pantry. Larger master bedrooms not only had sitting areas, his-and-her baths, and his-and-her dressing rooms but an area just for packing. Other McMansions features—his-and-her offices, conference rooms, libraries, bars, gyms, playrooms, home theaters, nanny and mother-in-law suites, massage and meditation rooms, even hair salons—could be compared to those found in a Newport "cottage," built during another era when space and money were for a relatively few Americans no object.[34]

Living in the city didn't preclude partaking freely in the beastly frenzy of conspicuous consumption. Nowhere was this more true than on New York's Upper East Side, a peculiar world to anyone who wasn't part of it but perfectly normal to those who were. Half the dads of kids in private schools there were or seemed to be investment bankers, their chauffer-driven Town Cars lined up at Dalton, Brearley, and Spence like a funeral procession every weekday morning and afternoon. Kids were wearing $3,000 watches and diamond necklaces to gym class; they never experienced the horror that was flying commercial. Two C-notes were often stuffed into birthday cards for friends, with boys or girls sometimes taking their whole class down to Disney World to celebrate. In their parents' circle, $100 million (nicknamed a "Hunge," while $1 billion was a "Bill") was now the measure for "real money." The simply well-to-do felt increasingly less secure and envious of their much richer neighbors.[35] "To be super-rich you need at least $100 million in assets and $10 million in annual income," concluded Dinesh D'Souza in his look at the cultural dynamics of wealth in 1999, arguing that people of this ilk represented a brand-new socio-economic group. In America, being merely "rich" meant having $10 to $100 million in assets and $1 to $10 million in annual income, an amazing leap in what it took to be considered wealthy over only twenty years.[36]

The arrival of so much New Money in one of the last bastions of Old Money did not go unnoticed. "Class Struggle on Park Avenue," announced *New York* magazine in 1999, as New Money gobbled up the best apartments on the famous street of dreams and, almost as worse, wore mink coats, stiletto heels, and copious amounts of jewelry. What was especially shocking was that these arrivistes had no desire to mingle with the shabby gentility; the idea that they could gain social status or perhaps learn a thing or two by doing so did not even occur to them. Since they didn't read, why would they emulate those who did, reasoned a long-time Park Avenuer, unapologetically bitter about the rocket-like ascendancy of the rich illiterati. Old Money found themselves complaining to their doctors about vague aches and pains and sexual impotency, their physical woes a direct result of spending inordinate amounts of time thinking about Mr. Big whisking his family down to the

Caribbean on a moment's notice or to their estate in Bedford for their regular weekend getaway.

Although they were hardly standing in line at soup kitchens, older money was seriously angry and depressed about its drop in the pecking order of life, especially within the few special acres of land where their families had typically lived for a couple of generations. Those who had read Edith Wharton in college were finding her class-obsessed writings of considerable therapeutic value, putting their own plight in historical and fictional perspective. Lily Bart, the heroine of *The House of Mirth*, was a particular delight. She had better taste and manners than her rich friends but precious little of their money, much like these Upper East Side ex–English majors holding onto their self-esteem for dear life. Some East Siders, conceding defeat, fled to the wilds of the Upper West Side to be around people more like themselves, the trek across Central Park a diaspora as emotional as for any immigrant displaced from his or her sacred homeland.[37]

RUINING IT FOR THE MILLIONAIRES

Much to the delight of less-than-super-rich East Siders and others who felt they had missed the high-tech boat, "the era of cyberbucks" was about to end rather abruptly. Start-ups, out of venture capital, entered the "nuclear winter" of the dot-com bust in the early 2000s; the bursting bubble rained on the Wall Street parade.[38] On the surface, the end of the run seemed to have a dampening effect, the frenzy of the late 1990s now over. In fact, the wealthy were spending as much money as ever, but to some, the buying spree seemed subtler than it had in recent and not so recent times. James W. Michaels and Victoria Murphy, for example, argued that consumption circa 2000 "equals anything seen during the gilded age of the late nineteenth century or the stock market boom of the 1920s," suggesting that the current rich were more "discreet."

David Brooks in *Bobos in Paradise* concurred, observing that, "It's hard to find signs of . . . outright decadence." Not so discreet, however, were the many new mansions that gave William Randolph Hearst's San Simeon a run for its money, nor the 300-foot aluminum yacht *Netscaper* James Clark was building that made J. P. Morgan's famed *Coursair* look like an old wreck. Foodies were still putting in not one but two or three Sub-Zero fridges, and those wanting their backyard to be a work of art installed mammoth fountains and giant boulders.[39] Newly planted but fully grown trees remained a common sight on the grounds of new mega-houses, their owners too impatient to wait for saplings to grow. In 2000, Alamo Rent-A-Car tycoon Michael Egan moved no less than 300,000 tons of dirt around to create a Frederick Law Olmstead-like vista of rolling hills, man-made streams, and bridges on his $25-million estate on Nantucket, dissatisfied with the landscaping put in by the original owner, George Vanderbilt. "New money is fast transforming Nantucket from New England paradise into Miami Beach north," said one reporter from *Forbes* that year; a not-so-funny joke on the island was that "the billionaires are ruining it for the millionaires."[40]

The billionaires were also ruining it for the millionaires on the Left Coast in 2000 by hogging all the best goods and services. Besides a major housing shortage that drove the prices for tract homes to half a million dollars, luxury cars, especially Beemers, were still virtually impossible to find in the Bay Area. Services catering to the wealthy were also a problem, with gardeners blowing off $10,000 jobs for $100,000 ones. The e-rich were flying to L.A. to have their taxes done and flying in contractors from Canada to install their home theaters, the waiting lists for locals to do each ridiculous.[41] If this was discreet, it would be hard to imagine what constituted blatant consumption.

With the possible exception of how the wealthy treated their pets, no aspect of consumer culture was more over the top at the turn of the millennium than that revolving around kids. For children of some of the American rich, it seemed, being born with a silver spoon in their mouths wasn't quite enough. Kate Spade, Versace, Burberry, Ralph Lauren, and Gucci all offered kid clothing and accessories—the latter an $865 diaper bag, $1,280 motorcycle suit, and $4,250 mink coat sold at Life Size, part of Fred Segal's, in Santa Monica. Cashmere booties, gloves, hats, and sweaters for little ones were available at Zitomer in New York, but these were mere trifles compared to what some celebrities were spending on their kids. Tahcrea O'Neal, Shaq's four-year-old daughter, wore three-carat diamond earrings and played in a $6,000 dollhouse, a Mini-Me version of the basketball star's lifestyle. A Hot Wheels wasn't quite luxe enough for two-year-old Christian Combs, so his dad Sean (a.k.a. Puffy, for the moment) special-ordered a $5,000 miniature Mercedes-Benz that looked and rode much like his old man's. When it came to having the finer things in life, it was clear that the acorn didn't fall very far from the wealthy tree.[42] "In an era when it's all about giving your child an 'edge,'" wrote Cynthia Hacinli for *Washingtonian* magazine in 2001, "no wonder pursuit of the best has become an Olympic sport." Baby chic could also be found in the form-counts-as-much-as-function realm of strollers, with the Italian Peg Perego and Swedish Emmaljunga leading the stylistic pack.[43]

Children weren't the only ones getting an "edge" in this era of you-can-have-it-if-you-want-it consumerism. In more and more arenas of life, privacy and exclusivity rapidly defined how the wealthy were getting an edge; their willingness to pay whatever it took to distance themselves from the public was powerful. For the clothes-obsessed, the fashion concierge replaced the between-the-wars dressmaker, postwar couturier, and personal shopper of the 1980s, thus allowing that woman on the go to forgo the dreadful shopping experience entirely. Boutiques, department stores, and even designers were hiring fashion concierges to pick out clothes they knew their clients would like and sending them (sometimes along with themselves) to these lucky women, most of them socialites or busy execs. Barneys had a concierge, of course, as did Bergdorfs, Neiman Marcus, Prada, and Gucci. Anyone who could afford such a service—often running into hundreds of thousands of dollars a year—was, essentially, being treated like a celebrity, cold cash now every bit as valuable as fame as social currency. Concierges for fashionistas were part of a growing trend—anytime, anywhere service for just about anything—for the wealthy, something that would grow into a key signifier of the American rich over the next decade.[44]

The economic slowdown in 2001, made even worse by 9/11, did little to impact the anytime, anywhere lifestyles of American wealth culture. Exclusivity was in fact fast becoming both demanded and expected by the wealthy as a distinct VIP subculture emerged in the early 2000s. Those without "juice" didn't have a prayer of getting into velvet rope clubs like the Candle Room in Dallas, Casa Casuarina in Miami, and Frederick's in New York—the result those with VIP privileges wanted. Even gyms were going exclusive. Memberships in places like Equinox's E in New York were limited to two hundred invitation-only guests (at $24,000 a year). "In a competitive social and economic environment, trading up—whether it's paying a premium so you can breeze past the bouncers or ponying up big bucks so you can cruise around in a Rolls-Royce Phantom—makes you look and feel like a playboy," explained Melissa Ceria of *Time* in 2004. Travel was also going VIP, with members of clubs like Exclusive Resorts given access to grand homes in more than twenty-five destinations from Aruba to Timbuktu (for up to $25,000 a year plus a $375,000 deposit).[45]

Not surprisingly, the uppermost end of the world of finance became as exclusive as it could get, with those able to utter any epithet they wanted with their money forming their own private investment clubs. The most elite of these was Tiger (The Investment Group for Enhanced Results) 21 (as in the century), a support group for the super-rich with chapters in New York, Los Angeles, San Diego, San Francisco, Palm Beach, and Miami. The mostly Old and Young Boys club (just a few women belonged) for the New Age required at least $10 million in investable assets to join and charged an annual fee of $25,000, a high enough financial hoop to keep the riffraff out. In 2007, eight years after the organization's founding in New York, the 145 members of Tiger 21 controlled about $10 billion in assets, about half of that their own money. One-half investment club, one-half therapy group ("Dr. Phil meets Morgan Stanley," said *Fortune*), Tiger 21 was a rare opportunity for members to share the juicy details of not just their portfolios but their lives. Members still meet for a full day once a month, when these extremely successful entrepreneurs (but not always successful investors) receive objective financial advice from their peers—something unavailable anywhere else.[46]

Celebrities also jumped on the exclusive bandwagon in the early 2000s, discovering there were fans out there who would pay enormous sums of money for a private audience with one of their heroes. The private show had always been part of show business, of course, a legacy of the European royal appearance and patronage system, but soon scads of celebrities started renting themselves out to the wealthy, realizing they didn't have to perform before hundreds or thousands of people to make the same amount of money. A private concert by Stevie Wonder could be had for $750,000 in 2002, for example; one's own stand-up show by Jerry Seinfeld was for sale for $550,000. Interested in talking about military strategy with a real pro? Norman Schwarzkopf was available for a hundred grand, while baseball fans could pick up some pointers from Tommy Lasorda for only half that much.[47] At least in terms of status, the billionaires (and mere centamillionaires) were ruining it for the millionaires, creating their own private playground in which only they were allowed and could afford to play. As hedge funders began to rule the rich roost in the mid-2000s, the spread between the mega-haves and the have-a-lots would grow into a chasm, putting the former into a league of their own.

THE SIMPLE LIFE

Interestingly, all this special treatment didn't do much to make the super-rich any happier than the rest of us who sit in the coach section of life. A study published in the *Journal of Personality and Social Psychology* in the mid-1990s found that money had little relationship to happiness, confirming the findings of a similar study from about a decade earlier. Genetics, these and other studies have shown, play the biggest role in determining one's level of happiness; a financial windfall can move the happy needle for just a short time.[48] Income had no bearing on workers' happiness level in a study done by corporate consultants Rich Foster and Greg Hicks and described in their 1999 book *How We Choose To be Happy*; this study also supported the "happiness set point" theory. If the rich truly weren't any happier than the rest of us, being envious of them was entirely unnecessary, research showed. This idea carried huge implications for life in America as we knew it.[49]

A mountain of research studies couldn't change the envy many Americans felt as they watched those around them stack their piles of cash like firewood, however. "In the midst of the longest sustained economic boom in history, many American families are experiencing an unprecedented sense of impoverishment," proposed Robert Frank in 2000. He believed we felt poorer not just because of the growing income gap but because, in our 24/7 media age, we were simply more aware of the tremendous wealth that surrounded us. Luxury fever among bobos in paradise wanting to trade up, to put it in a literary sense, was driving many middle-, upper-middle-, and even upper-class members crazy with unhappiness over not being invited to the big party going on next door.[50] This was ironic, to say the least, given the (over)abundance many Americans enjoyed, which was completely independent from the way their (not any happier) rich friends, neighbors, and co-workers were choosing to live their lives. "Class envy of the rich has always mystified me and makes less and less sense in today's world," said the eminent British historian and author Paul Johnson, a too-rare instance in which the whole concept of rich-is-better was challenged. "Amassing wealth has nothing to do with happiness, so why envy the rich?" he wondered, a question easy to ask but very difficult to answer.[51]

Besides not being any happier than po' folks, the American rich had other emotional issues to worry about, shrinks were finding. Although the business community had been generally gung ho about the escalating wealth of the mid-1990s, for example, there was concern about how it might be affecting the younger generation. "Affluenza is spreading," *Forbes* reported in 1995, the magazine suggesting that the perils of family money were now "becoming epidemic."[52] Five years later, sudden-wealth syndrome, another malady of the rich, was cause for concern. People with this condition were having trouble with the range of emotions that came with the territory. Usually male, under forty, and working for a dot-com, sudden-wealthers typically felt depressed, their life without meaning now that they had all the trappings of wealth at such a young age. Sudden-wealth syndrome was "the despair of people who have gotten what they want," according to Jacob Needleman, author of *Money and the Meaning of Life*. Sufferers were being treated at places like The Money Meaning and Choices Institute in Kentfield, California, conveniently located just north of Silicon Valley. Discomfort when thinking about money, guilt about having it, uncertainty about how to spend it, and uncontrollable fear of losing it were the major symptoms of the ailment; the most effective cure, according to therapists in the field, was the simple act of giving a lot of it away to someone who needed it more.[53]

The wealthy, or at least their therapists, might have been more careful about what they wished for. A wallop of a remedy was soon decreasing the angst associated with sudden-wealth syndrome—the plop-plop of the stock market and fizz-fizz of the dot-com bubble in 2001 provided, like Alka-Seltzer, instant relief. Therapists now, however, had a different problem to address with their clients: the loss of self-esteem that seemed to correlate precisely with one's net worth. "The anxiety is palpable," said one L.A. psychologist in October of that year about his very recently much richer clients. The mood was even worse in Silicon Valley, where young entrepreneurs had not only lost most or all of their paper millions but much of their social and personal identities as well. A fair share of the American rich were popping Xanax and Zoloft like M&Ms', hoping these quick fixes would tide them over while the bugs were shaken out of the New Economy.[54]

The emotional roller coaster of the American rich through the late 1990s and early 2000s seemed to run on a parallel course with their whale of a financial ride. There were 170 billionaires among the *Forbes* Four Hundred in 1997, thirteen times as many as in 1982 when the magazine published its first such list. If not quite tracking with Moore's Law (the power of computer chips doubles every eighteen months), the size of fortunes expanded at a startling rate, faster than ever before by a long shot. Although he was hardly representative of your ordinary millionaire, Bill Gates's personal wealth in 1996 grew by an incredible $400 million a *week*, on average, making the fortunes of Carnegie or Rockefeller, which each took decades to build, seem a little less impressive.[55] Indeed, it had taken Rockefeller twenty-five years to make his first billion by finding and then selling oil, while hardly legendary people like Gary Winnick were now joining the B-club in just a year or two (he did it in eighteen months simply by announcing his intention to build a global fiber-optics network).[56] More than half of *Forbes*'s 1999 list were billionaires, the first time that had occurred. The entire Four Hundred had a net worth of about $1 trillion—more than China's gross national product.[57]

With the upper class now rather suddenly cool, Hollywood eagerly embraced the semiotics of the rich to draw viewers to theaters. Geekworld may not have been able to make it in the movies but *fin de siècle* wealth could; luxurious lifestyles as pure eye candy were frequent backdrops on the silver screen in 1998, even when incongruous to plots. Michael Douglas, who had almost single-handedly defined 1980s-style wealth in *Wall Street*, was back with *A Perfect Murder*, his 10,000-square-foot New York apartment a veritable mountain of marble. In *Stepmom*, Susan Sarandon and Ed Harris make their way between their fabulous SoHo loft and gorgeous nineteenth-century colonial in the 'burbs in a Land Rover and BMW, not unlike what actual New Yorkers with money were doing but somehow a lot less prettily. Having no money didn't prevent the young couple in *The Parent Trap* from getting married on the *QE II*; they eventually take digs in a to-die-for winery in Napa Valley and a posh mansion in London, with butlers at the ready in each. (The movie also featured not one but two Ritz-Carltons, perhaps marking a new high—or low—in product placement.) And in *You've Got Mail*, Meg Ryan lives in a kick-ass apartment on the Upper West Side although her kids' bookstore is going down faster than the *Titanic*. Audiences responded well to all these films, suggesting that it was fun to hang out with the rich, if only for a couple of hours in a pretend world.[58] Two popular TV shows of the late 1990s—*Friends* and *Mad About You*—also blatantly skirted the realities of New York City real estate, their characters living in plush flats while holding down working-stiff jobs.[59]

Another product of Hollywood, however, cut to the chase, flaunting the superficiality of the American rich in all its glory. Although it might be painful to think of *The Simple Life* as a groundbreaking, even historically important, show, it wanted nothing to do with the faux worlds of movies and sitcoms and marked the crossover of reality TV from featuring people wanting to get rich to those who already were. Despite the fact that we were "at war" after invading Iraq in the spring of 2003, Americans' desire to watch the silly escapades of a couple of rich girls was no less diminished. For the show's first season, which debuted in late 2003, pampered princesses Paris Hilton and Nicole Richie reversed the direction of those rich television characters from the 1960s, the Clampetts, by moving from Beverly Hills to Arkansas. Inspired, if you could call it that, by another show from the sixties, *Green Acres*, which explored the wacky trials and tribulations of a fish-out-of-water wealthy couple, *The Simple Life* had the twenty-two-year-old party girls doing exactly what urbanites thought country folk did when they weren't on national television; i.e., plucking chickens and frying squirrels. *The Simple Life* was *King Lear*, however, compared to another show featuring rich girls, called, appropriately enough, *Rich Girls*. The MTV reality show starred Tommy Hilfiger's eighteen-year-old daughter Ally, offering viewers a peek into what life was supposedly like for your average limo-driven, Caribbean-vacationing high school student with a personal shopper.[60]

Blame Fox and MTV if you must, but television was, as usual, just using what was going on in the real world as entertainment fodder. Americans accounted for a disproportionate number of the richest people in the world in 2001, with eight of the top ten and twenty-three of the top forty wealthiest from the good old USA.[61] The collective net worth of the Forbes Four Hundred dropped from $1.2 trillion to $950 billion that year, however; this was only the third time in the history of the list that the richest Americans, as a group, had lost money. Individuals in Old Economy businesses like retailing and manufacturing had displaced a few dozen New Economy types on the Four Hundred; some semblance of sanity returned to the business arena after five years of raging dot-com fever.[62]

The 2002 class of the Four Hundred lost another $80 billion, the still-tanking stock market causing the super-rich, like ordinary Americans, to give back a good chunk of their windfall from the late 1990s.[63] In 2003, however, the Four Hundred rebounded by 10 percent. The group's total net worth received a spark from some newcomers working in the still rather mysterious investment field of hedge funds.[64] By 2005, it was clear the rich were back on track; the Forbes Four Hundred from that year picked up a tidy $125 billion in net worth. Of the Four Hundred, 374 were billionaires. Outside of hedge funds, the best ways to make a quick buck were good old real estate and oil.[65] Over the next few years, hedge funders would continue to invade *Forbes*'s list with a vengeance, in the process taking the wealthy elite to an entirely new level.

Low-cal Luxe

This era, in which the most money was made (and probably lost) in economic history, not surprisingly attracted some people who wanted to get a piece of the pie by meeting just the right person. Marrying for money was nothing new, of course, but the imperative for the rich to keep busy rather than wallow in opulent leisure had seeded a new kind of gold digger. "Gold digging, for the most part, has been sadly degraded," according to Freda Germaise. She recalled the good old days of decades past when women with a glint in their eyes went after Rich Uncle Moneybags purely to live the high life. "The old-time showgirl gold digger has given way to the aerobically conditioned bimbo leading a life of low-cal luxe with her sweet-'n-'lo daddy," she wrote for GQ in 1995, describing the hardworking, fundraising, dinner-party-throwing fortune seeker of the mid-1990s now as "a sad and isolated figure on her Stair-Master."[66] Rich men, and a few rich women, however, were taking no chances that they might be marrying a good old-fashioned gold digger. "Prenuptial agreements may seem like the ultimate mergers-and-acquisitions legacy of the 1980s," suggested Jan Hoffman of the *New York Times* that same year, citing a recent one that was seventy pages long, required five sets of lawyers to write, and cost more than $100,000. Not just family heirlooms but art collections, horses, and opera tickets were increasingly showing up in contracts, with a "pet clause" (detailing not only custody terms but dibs on potential offspring) a common item. Lawyers were also dealing with issues ranging from sexual expectations (just once a week, one man insisted) to weight level (no more than ten pounds over that of bridal night, another husband made clear), the prenup guaranteeing that the wealthy romantic received full value for his investment.[67]

Because of the rising popularity of prenups among the super-rich, gold diggers of the mid-1990s were also netting less gold when divorcing. In 1983, Revlon billionaire Ronald Perelman had to fork over $8 million to wife number one (Faith Golding) when they split up and $80 million to number two (Claudia Cohen) when they went separate ways in 1994. Two years later, however, it was going to cost fool-me-twice-but-don't-fool-me-thrice Perelman relative pocket change to make number three (Patricia Duff) go away, his "bulletproof" prenup saving the alimony day. Henry Kravis also had a bulletproof contract in hand, so he retained almost all of his nearly $1 billion estate when he said good-bye to Carolyn Roehm; John Kluge's ironclad agreement with his soon-to-be ex-wife was, legally speaking, a thing of beauty. Even Bill Gates, who once said he would never ask a potential fiancée to sign one, went prenup in 1994 when he married Microsoft colleague Melinda French. The Donald was eventually able to persuade a pregnant Marla Maples to sign on the dotted line just a week or two before they said "I do." Stowing money away in offshore trusts was a popular way for wealthy lover boys to protect assets should a bullet or two somehow pierce their contract; their lawyers were sure that bank officers from places like the Cayman Islands would never show up in a U.S. court.[68]

Much like a century and a half earlier, lots of gold diggers went west when men there started discovering big nuggets. The ratio of men to women in the tech world was seventy to thirty (about pi to one, in engineer vernacular) near the end of the boom in 2000, meaning "e-guys" would have to seek women outside the industry if they had romance on their big brains. Fortunately, almost as important as high-tech in Silicon Valley, public relations was an industry chock-full of young women very open to the idea of meeting a nice young man with more money than God. Potential mates were divided into two groups: millionaires on paper, or MOPs, and bona fide, gone-public millionaires, or GPMs, the latter of course much more desirable. Some women Googled guys they had met to find out how much they were worth before investing more time in the relationship; others actively attended benefits or what they referred to as "how-to-meet-a-rich-husband parties." Rich geeks' habit of avoiding suits and ties like the plague was a curve e-diggers had mastered, knowing very well that you can't tell a valuable book by its tattered cover. Although they'd never be mistaken for Pierce Brosnan and were unusually attached to their Palms, BlackBerrys, and Nokias, tech guys were viewed by most women on the hunt as sweet and decidedly uncadlike. "They call when they say they'll call and show up when they say they will," said one PR woman on the scene; she had no problem at all with industry men's preference to pursue courtships mostly via e-mail.[69] Others, however, were less kind about the pickin's for Bay Area gold diggers. "The odds are good but the goods are odd," went a popular saying, the more critical view being that engineers and programmers were much more interested in eBay and video games than learning the fine art of dating. Venture capitalists were considered far less nerdy but overwhelmingly self-absorbed, entirely capable of asking the proverbial question, "But enough of me—what do you think of me?"[70]

Meanwhile, back east, women of the new millennium were concentrating on minting their own gold, at least those who were already more than comfortable. Young ladies from Money, hardly just having lunch, were busy pursuing careers in, almost always, a creative milieu. Rather than immerse themselves in charity work like their grandmothers, mothers, and even older sisters did, Upper East Side thirtyish women like Lulu de Kwiatkowski, Aerin Lauder, Serena Boardman, and Hyatt Bass were throwing themselves into business, disdaining the "socialite" label (the "S-word"). "We're living in a culture— with cell phones and laptops and telecommuting and venture-capital madness—where work has become entertainment, as well as a kind of showy status symbol," wrote J. Van Meter for *Vogue* in 2000, reporting that women of a certain class were competing in an escalating battle of busyness. The dissing of the American rich in the late 1980s was a big part of the backlash against society among Park Avenue Princesses, very early twenty-first-century trust funders wanting, more than anything else, respect. Rather than just leaving things to chance, however, these young women relied heavily on a fundamental tool of society: publicity—provided, naturally, by the diva duo Lizzie Grubman and Liz Cohen themselves—to give their careers (and themselves) a boost. Dot-com launch parties and store openings had displaced charity galas as New York's social scene of the moment, the making of money considered cooler than giving it away.[71]

Ironically, and maybe a little perversely, the work-as-entertain-

ment phenomenon was an attempt for the younger generation of
Old Money to rebrand themselves as New. The New Economy was
making family money earned in the Old look dusty and musty,
an increasingly embarrassing anachronism. "People were doing it
[cashing in on new technologies] in the last century, and they're
doing it again at the end of this one," observed *Money* in 1997,
"[but] what's new is the acceleration of the chase—at warp or
warped speed." The status that used to come with having family
wealth for generations, that indefinable trait that separated the
true gentlemen from the nouveau boys and the true ladies from
the nouveau girls, was left mostly in the dust. "Old money is no
longer important," flatly stated David H. Konansky, the chairman
of Merrill Lynch, who knew of which he spoke, that same year.
"New wealth far outstrips old wealth," he made clear, the sheer
volume of money now being amassed making the number of years
one's family had it completely beside the point.[72] As Old Money
shrank further over the next decade, it became increasingly difficult
to tell who was rich and who was not. "There are simply so many
new millionaires and billionaires—from diverse backgrounds and
lifestyles—that the old signifiers of status have become obsolete,"
observed Robert Frank in 2007—nothing, from clothes to which
(Ivy League) college one went to, any longer a reliable indicator of
class.[73]

Even *Money* magazine, its mission to provide practical advice
on making and growing the green stuff, was now telling readers how
to become wealthy by marrying a billionaire. Forget the jewelry,
mansions, and other goodies to be gained by finding such a golden
goose, *Money* explained in 2007; snagging a sugar daddy meant no
more scrimping to contribute to your IRA or worrying about how
to pay for college for your kids. Luckily for fortune hunters in the
twenty-first century, there were now not only a considerable number of billionaires around (946 in the world, to be exact), but they
were much easier to find than in the past, thanks to good old
Google. Sure, most of them were married (and only thirty-eight
American women were among the bunch, with an average age of

sixty-three), but their numbers were growing as more centamillion-aires hit the Big B.[74]

So how exactly does one go about hooking up with a Mr. or Ms. UltraBig? Much the same way, it turns out, as Joanna Steichen recommended almost twenty years earlier, when a mere millionaire was enough—only the stakes are a thousand times higher. Most importantly, go to work for one, *Money* advised, having discovered that over half of the billionaires it tracked down had married a fellow employee. To that end, the magazine suggested, one should "get an M.B.A. ASAP," the degree offering a good way to have access to the boss. Naturally, finding a job in finance or investing offered the best chance to bump into that successful but lonely CEO, although media and entertainment, or even oil and gas, also had a decent number of billionaires riding the elevator. If one's GMAT scores just weren't up to snuff, other jobs that put one in contact with the very rich—high-end real estate or private jet or yacht sales, say—were the next best thing.[75]

Going to work for a B-Boy or one of the few B-Girls wasn't the only way to get close enough to shoot an arrow into his or her heart, however. (Madame de Pompadour sure didn't work for Louis XV when she reeled him in.) Moving into a tony neighborhood, even if it meant living in someone's attic, was a smart strategy, said *Money*, knowing that all roads eventually led to the local Starbucks. Museum receptions and gallery openings were also good bets, given that oil and watercolors ran through the veins of many a billionaire bachelor and bachelorette. Charity events also, of course, were a must, as was reading the *Chronicle of Philanthropy* to identify the causes du jour among top givers. (Party girl Mercedes Tavacoli had the good fortune to sit next to billionaire oilman Sid Richardson Bass at a charity event in England, reportedly throwing a dinner roll to liven things up. The bread trick worked, even though they were both married at the time.)[76] Should all these handy tips fail, there was always MillionaireClub123.com, which let women jump into its pool of eligibles for free (men paid anywhere between $10,000 and $150,000 in 2007 to find Ms. Poor-but-Right).[77]

THE MILLIONAIRE NEXT DOOR

All this effort may very well have been unnecessary, given that one was probably within spitting distance of a moneybags without even knowing it. Society divas, CEOs, star athletes, and Hollywood glitterati may have made the headlines, but the average person of wealth in America was, according to a new book in 1996, a self-employed businessperson living a very normal, even boring, some might say, life. Thomas Stanley's and William Danko's bestseller *The Millionaire Next Door: The Surprising Secrets of America's Wealthy* defused many of the myths surrounding the American rich by showing they were not private-school-educated snobs having high tea every afternoon but ordinary in every way, except for their high net worth. Of the 100 million households in the United States, 3.5 million held $1 million or more in assets; the overwhelming majority of the latter hadn't inherited their money but gradually accumulated it by saving, investing conservatively, and, of all things, being frugal.[78]

Ironically, in their research Stanley and Danko found relatively few millionaires in white-collar professions—doctors, lawyers, stockbrokers—because such people were a part of what the authors called "the high-consumption culture;" they had to look and act wealthy by joining country clubs, taking expensive vacations, and buying luxury cars.[79] On the other hand, those who lived below their means accounted for most of the millionaires, suggesting that those who played a good defense rather than a great offense had the better chance of getting rich in America.[80] Income and stuff were much different than wealth, *The Millionaire Next Door* showed. The book made a convincing case that being truly rich was, quite literally, money in the bank.[81] Investment bankers in New York were puzzled by the smash-hit's findings ("Where is this guy [the millionaire next door] from, Kansas?" asked one such big spender), but everywhere else in the country, people instantly recognized the rich-but-you-wouldn't-know-it archetype.[82]

After the success of *The Millionaire Next Door*, with wealth envy at an all-time high, other authors jumped on the how-to-get-rich bandwagon to make their own millions. "Millionaire mania has become the 'Harry Potter' of personal-finance publishing," *Newsweek* reported in 2000, as a string of advice books hit store shelves and online booksellers. Thomas J. Stanley followed up his own bestseller with another, *The Millionaire Mind*, and Brian O'Connell's *The 401(k) Millionaire* and Brian Koslow's *365 Ways to Become a Millionaire (Without Being Born One)* also showed readers how to get to Richville. *Who Wants To Be a Millionaire?* was the book version of the television show that was turning out to be a cultural phenomenon. (During one week in August 2000, the show finished second, third, and fourth in the Nielsen ratings, beaten only by *Survivor*, another show offering contestants the chance to win $1 million.)[83] Since the early nineteenth century, a million dollars held a special resonance, but now because of real estate values and the surging stock market, for many the magical number was within striking distance. About 4 percent of American households were indeed millionaires in terms of total assets (house included), clear evidence of the gradual "middleclassing" of wealth over the course of the twentieth century.[84]

Without a doubt, the persistent power of the "millionaire" has been and remains one of the most interesting aspects of the cultural dynamics of wealth. In pure financial terms, inflation has played a huge role in devaluing the status of being a millionaire—$1 million in 2005 was equivalent to just $86,000 in 1930—but the mythology is arguably as strong as ever. "There is something about the word 'millionaire' that continues to resonate," according to Andy Serwer in 2005, who correctly believed that, "It's still an entry point into a club that most folks hope to join." (Part of the popular appeal of America's most famous millionaire, President Bush—who had recently been reelected—was no doubt due to millionaire envy.) Serwer located about 40,000 books on Amazon.com with the word "millionaire" in the title (my own search in January 2009 revealed over 89,000), a good indicator of the term's still-potent cultural currency.[85] Hubert Herring of the

New York Times in 2006 felt similarly to Serwer, thinking that, "We still use the word 'millionaire' with reverential awe, with a sense that someone with such wealth lives in the rarefied world of the super-rich, the champagne flowing daily in an art-filled penthouse."

The fact was, however, that there were no less than 8.7 million millionaires in the world, according to a study from Merrill Lynch and Capgemini, their number nearly doubling in the past decade.[86] Millionaires had become commonplace over the decades ("Somewhere along the line, having $1 million—like the ability to diagram sentences, do math in your head, and the dollar itself—became devalued," observed Paul B. Brown of the *Times* in 2008), yet most people still wanted to be one.[87]

Moreover, much of the hostility held toward the rich in the 1980s had been defused during the tech boom, wealth as American as apple pie again, as in the postwar years. Interestingly, most of the how-to-become-a-millionaire books were making a solid case for "Old Economy" values like sacrifice, discipline, and hard work, exactly opposite from how many in the New Economy had, or at least appeared to have, gotten rich. "The frugal millionaire next door has emerged as the modern-day hero," *Newsweek* reported, he or she "embodying both money and morality." Suze Orman was going to town on this very idea in her blockbuster *The Courage to Be Rich*, a neo-1970s self-help take on the always ethically ambiguous pursuit of wealth. ("Money is attracted to people who are strong and powerful, respectful of it, and open to receiving it," went one of her courage boosters.) Inevitably, a new book appeared on the market—*How to Be a Billionaire: Proven Strategies from the Titans of Wealth*—the stakes raised now that millionaires were merely the guy or gal next door.[88] "Now we are divided between those people who have become rich in the past five years and those who haven't," thought Peggy Noonan in 2000, believing this gap had superseded previous national divisions of race and class.[89]

By midway through the first decade of the twenty-first century, the millionaire drizzle had turned into a downpour. Stanley had followed up his sequel with another, *Millionaire Women Next Door*, but it was David Bach's *The Automatic Millionaire: A Powerful One-Step Plan to Live and Finish Rich* that blew the doors off the how-to-get-rich genre. Understanding that readers didn't really want to work that hard to get wealthy, authors took the roads-are-paved-with-gold idea even further with books like *One Minute Millionaire, Lunchtime Millionaire,* and *The Accidental Millionaire.* Speed was of the essence, with *Millionaire by 40* outdone by *Millionaire by 26* outdone by *How to Be a Teenage Millionaire* outdone by *Discovering the Millionaire in Every Child.* It was surprising a book called *How to Conceive a Millionaire* had not yet been published.[90]

It wasn't a book about how to become a millionaire that most emphatically celebrated wealth in the early 2000s, however, but the first Millionaire Fair, which was held in the Netherlands in 2002, also making stops in Cannes, Shanghai, and Kortijk, Belgium. By 2005, the annual event included the city that was well on the way to becoming the world capital of conspicuous consumption—Moscow. Twenty-five thousand people spent a total of $600 million at that year's fair in Moscow, and 40,000 showed up the next year to buy everything from a $150,000 GoldVish cellphone (gold-plated charger included) to a 1.3 million euro Bugatti. (One jeweler was selling a gold-plated pacifier, and villas off the coast of Dubai were offered for the taking.) Russian oil barons, businessmen, and others who had made their millions or billions in ways best not known were basking in what was known as "palace style," a form of over-the-top luxury unique to their country (think chandeliers in the bathrooms). In 2003, Russia's 88,000 millionaires and twenty-five billionaires were apparently looking to Arabian oil sheiks as role models; one dismantled an Orthodox church in Russia and re-assembled it in Cannes for the perfect ($40 million) wedding.[91]

Indeed, in a culture in which the idea of saving one's money for a rainy day was peculiar at the very least, rich Russians were seizing their day, putting Americans to shame when it came to spending their fortunes. The globalization of wealth would only accelerate in the next few years, East challenging West not in a space race or arms race but in perhaps the ultimate contest—the race to be rich. The 2007 Millionaire Fair in Moscow was an even more over-the-top affair, with more than 200 luxury marketers showing off their stuff to some of Russia's 103,000 millionaires and fifty-three billionaires. As had the Saudis in the 1970s and the Japanese in the 1990s, the Russians clearly ruled the global new money roost, still not very well acquainted with luxury brands but learning fast. Buying Escalades and custom rims like they were going out of style, the Russian arrivistes were making American show-offs look like the millionaire next door.[92]

TED'S EXCELLENT DONATION

How the rich could and should get rid of their money also redefined wealth culture in the last decade of the twentieth century and the first decade of the twenty-first. With the decline of Old Money, one of the cornerstones of society—the charity gala—was on the ropes, a bit worn at the seams after a hundred years or so. Even Brooke Astor, at ninety-three still the reigning queen of philanthropy in New York and, perhaps, the world, was dreading the upcoming benefit season in fall 1995. "Just hearing the word 'benefit' is like having around your neck a large collar, which has snapped on to it a long leash," she revealed in *Vanity Fair*, fully aware that those she was about to implore to attend one felt exactly the same way. In her research for *Why the Wealthy Give: The Culture of Elite Philanthropy*, Francine Ostrower indeed found that the wealthy elite went to benefits not for fun but for social climbing and networking, willing to endure yet another boring affair simply because, as one swell put it, "There are a lot of people like me there."[93]

One rich man—Ted Turner—was about to change the entire landscape of philanthropy, in his inimitable style spearheading a much more compelling way of giving away money than the been-there, done-that benefit circuit. Turner believed the annual *Forbes* list was hurting philanthropic efforts as the Four Hundred jockeyed for position in what he called "their Super Bowl," the very wealthy reluctant to part with significant amounts of money out of sheer ego. "These new super-rich won't loosen up their wads because they're afraid they'll reduce their net worth and go down on the list," Turner said in 1996, adding that the current batch of "ole skinflints" were doing nothing less than "destroying our country." At the time, Turner, through his foundation, was giving about $7 million a year to environmental and other causes, which represented about 7 percent of his net worth. Turner had pledged lots more money to his alma maters and his own foundation but hadn't yet come up with the actual goods, something that only added to his reputation as "the Mouth of the South."[94] Turner's call for a new list—one that ranked the biggest givers rather than the biggest getters—made a lot of sense, and soon such a list was making headlines. The *Slate* 60, published by the (Microsoft-owned) online magazine, listed the largest charitable donations made by an American family or individual in 1996; Samuel and Aline Skaggs came in as most generous (their $100-million gift went to the Scripps Research Institute). Interestingly, *Slate*'s research revealed that the richest one-half of one percent of households accounted for 11 percent of all charity, evidence enough to dismiss the notion that the wealthiest Americans were "ole skinflints."[95]

Whether it was true or not, the belief that the new techno-rich in particular held onto their money like Jack Benny was a persistent one. Some blamed the libertarian streak that ran through Silicon Valley for the locals' lack of philanthropy, while others thought their money was simply too new to seed an ethos of noblesse oblige. The volatility and insecurity of their business—the digital bubble could suddenly burst—certainly played a role in their reluctance to give, while the geeks themselves said they were just too busy to find the time for philanthropy. Without a doubt, the gold rush feeling of the technology boom played a key role in preventing software millionaires from being more generous. Among them was the common belief that one should make as much money as possible while the circus was in town and think about how to best give it away when it eventually left town, sometime in the future. The richest man in the world, Bill Gates, felt that way; his plan was to give all but a fraction of his wealth away "much later" in life. Gates seemed to be following in the footsteps of the leader of the last technological revolution, Henry Ford, who had been making cars for almost four decades before he started his foundation and gave buckets of his money away.[96]

This promise wasn't good enough for those in philanthropic circles, however, and Gates was widely criticized for not giving away even one percent of his net worth a year.[97] "Bill Gates, who is worth $18.5 billion, shows no sign of using it for anything but making more money," complained Michael Lewis in 1996, obviously not a fan of the man. "He is best motivated by clearly defined goals (destroying Netscape, requiring the whole world to own Windows 95)," Lewis continued, a view many shared.[98] "If his mother were alive, she would paddle him," Paul Saffo, director of the Institute for the Future, said of Gates in 1996, a sentiment leading *People* magazine to label the man "the Rodney Dangerfield of the American Dream."[99] In a few years, Gates would get even less respect, when the U.S. Justice Department charged his company with a range of monopolistic practices that, if true, would give him the paddling many felt he deserved.

Ted Turner himself would soon make not just Gates but all of those on *Slate*'s list of benefactors look like cheapskates, however. While reportedly looking over some financial statements on a flight to New York to address a group at the United Nations in September 1997, Turner noticed he was worth $3.2 billion—a full billion more than he claimed he realized. The Mouth of the South decided on the spot to give his billion-dollar windfall—"the big one," as he called it—to the U.N. over ten years, assuming his wife Jane Fonda was on board with the idea. ("She burst into tears" of joy over dinner at the Waldorf-Astoria, he later said.) Soon Turner was at the U.N. announcing his decision, stunning an audience that included Secretary-General Kofi Annan. Although the gift was in Time Warner stock versus cash (and thus could—and would—fluctuate based on the company's share price), it was by far the largest single donation ever made, marking a new era in the annals of philanthropy.[100] Turner's largesse threw a gauntlet down at the feet of super-rich holdouts, principally Gates and Warren Buffett. "I just hope this giving thing is contagious," the man said after his showstopping performance, challenging his peers to put their billion-dollar egos aside and be equally generous.[101]

Virtually as soon as Turner pledged the $1 billion, rumors flew as to his real motivation for parting with almost a third of his wealth. Those who knew Turner well thought the huge gift had much to do with his obsession with *Citizen Kane* (he had seen the film more than a hundred times) and the tycoon's worst fear that he would end up lonely and despised like that quasi-fictional media mogul. Critics, however, thought a thirst for power lurked beneath the gift, his ties with the U.N. a way to colonize his television empire around the world. The tax benefits Turner gained by the donation were also enormous, making other skeptics believe it was, as much as anything else, a brilliant financial move. Still others were convinced that the whole thing was simply his latest and most ambitious effort to win a Nobel Peace Prize, a dream he had revealed to his closest friends. Whatever the reason for it, "Ted's Excellent Donation," as *USA Today* called it, was a wake-up call for all rich folks to seriously consider spreading their wealth around.[102]

Although Turner was goading those who were, like him, in the upper stratosphere of wealth to give more money to worthy causes, the fact was that the wheels of a different kind of philanthropy were already in motion. "There is a brand new philanthropic movement emerging from the 1980s and 1990s wealth boom," *Business-Week* noted just a couple of weeks after the media mogul made his Carnegie-esque announcement, as "a new generation of entrepreneurs, entertainers, financiers, and executives finally start to give its money away." Charitable donations over the past couple of years were indeed up, after being flat for almost a decade, leading one top adviser to the wealthy to claim that, "We're on the cusp of something big." Rather than write a check, however, many American rich were acting as "investor donors," viewing philanthropy as a business that should be run like one and be held accountable for its actions. Entrepreneurialism and the ability to create positive change was fast replacing simply writing a check as the business model of philanthropy, a function of New Money's hands-on approach to everything.[103]

The emergence of the "social venture" school of philanthropy would crystallize this new philosophy of giving away money that had been bubbling up alongside the West Coast tech boom. In 1997, Paul Brainerd, a software millionaire, founded Social Venture Partners (SVP), an organization designed to help those wanting to be part of this new brand of philanthropy, which relied on, go figure, tried-and-true business practices in the decision-making process. "The idea is to look at the giving away of money in a paradigm that people in our industry are used to looking at," said Ida Cole, one of SVP's charter members, "from a point of view where you can recognize budgets and deliverables."[104] Others in the field, seeing which way the big money was blowing, were soon talking the same kind of talk and walking the same kind of walk. "We have a venture capital attitude toward charity," echoed Robin Hood Foundation executive director David Saltzman, the elite philanthropic organization also taking a "tough love" approach to how its donors' money was used.[105]

Now aligned with business, and notably with the cooler-than-cool world of high-tech, philanthropy had in just a couple of years moved a long way from reliance on Brooke Astor's universally dreaded round of benefits. "If the stock market stays buoyant, 1997 may be remembered as the year it became hip to be philanthropic," *Newsweek* proposed at the end of that year; "Suddenly any self-respecting millionaire who isn't giving lots of it away is in danger of being labeled a Scrooge."[106] "Nowadays, giving money away is trendy—almost as sexy as making it," *Fortune* agreed in 1998, something not said regarding the philanthropic deeds of men like

Mellon or Morgan, no matter how impressive.[107] Even Michael Milken, that bad boy of the 1980s, was now dedicating his life to philanthropic ventures, his father's and his own bouts with cancer
giving him a much different set of values and sense of purpose.[108]
"Giving is good," a more evolved Gordon Gekko might have said
in a 1999 sequel to *Wall Street*, recalling the ethos of very wealthy
men raised in the Calvinist tradition, like Andrew Carnegie and
John D. Rockefeller. When it came to the rich giving their money
away, the wealthy elite had, by the end of the twentieth century,
come full circle.

Bill Gates had also gotten religion; at least he started delivering
on his promise to be more philanthropic in the future. In 2004,
Gates had in fact lost half of his 1999 net worth of $100 billion,
but only part of this was due to Microsoft's stock having dropped
more than 50 percent from its high. Gates had over the past three
years donated $23 billion of the company's stock to his foundation,
silencing critics' complaints that the man didn't give nearly enough
money away. Now Warren Buffett deserved the maternal paddling,
having given less than one percent of his $41 billion away—a mere
$321 million.[109] Soon Buffett would join Gates in pledging billions
to philanthropy, however, confirming the sea change that was taking place in the upper strata of philanthropy. Buffett's pledge to
give 85 percent of his now $44 billion fortune to Gates's foundation
starting in 2006 began, like Gates's own philanthropic initiative,
earlier than previously promised, perhaps a sign that each man
wanted to watch his money work its magic.[110] "These are exciting
times in the traditionally quiet world of philanthropy, as a growing
cadre of the newly wealthy promises to change the world—as well
as the face of charitable giving," noted Jane Lampman of the
Christian Science Monitor in 2006, citing as very healthy signs for
the future not just the recent blockbuster donations but an increase in family foundations and personal commitments to make a
difference.[111]

Indeed, it appears that we are on the cusp of a golden age of
giving, as more American rich commit to what Paul Schervish of

the Center on Wealth and Philanthropy at Boston College called a "philanthropic vocation." In 1999, Schervish predicted that $21 trillion would be given to charity over the next half century, and, barring a total economic meltdown, his forecast remains quite plausible. Schervish found in his research that engaging in philanthropy not only provides a sense of purpose and makes one happy but often creates relationships much like those of a family. Rich boomers, wanting to leave a legacy, will give away much if not most of their money before heading to the big Woodstock in the sky. The current obsession among celebrities with causes of every stripe will also no doubt continue, as will corporations' desire to partner with them to generate consumer goodwill.[112]

Encouragingly, the social venture model of philanthropy also continues to accelerate, as more foundations pay attention to whether their giving is truly making a difference or, in current lingo, creating "sustainable change." Metrics and ROI models are increasingly being applied to philanthropy, as more Wall Streeters (such as the Robin Hood Foundation, started by New York hedge fund managers) think of giving in terms of maximizing the impact of an investment portfolio. Google's model of philanthropy, in which one percent of the company's equity and profits are set aside for giving (creating a budget of about $1 billion), is exciting, allowing all 16,000 Googlers to be part of the action rather than just the two founders with their personal fortunes. Even more exciting, perhaps, is the trend of young heirs to give away good chunks of their inheritance to pursue what is called "social justice philanthropy." Driven by equal parts guilt and altruism, these trust fund babies in their twenties and thirties are choosing small nonprofits as their causes, trying to create sustainable change at the grassroots level. As a new generation of plutocrats tackles some of our major, institutional problems head-on, it's clear that the American rich is on the brink of yet another twist and turn, literally invested in the unlimited possibilities of tomorrow.[113]

Without a doubt, one of the most interesting stories yet to unfold has to with the future of the fortunes of today's rich. How these great fortunes will be put to use—decisions that will affect millions of people's lives—is of the utmost importance. Will the American rich continue on their luxury-mania path, interested in wealth for wealth's sake—for the pleasures it can afford and as a way to know they are winning the game? Or will they take a path similar to the one chosen by many of the rich of the last Gilded Age, who returned most of their fortunes to those who had made wealth possible? With more people with more money than ever before in history, and still more to come, the era of wealth that we're currently entering is perhaps *the* most important in terms of how the course of the future will be shaped and the potential impact on individuals, the nation, and the world.

Happily, signs look very promising that a good share of the richest of the American rich will choose the latter path and put their money back into the system where it belongs. As they evolve over time and their assets continue to grow, many millionaires are becoming what I call Willionaires (see Appendix), a trend that I believe will only accelerate in the years and decades ahead. Quite fittingly, for example, on his seventieth birthday in 2007, Sandy Weill, one of the richest persons in the world, gave a fund-raising party for Carnegie Hall at the famous building that its namesake (and original Willionaire) Andrew Carnegie had built in 1890. Weill and others pledged $30 million to improve the concert hall, an example of noblesse oblige that neatly bridged one Gilded Age to another, suggesting that today's financial barons may turn out to be just as generous as the robber barons were.[114] As a more personalized and passionate brand of philanthropy grows into nothing less than a social movement, the line between business and charity, profit and nonprofit is becoming increasingly blurry, a win-win situation for all. Best of all, philanthropy has become unquestionably cool, infused with boomer- and youth-centric values hearkening back to their idealistic countercultural days. We are clearly at another tipping point in the history of the rich, a new, exciting narrative grounded in social responsibility offering us good reason to be optimistic about where American wealth culture may be headed.

CONCLUSION

THE BECKONING OF ANOTHER GOLDEN AGE OF PHILAN-
thropy is just one example of how the more the American
rich have changed over the past century, the more they have remained the same. Many of the themes central to American wealth
culture—the quest to crack the get-rich code through how-to
schemes, the enduring power of the millionaire, and the difficulty
in getting good help these days, to name just a few—remain as
relevant as ever, suggesting things today may not be as different as
they often appear. The American love-hate relationship with the
rich certainly continues, of course, as does our common desire to
join the club, despite research showing that money and happiness
are two very different things. All this shouldn't come as too much
of a surprise, given that observers of the scene as far back as de
Tocqueville and Veblen knew very well that money and America
went together like a horse and carriage.

Still, it would be impossible to ignore the major transformation

of the American rich since the end of World War I, the most notable development being the rise of the first mass-affluent class in
history. Essentially a cheap knockoff of European aristocracy for a
couple of centuries, the American rich over time created its own
identity, eventually discarding the foreign concepts of entitlement
and family dynasty. Out of the ashes of Old Money rose a much
larger and much more diverse American rich, truer to our ideals of
democracy and meritocracy, a transformation that is, from a historical view, nothing short of extraordinary. How fortunes were, and
continue to be, made has also changed, of course, as the emergence
of an information-based economy displaces the industrial-based
version of yesterday. Other significant developments—the flattening of the world, the reconciliation of wealth with Christian morality, and the moving in of "the billionaire next door"—have also
helped to reconfigure the cultural dynamics of wealth in America.

As the nation and the world endure a recession or perhaps even
the "great unraveling," American wealth culture is embarking on
yet another era in its fascinating history. As in previous tough
times, the rich in early 2009 are cutting back on luxury goods and
services, their conspicuous consumption for the moment considerably less conspicuous. Yacht sales are on the rocks, for example, as
are those for expensive jewelry. High-end art is still selling well—
justified as a good investment—but works by lesser-known artists
are remaining in galleries, another casualty of Wall Street jitters.
The wealthy are also currently not above going to Men's Wear-
house to get that Armani pinstripe suit instead of a boutique to
shave a couple of grand off the price. At least one member of the
Forbes Four Hundred has put his two jets on the market, hoping
he'll fetch $108 million for the pair.[1] Some of the very well-to-do
are putting off plastic surgery for themselves (and their children,
rather frighteningly), substituting a $1,200 Botox treatment for a
$15,000 facelift.[2] Even the Russian ultra-wealthy are pinching their
rubles as the price of oil has plummeted, forgoing that antique
Rolls-Royce or Luxembourg-sized mansion.[3]

A reality check is helpful before we start feeling sorry for the rich (or celebrate their downfall). Rather than $20 million as in 2007, a high-earner may now pull in only $2 million, not exactly the dire stuff of a Charles Dickens novel. Many will have lost 20 percent or 30 percent of their $10 million or $100 million investment in stocks, again not what you would call a worst-case scenario.[4] Although seeing one's net worth go south may take a psychic toll, it's hardly the end of the world as we know it for the American rich. The recent global economic crisis has many thinking that the glory days of the rich are over, however, and that the wealthy elite may very well be an endangered species. "Goodbye To All That," ran the headline of a *New York Times* article in October 2008; the reporters suggested that the biggest source of wealth— Wall Street—may have dried up for good. Even historians who should know better have predicted that the sky is falling ("It's the end of the era of conspicuous displays of wealth," fretted Steve Fraser, author of *Wall Street: America's Dream Palace*).[5]

The history of American wealth culture suggests otherwise. These Chicken Littles ignore the time-proven fact that the rich are incredibly adaptive, quite familiar with the natural ebb and flow of economic cycles and how to ride them out. The affluent class has historically behaved much like the stock market, continuing to rise over the decades while experiencing the occasional "correction" and even the rare cataclysm, such as the recent Bernie Madoff scandal. In our economic environment, grounded in survival of the richest, some of today's wealthy will no doubt become extinct, but others will emerge, as in the past. As in previous lean times like the 1930s and 1970s, the American rich will continue to cut back and economize like the rest of us, putting major expenditures (like that cute island off Georgia) on hold. (Spending on luxury goods is always the first to take a hit, another reason marketers to the wealthy should look beyond their material or even experiential desires.) Also like these periods, a shaky economy will no doubt hurt the Little Rich (who I define today as having $1 to $10 million in net worth) and some of the Medium Rich ($10 to $100 million) but precious few of the Big Rich ($100 million plus).

Finally, a deep recession or even depression will likely further separate the have-a-lots from the haves, with the most elite of the ultra-rich (who University of Michigan economics professor Joel Slemrod recently and humorously called the "Fortunate 400") pulling further away from the merely rich pack.[6] Like insects, the very rich, or at least their money, will be around long after the rest of us have disappeared, ensuring that another chapter in their history remains to be written.

APPENDIX

A S A RECENT HISTORY OF THE RICH SUGGESTS, THE CONTIN-
ual raising of the bar of what constitutes being wealthy has
made efforts to understand high net worths as a market a particularly challenging pursuit. Rather than the traditional distinction between Old versus New Money, today's American rich comprise a
complex subculture, a far richer, so to speak, group of people than
has ever existed—or could have existed in Fitzgerald's time. The
trope of Old versus New Money is thus a tired one, relevant a century or half century ago but now a distinction that means little
since the previously defining characteristics of the American rich
have virtually completely eroded. "Old Money" certainly exists, especially in established epicenters of wealth like New York and Boston, but, four or five generations after their turn-of-the-century kin
made their millions (when a million was really a million), most
family wealth has been scattered (and squandered). The American
rich is today much more fragmented and tribal than that of dec-

ades past, but the mythology of Old Money is remarkably persistent, making many of our assumptions and beliefs about the wealthy flawed and misleading. As well, the dynamics of wealth are heavily obscured by our absurd obsession with "luxury," that overused, under-delivered term that many mistakenly define as the sole interest of the rich. Net net, the great diversity within the wealth market from a values standpoint, combined with the giant disparity in assets, makes understanding it challenging, to say the least, demanding new and different research tools.

To that end, on behalf of my clients, I along with my network of "cultural stringers" around the country have ventured into the wilds of the American rich, documenting how these individuals spend their time and money by applying the classic methods of cultural anthropology. Rather than what people say, think, or say they think—the focus of attitude-based, opinion-oriented traditional market research—I hold that it is only what people do that really matters, hence the need for an anthropological approach. (*Slate.com* rather flatteringly called my work "the anthropology of plutocrats aim[ing] to do for the American wealthy what Margaret Mead did for the Samoans" after the findings of my Wealthology™ study for JP Morgan were reported in the media. *Worth* was a bit less kind, considering my habit of chatting up doormen, pretending to be shopping for a $100,000-plus car or $1,000,000-plus boat, hanging out at private schools, and getting thrown out of the occasional country club "invasive techniques.") This kind of approach is exactly what's needed to understand today's rich, however, something more businesspeople are realizing. "In hot pursuit of the affluent, more financial advisers are focusing on the passions and motivations of their clients rather than just the size of their wallets," said the *Wall Street Journal* in its own report of my work for JP Morgan, concluding that it "no longer suffices merely to know clients' favorite sports teams and the ages of their children."

After spending years tracking the wealthy in their native habitats (a dirty job, need it be said, but somebody has to do it), my research suggests there are now five different types of rich Americans (defined as those having investable assets of at least $5 million), each kind comprising a subculture all its own—see my Web site, www.cultureplanning.com, for more on my Wealthology™ study). I call the first kind of millionaire Thrillionaires, wealthy people who subscribe to the idea that money exists principally to use. Thrillionaires have a profound desire to enjoy the things and experiences that wealth can buy; their wealth serves as a confirmation of their success in life. They have a keen interest in both quality and quantity and view first class not as special but as a 24/7 lifestyle. For them, wealth is the means to privacy, exclusivity, pleasure, and highly memorable experiences.

However, my Wealthology™ findings indicate that, over time and with more money, the American rich fall into a kind of hierarchy based on what I believe is the driving force in contemporary American society—finding meaning and purpose in one's life. Riffing on Maslow's hierarchy, my hierarchical pyramid suggests there is an evolutionary ladder within this subculture, with values associated with some millionaires falling "lower" on a scale of meaning and purpose than those of other millionaires. This important idea emerged out of my fieldwork indicating that most of the American rich are a "work in progress," as they attempt to evolve as human beings away from personally defined interests and needs toward those of others. Those folks who have found a "higher" purpose in their lives are infinitely happier and more secure (richer, so to speak) than those interested in the acquisition of things or even experiences, a finding that poses enormous implications for how we all might choose to live our lives. Despite their often being the wealthiest of the wealthy, I (subjectively, of course) argue that Thrillionaires represent the entry level to the American rich in terms of both their values and contentment, their priority— superficial, hedonistic pleasures (i.e., "luxury")—ultimately unfulfilling.

The second kind of millionaire I identified in my anthropological study of the American rich are dubbed Coolionaires, who view aesthetics as the essence of life. Coolionaires have a deep desire to

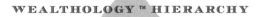

WEALTHOLOGY ™ HIERARCHY

ARCHETYPE #5: WILLIONAIRES

ARCHETYPE #4: WELLIONAIRES

TIME AND
MONEY

ARCHETYPE #3: REALIONAIRES

ARCHETYPE #2: COOLIONAIRES

ARCHETYPE #1: THRILLIONAIRES

Source: Culture Planning LLC

surround themselves with beautiful things and experiences, viewing their wealth as the opportunity to express their status as a person of refinement and sophistication. They share a proactive
pursuit of sensory and stylistic environments of all kinds, with arts
and artistry the cornerstone of their personal identity. For them,
wealth is the means to consume beauty if they can't actually create
it and a way to dwell in and show off their personal aesthetics and
taste. Although Coolionaires are undoubtedly the coolest of the
American rich, I suggest, they compose the second tier of my five-
tiered hierarchy of the wealthy elite.

The third kind of millionaire, Realionaires, stand as evidence
that less can indeed be more. They have a natural inclination (versus a conscious effort) to stay under the radar of the trappings of
wealth and view their affluence as an indicator of their status as a
person of uncommon common sense. Realionaires share a willingness to spend big money on things that matter but also show a firm
resolve to save on things that don't, finding pride in being well
informed and a smart consumer. For them, wealth is simply a

means to be oneself, having earned that privilege through their practicality and determination to get the biggest bang for their buck. Realionaires are smack-dab in the middle of my hierarchical pyramid, more evolved than Thrillionaires and Coolionaires but less so than Wellionaires and Willionaires.

The fourth kind of modern millionaire, Wellionaires, pursue "360-degree" wellness through their commitment to look good, feel healthy, and think positively. They use their wealth to convey to themselves and others that they are living lives in and of balance, and they have discovered an underlying spirituality in Eastern and New Age philosophies and therapies. For them, wealth is the means to keep one's body and the Earth as natural and green as possible, perceiving a symbiotic relationship between themselves and the planet. As highly evolved people looking for deep purpose and meaning in life, Wellionaires are near the top of my values-based hierarchy of the rich.

The final type of millionaire, Willionaires, focus on their privilege and responsibility to try to make the world a better place. They are determined to give back and, in doing so, make a mark and ultimately be remembered. They view their wealth as a way to tell others and remind themselves that life should have purpose and meaning. Willionaires recognize their good fortune, literally and figuratively, to maintain traditions and strengthen the bonds of their family and community. For them, the concept of philanthropy is not charity but a way of life, and wealth is the means to be a social entrepreneur in avenues they feel are important. Heavily invested in improving the lives of others (in more ways than one), Willionaires are A-number-one, top of the heap in terms of finding meaning and purpose in their lives, an achievement we less-than-rich (Nilionaires?) might strive for.

NOTES

Introduction

1 "Millionaire No Distinction," *Los Angeles Times*, July 19, 1929, 18.

2 Dinesh D'Souza, "The Billionaire Next Door," *Forbes*, October 11, 1999, 51; Russ Alan Prince and Lewis Schiff, *The Middle-Class Millionaire: The Rise of the New Rich and How They Are Changing America* (New York: Currency, 2008).

3 "TNS Reports Another Record-Breaking Year for Millionaire Households," PR Newswire, May 5, 2008.

4 N. Gregory Mankiw, "The Wealth Trajectory: Rewards for the Few," *New York Times*, April 20, 2008, BU9.

5 Rob Haskell, "What's Rich Now?" *Harper's Bazaar*, October 2007, 305–306.

6 Stefan Theil, "Shining in the Gloom," *Newsweek*, May 26, 2008, 52–55; David Rothkoph, *Superclass: The Global Power Elite and the World They are Making* (New York: Farrar, Straus and Giroux, 2008).

7 Steven Winn, "The Rich are Feeling Cheap," *San Francisco Chronicle*, March 1, 2009, E1.

8 Lily Bart, "Some Reflections on the Rich," *Mademoiselle*, December 1965, 130.

9 Alexis de Tocqueville, *Democracy in America*; Russell Kirk, "The Wealthy American Bum," *National Review*, March 12, 1963, 198.

10 "A Century of Wealth," *Forbes*, October 11, 1999, 112; In 1999, Ben Pappas of *Forbes* did yeoman work by tracking down every American movie with the term "million" or "millionaire" in its title. The term was far more popular in the first half of the century, with Hollywood using the terms just once in the 1900s, thirty-one times in the 1910s, twenty-six times in the 1920s, twenty-eight times in the 1930s, nine times in the 1940s, six times in the 1950s (in addition to *The Millionaire* television show), eight times in the 1960s, twice in the 1970s, three times in the 1980s, and four times in the 1990s (plus the *Who Wants to Be a Millionaire?* TV show). "The Forbes 400," *Forbes*, October 11, 1999, 398.

11 Cleveland Amory, "About Millionaires: Past, Present, and Future," *New York Times*, March 22, 1959, SM14.

12 Ruth West, "The Care and Feeding of the Very Rich," *McCall's*, August 1969, 56.

13 "Gay Old Days of High Living," *Life*, December 28, 1959, 12–29.

14 "The Care and Feeding of the Very Rich."

15 John Berendi, "The Quiet Rich," *Esquire*, February 1990, 28. See Charles R. Morris's *The Tycoons: How Andrew Carnegie, John D. Rockefeller, Jay Gould, and J. P. Morgan Invented the American Supereconomy* for an examination of the tremendous impact of the four principal robber barons of post–Civil War America.

16 David E. Green, "So You Want To Get Into the Social Register," *Cosmopolitan*, October 1959, 32.

17 Stephen Birmingham, "Cupid With the Golden Arrow," *Cosmopolitan*, January 1961, 62.

18 *Who Killed Society?*; "The Careful Conversion of the Nouveau Riche," *Esquire*, November 1961, 104–105 +.

19 Edith Wharton, *The Age of Innocence* (New York: Modern Library, 1999); "The Careful Conversion of the Nouveau Riche."

20 Jesse Kornbluth, "The Working Rich," *New York*, November 24, 1986, 30.

21 "Wall Street Journal Straws," *Wall Street Journal*, June 20, 1929, 2.

22 Adam Smith, "You Ought to Get Rich," *Esquire*, February 1985, 92.

23 Arthur Train, "The Billionaire Era, Part I," *Forum & Century*, November 1924, 616–628.

24 Arthur Train, "The Billionaire Era, Part II," *Forum & Century*, December 1924, 746–759.

25 "The Quiet Rich."

26 "The Billionaire Era, Part I."

27 Hoffman Nickerson, "The Rich Man in American History," *American Mercury*, September 1929, 113.

28 "The Billionaire Era, Part II."

29 Silas Bent, "Million-a-Year Men Increasing in Number," *New York Times*, July 13, 1924, XX4.

30 "Millionaire Crop Flourishing," *Los Angeles Times*, February 15, 1928, 7.

31 "Soar in Report," *Los Angeles Times*, November 4, 1929, 1.

32 "Millionaire No Distinction," *Los Angeles Times*, July 19, 1929, 18.

33 "Millionaires in Politics," *Chicago Daily Tribune*, September 20, 1927, 10.

34 "The Senate and the Needle's Eye," *New York Times*, September 26, 1929, 28.

35 Montgomery Evans, "On Prodigal Sons," *Forum & Century*, August 1927, 261–268.

36 John T. Flynn, "The Dwindling Dynasties," *North American Review*, December 1930, 646.

37 "Number of Millionaires," *Chicago Daily Tribune*, May 21, 1944, A5.

38 "Wallace Declares All Must Share in Post-War Wealth," *Chicago Daily Tribune*, April 20, 1943, 6.

39 Joseph Nolan, "How to Make a Million," *New York Times*, July 10, 1955, SM13.

40 Alvin Shuster, "Our 398 Millionaires—A New Breed," *New York Times*, September 15, 1963, 237.

41 Katherine Betts, "The New Rich," *Vogue*, April 1999, 389.

42 Robert Trumbull, "Gifted Displacing Rich at Ivy 'Big 3,'" *New York Times*, March 14, 1964, 25.

43 Charles McGrath, "The Decline of WASP Reserve," *New York Times*, November 15, 1998, SM67.

44 Ferdinand Lundberg, *The Rich and the Super-Rich* (New York: Bantam, 1969).

45 Nelson W. Aldrich, Jr., *Old Money: The Mythology of America's Upper Class* (New York: Alfred A. Knopf, 1988); Joseph Nocera, "The Arriviste Has Arrived," *New York Times*, November 15, 1998, SM68.

46 Michael Lewis, "The Rich," *New York Times*, November 19, 1995, SM65.

47 "The Decline of WASP Reserve."

48 Joseph Nocera, "The Arriviste Has Arrived," *New York Times*, November 15, 1998, SM68.

49 Ray Boshara, "The $6,000 Solution," *Atlantic Monthly*, January–February 2003, 91.

50 Daphne Merkin, "Money Always Talks," *New York Times*, October 14, 2007, 110.

51 Romesh Ratnesai, "The New Rich Man's Club," *Time*, December 1, 1997, 50.

52 Allan Sloan, "The New Rich," *Newsweek*, August 4, 1997, 50.

53 "Does Money Buy Happiness?" *Forbes*, April 21, 1997, 394.

CHAPTER 1

1 Cornelius Vanderbilt, Jr., "The Future of the American Dynasties," the *Saturday Evening Post*, January 8, 1927, 10–11+.

2 "The Future of the American Dynasties"; Susan Strasser, *Satisfaction Guaranteed: The Making of the American Mass Market* (New York: Pantheon, 1989).

3 Edwin Lefevre, "The Annoyance of Being Rich To-day," the *Saturday Evening Post*, January 31, 1920, 19+.

4 "The Annoyance of Being Rich To-day."

5 E. Alexander Powell, "The Lap of Luxury," *Woman's Home Companion*, June 1927, 25–26. See Rockwell Stensrud's *Newport: A Lively Experiment 1639–1969* for a full history of the "Queen of Resorts."

6 "The Annoyance of Being Rich To-day."

7 "The Annoyance of Being Rich To-day."

8 "The Annoyance of Being Rich To-day."

9 "The Annoyance of Being Rich To-day."

10 "The Annoyance of Being Rich To-day."

11 "The Annoyance of Being Rich To-day"; German butlers, at least the one hired in the early 1920s by the artist Rube Goldberg, did not quite stack up to the British variety. The butler, an ex-admiral in the German navy, "did everything but work," according to Goldberg, so much so that "our friends often mistook him for a new piece of statuary in the hallway." Rube Goldberg, "What I Have Found Out About Money," *Good Housekeeping*, October 1924, 30–31+.

12 Elizabeth Barbour, as told to Brenda Ueland, "How to Keep House on a Million Dollars a Year," the *Saturday Evening Post*, March 19, 1927, 13–14+.

13 "The Annoyance of Being Rich To-day."

14 "The Annoyance of Being Rich To-day."

15 Albert W. Atwood, "The Rockefeller Fortune," the *Saturday Evening Post*, June 11, 1921, 21+. See Ron Chernow's *Titan: The Life of John D. Rockefeller, Sr.* for a (titanic) biography of history's first billionaire and the patriarch of America's most famous dynasty.

16 "The Rockefeller Fortune."

17 "The Rockefeller Fortune."

18 "The Rockefeller Fortune."

19 "The Rockefeller Fortune."

20 Albert W. Atwood, "What Becomes of the Rich Man's Income?" the *Saturday Evening Post*, October 4, 1924, 8+.

21 "What Becomes of the Rich Man's Income?"

22 Albert W. Atwood, "What Becomes of the Rich Man's Income?" the *Saturday Evening Post*, October 25, 1924, 27+. See Steven Watts's *The People's Tycoon: Henry Ford and the American Century* for much more about the business legend.

23 "Given Away—The Duke and Eastman Millions," the *Literary Digest*, December 27, 1924, 36–44. Elizabeth Brayer's *George Eastman: A Biography* is a fascinating account of the camera and film tycoon.

24 Bruce Barton, "How Much Money Do You Want?" *Good Housekeeping*, October 1926, 20–21.

25 Frederick Palmer, "You Cannot Buy It All," *Harper's Monthly Magazine*, August 1924, 305–310.

26 Rheta Childe Dorr, "How to Get Rich," *Collier's*, July 17, 1926, 10.

27 "Our 11,000 Millionaires," the *Literary Digest*, September 29, 1926, 14.

28 Oswald Garrison Villard, "A New Adventure for Millionaires," *Harper's Monthly Magazine*, September 1927, 469–474.

29 "Broad Street Gossip," *Wall Street Journal*, May 3, 1926, 2.

30 "Millionaire Crop Flourishing," *Los Angeles Times*, February 15, 1928, 7.

31 Samuel Crowther, "How Do They Get Their Money?" the *Saturday Evening Post*, March 9, 1929, 6–7.

32 "Specialty Shops Carry Wealth of Ideal Gifts," *Los Angeles Times*, November 13, 1929, B1.

33 Samuel G. Blythe, "First Aid for Mere Millionaires," the *Saturday Evening Post*, July 20, 1929, 8–9.

34 Stuart Chase, "Park Avenue," the *New Republic*, May 25, 1927, 9–11; See Michael Gross's *740 Park Avenue: The Story of the World's Richest Apartment Building* for a window into the premier building on the premier avenue.

35 Maurice Merney, "Croesus's Sixty Acres," *North American Review*, January 1929, 1–7.

36 "Croesus's Sixty Acres."

37 "Park Avenue."

38 "Cardinal O'Connell Denies Bible Simile," *New York Times*, February 21, 1926, 15.

39 "How Much Money Do You Want?" Bruce Barton, *The Man Nobody Knows* (Indianapolis: Bobbs-Merrill Company, 1925).

40 "Billionaires," the *Saturday Evening Post*, June 11, 1927.

41 Montgomery Evans, "On Prodigal Sons," *Forum & Century*, August 1927, 261–68.

42 Samuel Strauss, "Rich Men and Key Men," *Atlantic Monthly*, December 1927, 721–729.

43 Governor Albert C. Ritchie, "The Imperialism of the Dollar," *Atlantic Monthly*, May 1928, 587–93.

44 "First Aid for Mere Millionaires."

45 Hoffman Nickerson, "The Rich Men in American History," *American Mercury*, September 1929, 102–113.

46 "Rich Men and Key Men."

47 "Millionaires in Politics," *Chicago Daily Tribune*, September 20, 1927, 10.

48 Laurence Todd, "Government by Millionaires," *The Nation*, March

27, 1929, 367–68. David Cannadine's *Mellon: An American Life* is a superb study of the financial giant and founder of the National Gallery of Art.

49 "First Aid for Mere Millionaires."

50 Oliver McKee, Jr., "The Poor Man in Politics," *North American Review*, August 1929, 185–92.

51 John B. Kennedy, "His Money Makes Him Work," *Collier's*, December 19, 1925, 26.

52 Cornelius Vanderbilt, Jr., "It is Hard to Be a Rich Man's Son," the *Saturday Evening Post*, December 4, 1926, 8–9 + .

53 "It is Hard to Be a Rich Man's Son."

54 "How to Keep House on a Million Dollars a Year."

55 "How to Keep House on a Million Dollars a Year."

56 Cornelius Vanderbilt, Jr., "Does Society Mock at Marriage?" the *Saturday Evening Post*, April 23, 1927.

57 "The Rich Men in American History."

58 Maude Parker, "Nomads De-Luxe," the *Saturday Evening Post*, October 5, 1929, 16–17.

59 "Nomads De-Luxe."

60 "Nomads De-Luxe."

61 "Nomads De-Luxe."

62 "Does Society Mock at Marriage?"

63 Maude Parker, "Children of Croesus," the *Saturday Evening Post*, November 9, 1929, 10–11.

64 "Nomads De-Luxe."

65 "Nomads De-Luxe."

66 Maude Parker, "Where Are the Idle Rich?" the *Saturday Evening Post*, November 23, 1929, 22–23.

67 "Where are the Idle Rich?"

68 "Where are the Idle Rich?"

69 "Where are the Idle Rich?"

70 "Where are the Idle Rich?"

CHAPTER 2

1 Croswell Bowen, "I Was a Rich Man's Son," *Forum*, January 1935, 34–38.

2 "The Plutocrats of Yesteryear," *Literary Digest*, February 22, 1930, 13. See Amity Shlaes's *The Forgotten Man: A New History Of The Great Depression* for a alternative take on the economic crisis.

3 "Why Millionaires Don't," the *Saturday Evening Post*, May 17, 1930, 28+.

4 "Pitiful Rich," *The Nation*, August 6, 1930, 142.

5 Nancy Hill, "Poverty in Park Avenue," *Outlook*, October 21, 1931, 240–41+.

6 "Poverty in Park Avenue."

7 "Poverty in Park Avenue."

8 "Poverty in Park Avenue."

9 Walter Lippman, "The Almighty Dollar," *Women's Home Companion*, November 1931, 26–27.

10 "No Rich Men Today, Says Mr. Schwab," *Los Angeles Times*, April 20, 1932, 1; "No Rich Men Now, Schwab Declares," *New York Times*, April 20, 1932, 25.

11 "No Rich Men Left?" *Literary Digest*, May 7, 1932, 10. Schwab made his remark the very same day that President Hoover had issued a statement on the "evils of hoarding," so the former was likely a response to the latter. Morrow Mayo, "Croesus at Home," *American Mercury*, October 1932, 230.

12 "These They Cannot Take," *The Nation*, March 22, 1933, 304.

13 "Civilization Lost, Darrow Declares," *New York Times*, January 20, 1934, 16.

14 Howard Wood, "Margin Calls, Taxes Wiping Out Old Rich," *Chicago Daily Tribune*, July 12, 1932, 21.

15 "Our Next Crop of Millionaires," *Literary Digest*, January 14, 1933, 42.

16 D. W. Brogan, "Paradise Lost—Or Mislaid?" *Harper's*, December 1934, 26–36.

17 "The Rich Get Richer," the *New Republic*, August 28, 1935, 68–72.

18 "The Rich Get Richer."

19 "Norris Asks Rich to Pass Wealth Back to People," *Chicago Daily Tribune*, November 17, 1933, 10.

20 "Long Would Share All Types Wealth," *New York Times*, March 9, 1935, 9. Richard White's *Kingfish: The Reign of Huey P. Long* is a good study of the man FDR considered "one of the two most dangerous men in the country."

21 "Let's Not Go Goofy," *Collier's*, June 29, 1935, 58.

22 Jonathan Daniels, "The Rich Begin to Pay," *Forum*, September 1935, 139–144.

23 Garet Garrett, "The Wealth Question," the *Saturday Evening Post*, August 31, 1935, 5–7 +.

24 "Henry Ford, Jim James, and Taxes," *Literary Digest*, August 17, 1935, 5–6.

25 "Taxation, Advice and Family Trust," *Literary Digest*, August 24, 1935, 4–5.

26 "Pittsburgh Hails Carnegie Gifts," the *Christian Century*, December 11, 1935, 1604. David Nasaw's massive *Andrew Carnegie* tells the full story of the man who rose from poverty to become the richest person in the world.

27 "Taxation, Advice and Family Trust."

28 "The Wealth Question."

29 "Making Wealth Pay," the *Saturday Evening Post*, May 16, 1933, 22.

30 "Without Maecenas," *The Nation*, April 18, 1934, 432.

31 "Employees of the Luxury Trade," the *Saturday Evening Post*, January 12, 1935, 22.

32 Albert W. Atwood, "The Passing of Great Fortunes," the *Saturday Evening Post*, February 27, 1937, 23 +.

33 "Henry Ford, Jim James, and Taxes."

34 Raymond Moley, "Perspectives," *Newsweek*, October 31, 1938, 44.

35 "Let's Not Go Goofy."

36 "My Lady Poverty," *Atlantic Monthly*, September 1931, 385–88.

37 "The Rich Begin to Pay."

38 "The Old Guard Never Surrenders," the *New Republic*, January 2, 1935, 216–218.

39 Bernard Kilgore, "Revenue and Reform," *Wall Street Journal*, June 21, 1935, 3; Frank R. Kent, "The Great Game of Politics," *Wall Street Journal*, June 24, 1935, 2; Howard Wood, "'Soak the Rich' Tax Held Blow at 'Little Man,'" *Chicago Daily Tribune*, June 26, 1935, 4; "Reed Attacks 'Soak the Rich' Plan as 'Theft,'" *Chicago Daily Tribune*, July 1, 1935, 17; "Soak the Rich Share-Wealth Hearing Flops," *Chicago Daily Tribune*, July 12, 1935, 6; "Senate Passes Tax Bill to Soak the Rich," *Chicago Daily Tribune*, August 16, 1935, 1; "Roosevelt Signs Bill to Tax Rich," *Los Angeles Times*, August 31, 1935, 1.

40 "The Passing of Great Fortunes."

41 Robert Hale, "But I, Too, Hate Roosevelt," *Harper's*, August 1936, 268–273.

42 Marquis W. Childs, "They Hate Roosevelt," *Reader's Digest*, July 1936, 9–14. Jean Edward Smith's *FDR* captures the essence of the president's complex and compelling life.

43 "Era of Big Estates Past, Say Bankers," *New York Times*, February 17, 1938, 12.

44 "Parties and Breadlines," *Literary Digest*, January 17, 1931, 10.

45 "The Fortune Survey," *Fortune*, July 1935, 66.

46 "Henry Ford, Jim James, and Taxes."

47 "The Rich Begin to Pay."

48 "Paradise Lost—Or Mislaid?"

49 "Croesus at Home."

50 "A Widow's Wealth," the *Saturday Evening Post*, August 12, 1933, 23–24+.

51 "Women, Owners of America," *Literary Digest*, August 21, 1935, 29.

52 "Richest U.S. Women," *Fortune*, November 1936, 115–120+.

53 "Cinema People Doubt Success of Rich Girls," *Chicago Daily Tribune*, March 18, 1934, D8.

54 "Art in the Higher Brackets," *New York Times*, January 23, 1940, 16.

55 "How the Rich Live," *BusinessWeek*, March 18, 1939, 16–18.

56 Isabel Lundberg, "The Millionaire Lunatic Fringe," *American Mercury*, September 1939, 92–98.

57 "The Millionaire Lunatic Fringe."

58 "The Millionaire Lunatic Fringe."

59 "The Millionaire Lunatic Fringe."

60 "The Millionaire Lunatic Fringe."

61 "The Millionaire Lunatic Fringe."

62 "The Millionaire Lunatic Fringe."

63 "The Millionaire Lunatic Fringe."

64 "The Millionaire Lunatic Fringe."

65 "The Millionaire Lunatic Fringe."

66 "Rich Refugees," *Fortune*, February 1941, 80–82+.

67 S. F. Porter, "Refugee Gold Rush," *American Magazine*, October 1942, 46–47 + .

68 "Refugee Gold Rush."

69 "Rich Refugees."

70 "Refugee Gold Rush."

71 "Rich Refugees."

72 "Rich Refugees."

73 "Refugee Gold Rush."

74 "Refugee Gold Rush."

75 "Refugee Gold Rush."

76 "Rich Refugees."

77 Lucy Greenbaum, "Generals Take Over Resort Hotel To Watch Carolina Maneuvers," *New York Times*, November 19, 1941, 8.

78 Norma Lee Browning, "Battle Scarred Air Corps Yanks Bask in Luxury," *Chicago Daily Tribune*, October 7, 1945, 3.

79 "Luxurious Club to Bow to 3 R's," *New York Times*, October 3, 1941, 25.

80 "$1,000,000 Club Is Closed by War; Relic of Pre-Depression Grandeur," *New York Times*, January 22, 1943, 21.

81 "$1,000,000 Club Is Closed by War; Relic of Pre-Depression Grandeur."

82 Clarence E. Lovejoy, "U.S. Backs Boating as Wartime Asset," *New York Times*, April 12, 1942, S4.

83 "Millionaire Gould Peels Potatoes in Sydney Camp," *Los Angeles Times*, April 13, 1942, A.

84 "A Millionaire is Promoted to $60 a Month," *Chicago Daily Tribune*, May 22, 1941, 26.

85 George Waller, "Soldiers Feast on Rare Dish," *Los Angeles Times*, September 3, 1942, 3.

86 "WMC 'Crack-Down' To Get Nurses Seen," *New York Times*, December 30, 1944, 11.

87 "ODT Considers New Travel Curbs in 'All Categories,' Says Director," *New York Times*, July 13, 1945, 11.

88 Alma Whitaker, "'Riveter Rosie' Doesn't Wear Wealth Genteelly," *Los Angeles Times*, December 19, 1943, D1.

89 Frederick Lewis Allen, "Who's Getting the Money?" *Harper's Magazine*, June 1944, 1–10.

CHAPTER 3

1 Robert Daley, "Auto Pros Take Over," *New York Times*, May 12, 1959, 46.

2 "Land of the Big Rich," *Reader's Digest*, September 1948, 20–22.

3 "Southwest Has a New Crop of Super Rich," *Life*, April 5, 1948, 23–27. Texaholics may want to check out Sandy Sheehy's *Texas Big Rich* for a frothy history of cowboy capitalists.

4 Stanley Walker, "Growing Legend of the Texas Millionaires," *New York Times*, March 8, 1953, SM14.

5 "The 'Nays' of Texas," *Wall Street Journal*, April 11, 1961, 16.

6 "Southwest Has a New Crop of Super Rich."

7 "Land of the Big Rich."

8 "Land of the Big Rich."

9 Clarence Woodbury, "Boom Towns of the New Frontier," *The American Magazine*, September 1948, 133–134.

10 "Shirtsleeve Millionaires," *Life*, September 3, 1951, 105.

11 Robert E. Bedingfield, "The World's Richest Men," *New York Times*, October 20, 1957, SM34.

12 "The World's Richest Men."

13 "The World's Richest Men." See Harry Hurt III's *Texas Rich: The Hunt Dynasty from the Early Oil Days Through the Silver Crash* for more on H. L. and his children.

14 "Death and a Changing Industry Thin Oil's Multimillionaires," *BusinessWeek*, October 10, 1959, 30–32.

15 Stanley Walker, "Strange Gushings of Oil Money," *New York Times*, November 22, 1959, SM29.

16 "The Super-American State," the *New Yorker*, April 8, 1961, 62–64+.

17 "'That So Necessary Ingredient,'" the *Saturday Evening Post*, September 5, 1964, 56–59.

18 David E. Green, "So You Want to Get Into the Social Register," *Cosmopolitan*, October 1959, 32.

19 "So You Want to Get Into the Social Register."

20 "So You Want to Get Into the Social Register."

21 "So You Want to Get Into the Social Register."

22 Cleveland Amory, "About Millionaires: Past, Present, Future," *New York Times*, March 22, 1959, SM14.

23 "The Super-American State."

24 "So You Want to Get Into the Social Register."

25 "Mystery Man Throws Lavish Masked Party," *Chicago Daily Tribune*, September 4, 1951, 1.

26 Richard Gehman, "The World's Most Exclusive Bedrooms," *Cosmopolitan*, October 1959, 76–82.

27 Stephen Birmingham, "Cupid With the Golden Arrow," *Cosmopolitan*, January 1961, 60–64.

28 "The Super-American State."

29 William Letwin, "Money Matters," *The Reporter*, February 15, 1962, 47.

30 "The Careful Conversion of the Nouveau Riche," *Esquire*, November 1961, 104–105 +.

31 "The Careful Conversion of the Nouveau Riche."

32 "The Careful Conversion of the Nouveau Riche."

33 Helen Hill Miller, "American Culture In Search of Angels—I," the *New Republic*, March 3, 1958, 7–8.

34 Russell Kirk, "The Wealthy American Bum," *National Review*, March 12, 1963, 198.

35 Richard Austin Smith, "The Fifty-Million-Dollar Man," *Fortune*, November 1957, 176–180 +.

36 Richard Schickel, "The Credit-Card Millionaires," *The Nation*, February 29, 1959, 186.

37 "The Credit-Card Millionaires."

38 "Elegance Can Be Rented," *Cosmopolitan*, October 1959, 52–56.

39 David Cushman Coyle, "Millionaires are Made, Not Born," *New York Times*, August 26, 1951, SM8.

40 "The New Rich," *Fortune*, January 1952, 60.

41 Vance Packard, "How To Make a Fortune . . . New Style," *Ladies' Home Journal*, January 1959, 86.

42 "About Millionaires: Past, Present, Future."

43 Leonard Gross, "Money," *Look*, February 14, 1961, 18–19.

44 "Money."

45 "Money Matters."

46 Robert Trumbull, "Gifted Displacing Rich At Ivy 'Big 3,'" *New York Times*, March 14, 1964, 25.

47 "The New Rich."

48 Jack Pollack, "Want to Make a Million?" *Science Digest*, May 1948, 61; Andrew Tully, "Today's Millionaires are Pikers!" *Coronet*, December 1955, 37–41.

49 Cleveland Amory, "The Last Stand of the Rich," the *Saturday Evening Post*, November 1, 1952, 32–33 +.

50 "The Last Stand of the Rich."

51 "The Last Stand of the Rich."

52 "The Fifty-Million-Dollar Man."

53 "The Fifty-Million-Dollar Man."

54 "The Fifty-Million-Dollar Man."

55 "The Egghead Millionaires," *Fortune*, September 1960, 172–178.

56 "Rich Get Richer—But Not for Long," *BusinessWeek*, January 27, 1962.

57 "One Thing in Common," *Newsweek*, June 19, 1961, 102.

58 William Letwin, "Wealth Springs Eternal," *The Reporter*, September 14, 1961, 62–63.

59 Gilbert Burck and Sanford S. Parker, "The Wonderful, Ordinary Luxury Market," *Fortune*, December 1953, 117–119 +.

60 "The Wonderful, Ordinary Luxury Market."

61 "The $250,000 House," *Fortune*, October 1955, 133–142 +.

62 Laura Date Riley, "America's 10 Richest Women," *Ladies' Home Journal*, September 1957, 60–61 +.

63 "The $250,000 House."

64 "The Rich Come Out of Hiding," *BusinessWeek*, November 15, 1958, 58–60 +.

65 "The Rich Come Out of Hiding."

66 "The Rich Come Out of Hiding."

67 Willard Edwards, "7 Years in White House Make Truman Rich," *Chicago Daily News*, January 13, 1953, 1.

68 "Are Millionaires Running Washington?" *U.S. News & World Report*, October 30, 1953, 17–21.

69 E. Digby Baltzell, "Rich Men in Politics," *The Nation*, May 31, 1958, 493–95.

70 "Rockefellers Outspend Harrimans in Campaign," *Wall Street Journal*, October 30, 1958, 19.

71 Edwin A. Roberts, Jr., "Rockefeller: His Way to Victory," *Wall Street Journal*, November 6, 1958, 12.

72 W. H. Lawrence, "Humphrey Cites Wealth of Foes," *New York Times*, April 26, 1960, 28.

73 Louis M. Kohlmer, "The Johnsons' Balance Sheet," *Wall Street Journal*, August 20, 1964, 2.

74 "Goldwater Store Source of Wealth," *New York Times*, July 16, 1964, 16.

CHAPTER 4

1 "Chewing for Dollars," *Time*, November 28, 1977, 107.

2 "How to Become a Millionaire (It Still Happens All the Time)," *Time*, July 9, 1965, 87–89.

3 "How to Become a Millionaire (It Still Happens All the Time)."

4 "Millionaires: How They Do It," *Time*, December 3, 1965, 88–92 + .

5 "Now There are 90,000 Millionaires in U.S.," *U.S. News & World Report*, October 11, 1965, 119–120.

6 Herman M. Miller, "Non-Poverty Program: Millionaires Are a Dime a Dozen," *New York Times*, November 28, 1965, SM50–51 + .

7 "Non-Poverty Program: Millionaires Are a Dime a Dozen."

8 "Yes, You Can Make a Million: Here's the Way It's Done Today," *U.S. News & World Report*, May 16, 1966, 111.

9 "Richest of the Rich," *Time*, May 3, 1968, 72.

10 "On Being Very, Very Rich," *Time*, July 12, 1968, 30–31.

11 Kenneth L. Woodward, "Secrets of the Very Rich," *Newsweek*, October 7, 1974, 78.

12 G. William Donhoff, "A Blast at Everyone," *The Nation*, August 19, 1968, 121–122; Isadore Silver, "Making It," the *New Republic*, October 12, 1968, 41–45.

13 John K. Hitchens, "One Thing and Another," *Saturday Review*, November 2, 1968, 32–33.

14 Colman McCarthy, "The Hard-Core Rich," the *New Republic*, March 15, 1969, 14–15. Ronald Kessler's *The Season: The Secret Life of Palm Beach and America's Richest Society* is a dishy expose on this town that "makes *Dynasty* and *Dallas* look like nursery tales."

15 "The Hard-Core Rich."

16 "The Hard-Core Rich."

17 Ruth West, "The Care and Feeding of the Very Rich," *McCall's*, August 1969, 56–57 + .

18 "The Care and Feeding of the Very Rich."

19 "The Care and Feeding of the Very Rich."

20 "The Care and Feeding of the Very Rich."

21 "The Care and Feeding of the Very Rich."

22 "The Care and Feeding of the Very Rich."

23 Shirley Lord, "Nouveau vs. D'Habitude," *Harper's Bazaar*, August 1969, 196.

24 "Nouveau vs. D'Habitude."

25 "How to Make a Million," *U.S. News & World Report*, December 15, 1969, 58–61.

26 Stephen Birmingham, "How the Rich Stay Young and Beautiful," *McCall's*, April 1968, 11–13 + .

27 "How the Rich Stay Young and Beautiful."

28 "How the Rich Stay Young and Beautiful."

29 "How the Rich Stay Young and Beautiful."

30 "How the Rich Stay Young and Beautiful."

31 Willi Frischauer, "Onassis: The Yachtsman Who's Had Them All Aboard," *Ladies' Home Journal*, March 1968, 90–91 + ; The *Christina* was the biggest yacht in the world but, as a converted tanker, not the biggest privately built one. That honor belonged to Charles Revson's *Ultima II*, which required a crew of thirty-six, including three chefs—French, Italian, and Chinese—and two doctors ("The Care and Feeding of the Very Rich"). See Peter Evans's *Ari: The Life & Times of Aristotle Socrates Onassis* for much more about the yachtsman.

32 Stephen Birmingham, "The Good, Good Life of the Alpine Set," *McCall's*, January 1970, 46–47 + .

33 "The Good, Good Life of the Alpine Set."

34 "The Good, Good Life of the Alpine Set."

35 "The Girl Who Has Everything Plus," *Newsweek*, August 27, 1973, 53–54 + .

36 "The Girl Who Has Everything Plus."

37 "The Girl Who Has Everything Plus."

38 "The Girl Who Has Everything Plus."

39 "Boom in Millionaires," *U.S. News & World Report*, July 26, 1976, 40.

40 "Recession and the Rich," *Time*, December 16, 1974, 102.

41 "Recession and the Rich."

42 W. Hamilton, "Our Neglected Rich," *Newsweek*, March 31, 1975, 12.

43 "A Yen for a Renoir or Gucci," *Newsweek*, April 16, 1973, 42–43.

44 "A Yen for a Renoir or Gucci."

45 "A Yen for a Renoir or Gucci."

46 "Now It's Young People Making Millions," *U.S. News & World Report*, February 25, 1974, 47–50.

47 Claire Safran, "Rags-to-Riches Female Style," *Today's Health*, March 1974, 36–37 + .

48 "How to Become a Millionaire: New York Businessman Shares Secrets of his Success," *Ebony*, October 1975, 72–74.

49 Carlyle Douglas, "How to Become a Millionaire: Al Johnson Shows That It Can Be Done," *Ebony*, December 1975, 149–152 + .

50 Carlyle C. Douglas, "How to Become a Millionaire: Never Buy Other People's Paint," *Ebony*, February 1976, 132–134.

51 Claire Safran, "All Right! I Won a Million Bucks. Now What Do I Do With It?" *Today's Health*, November 1974, 56–61.

52 "All Right! I Won a Million Bucks. Now What Do I Do With It?"

53 "All Right! I Won a Million Bucks. Now What Do I Do With It?"

54 "The New Millionaires," *Newsweek*, May 19, 1975, 72.

55 Peter Barnes, "The Rich Boys of Summer," the *New Republic*, April 27, 1974, 25.

56 "Boom in Millionaires."

57 Allen J. Mayer, "The Richest Men in America," *Newsweek*, August 2, 1976, 56–59.

58 "The Richest Men in America." See Ray Kroc's *Grinding It Out: The Making of McDonald's* for the inside scoop on the burger man's success story.

59 "The New Rich," *Time*, June 13, 1977, 72–76 + .

60 "The New Rich."

61 "The New Rich."

62 Kenneth Lamott, "The Money Revolution," *Human Behavior*, April 1978, 18–23.

63 "The Money Revolution."

64 Andrew Tobias, "Getting By on $100,000 a Year," *Esquire*, May 23, 1978, 21–24.

65 Greg Mitchell, "Robin Hood Was Right!" *Crawdaddy*, December 1978, 28–31.

66 "Robin Hood Was Right!"

67 Tara Korenblum, "Waifs of the Golden Ghetto," *Maclean's*, October 16, 1978, 54–55.

CHAPTER 5

1 Donald R. Katz, "Reasons for Getting Rich," *Esquire*, March 1986, 51–52.

2 Firth Calhoun, "What It Takes To Be (Truly) Rich Today," *Money*, March 1986, 186–196.

3 Michael Eisenberg, "Getting Rich in America," *Money*, July 1986, 49–53.

4 Susanna McBee, "Flaunting Wealth," *U.S. News & World Report*, September 21, 1981, 61–64.

5 William K. Stevens, "Dallas Watches Nation Watch 'Dallas,'" *New York Times*, November 21, 1980, A16.

6 Michael Doan, "There's No Recession In the Luxury Market," *U.S. News & World Report*, November 23, 1981, 53–54.

7 Harold Seneker, "The Forbes Four Hundred," *Forbes*, September 13, 1982, 100.

8 "Ranking America's Richest," *Newsweek*, September 13, 1982, 70.

9 N.R. Kleinfield, "Forbes Hunt for Richest 400," *New York Times*, September 11, 1982, 35. In their *All the Money in the World: How the Forbes 400 Make—and Spend—Their Fortunes*, editors Peter W. Bernstein and Annalyn Swan explore the extremely successful habits of the super-rich who made it onto the prestigious list.

10 Harold Seneker, "On the Art of Becoming Rich," *Forbes*, September 27, 1982, 43–44 +.

11 "Reaction to the Forbes Four Hundred Richest Americans," *Forbes*, October 11, 1982, 28–29.

12 "Reaction to the Forbes Four Hundred Richest Americans."

13 William Berry Furlong, "N.Y. School Teaches 'How to Marry Money,'" the *Saturday Evening Post*, December 1981, 24+.

14 Lynda Scher, "How to Marry a Millionaire," *Mademoiselle*, April 1982, 178–179+.

15 Leslie Dormen, "Can You Bank on a Rich Man?" *Mademoiselle*, March 1984, 124–125+.

16 Dawn MacDonald, "Matchmaker to the Rich," *Maclean's*, December 5, 1983, 56.

17 Susan Bidel, "Millionaire Bachelors," *Harper's Bazaar*, January 1989, 46+.

18 Barbara Crossette, "In Brunei, Even the Subjects Can Live Like a King," *New York Times*, February 1, 1986, A2.

19 Marlys Harris, "How to Divorce a Millionaire: In This Game, Nothing is For Keeps Except a Big Settlement," *Money*, June 1983, 180.

20 "How to Divorce a Millionaire: In This Game, Nothing is For Keeps Except a Big Settlement."

21 David Oliver Relin, "When Greed Was Good: The 1980s Will Go Down in History as a Decade of Excess," *Scholastic Update*, March 8, 1991, 14.

22 Harry F. Waters, "An Embarrassment of Riches," *Newsweek*, April 2, 1984, 74–75.

23 Lance Morrow, "The Shoes of Imelda Marcos," *Time*, March 31, 1986, 80.

24 "An Embarrassment of Riches."

25 Stephen Drucker, "Psyching It Out," *Vogue*, January 1987, 208–09+.

26 Judy Romberger, "Lifestyles Of Rich 'N Famous Teens," *Teen*, September 1988, 66–68+.

27 Jeff Jarvis, "Reveling in the Lap of Luxury ('Clothesaholic' Celebritics)," *People Weekly*, March 21, 1983, 64.

28 "Stoking the Impulse to Spend Big," *Fortune*, June 11, 1984, 66–73.

29 "The 400 Richest People in America," *Forbes*, October 1, 1984, 70.

30 Loudon Wainwright, "A Little Filthy Lucre Buys a Lot of Envy," *Life*, November 1984, 7.

31 "Reveling in the Lap of Luxury ('Clothesaholic' Celebrities)."

32 "Reveling in the Lap of Luxury ('Clothesaholic' Celebrities)."

33 "What It Takes To Be (Truly) Rich Today."

34 Eloise Salholz, "Rummage Sales for the Rich," *Newsweek*, September 2, 1985, 72.

35 Mary-Margaret Wantuck, "Marketing to the Big Spenders," *Nation's Business*, August 1985, 42–45.

36 C. D. B. Bryan, "Flaunting It," *Esquire*, June 1985, 282–97.

37 "When the Well-To-Do Deal in Drugs," *U.S. News & World Report*, November 1, 1982, 7.

38 Anthony Haden-Guest, "The Young, the Rich, and Heroin," *Rolling Stone*, July 7, 1983, 20 + .

39 Andrew Reede, "Blood Lines," *New York*, July 21, 1986, 36–38.

40 John Sedgwick, "Aren't They Rich?" *Mademoiselle*, October 1985, 202–03 + .

41 David Handelman, "The Aristobrats," *Mademoiselle*, April 1987, 230–31 + .

42 Warren Cook, "The Cash Splash," *Harper's Bazaar*, August 1986, 118–120 + .

43 Hugh Sidney, "Affluence in Pursuit of Influence," *Time*, November 4, 1985, 24.

44 "The Cash Splash."

45 Ellen Hopkins, "Our Ladies of Charity," *New York*, October 13, 1986, 48–53.

46 Sharon Churcher, "Making It By Doing Good," *New York Times*, July 3, 1988, A16.

47 Brad Edmondson, "Sampling the Upper Crust," *American Demographics*, September 1990, 47.

48 "The 400 Richest People in America," *Forbes*, October 28, 1985, 108.

49 "The 400 Richest People in America," *Forbes*, October 27, 1986, 106–107.

50 Lawrence Minard, "You've Got to Work At It," *Forbes*, October 26, 1987, 6. Sam Walton's own *Sam Walton: Made In America* explains in considerable detail how the man from Arkansas became the king of retail.

51 "The Cash Splash."

52 Robert J. Samuelson, "The Discovery of Money," *Newsweek*, October 20, 1986, 58.

53 Jesse Kornbluth, "The Working Rich," *New York*, November 24, 1986, 30–37.

54 "Psyching It Out."

55 Holly Brubach, "Flaunting It," *Vogue*, January 1987, 204–05 +.

56 "Psyching It Out."

57 Edward F. Cone, "How the Nouveaux Riches Got That Way," *Forbes*, October 24, 1988, 105–106.

58 Nick Ravo, "Bored With Tennis, 'New Breed of Wealthy' Turns to Polo," *New York Times*, May 22, 1987, B1.

59 Lisa Robinson, "Spoofing It," *Vogue*, January 1987, 207.

60 "Flaunting It."

61 "Psyching It Out."

62 Dinitia Smith, "Art Fever," *New York*, April 20, 1987, 34–43.

63 "The 400 Richest People in America," *Forbes*, October 26, 1987, 106, 110; Peter Newcomb, "The Rich Got Poorer," *Forbes*, November 16, 1987, 41 +.

64 "The 400 Richest People in America," *Forbes*, October 24, 1988, 142–46. See any of Trump's many books to, as his most recent effort put it, *Think BIG and Kick Ass in Business and Life*.

65 Margot Dougherty, "Ali-Dada's Arabian Night," *People Weekly*, September 4, 1989, 34.

66 Jennet Conant, "Billionaire Bashing," *Newsweek*, May 30, 1988, 66–67.

67 Glenn Collins, "Now, a Look at the Life Style of Robin Leach," *New York Times*, December 2, 1990, A35.

68 "Billionaire Bashing."

69 Thomas Sowell, "Galbraith Strikes Again," *Forbes*, May 25, 1992, 140.

70 "Leona Helmsley, and the Iniquitous 1980s," *The Economist*, April 25, 1992, A28.

71 Kevin P. Phillips, "A Capital Offense: Reagan's America," *New York Times*, June 17, 1990, A26.

CHAPTER 6

1 "Hazards of New Fortunes," *New York Times*, May 30, 2004, 13.

2 Peter Newcomb, "Land O' Plenty," *Forbes*, October 16, 1995, 107.

For a critical look at the wild and wooly dot-com days, see John Cassidy's *Dot.con: How America Lost Its Mind and Money in the Internet Era.*

3 Ann Marsh, "Meet the Class of 1996," *Forbes*, October 14, 1996, 100–104.

4 James Collins, "High Stakes Winners," *Time*, February 19, 1996, 42–47.

5 "High Stakes Winners."

6 David A. Kaplan, "Cyber Toy Story," *Newsweek*, August 4, 1997, 56–59.

7 Amy Cortese, "My Jet Is Bigger Than Your Jet," *BusinessWeek*, August 25, 1997, 126.

8 David A. Kaplan, "Silicon Heaven," *Newsweek*, June 14, 1999, 48–51.

9 Robert Frank, "The Wealth Report," *Wall Street Journal*, June 22, 2007, W2.

10 Joseph Nocera, "The Arriviste Has Arrived," *New York Times*, November 15, 1998, SM68.

11 Ben Pappas, "Cathedrals to Sunglasses and Other Fantasies of the Very Rich," *Forbes*, October 13, 1997, 90–91.

12 Joe Queenan, "Why Can't Billionaires Grow Up?" *Forbes*, October 13, 1997, 46–47.

13 Joe Queenan, "If You've Got Dough, Act Like It," *Forbes*, October 11, 1999, 128.

14 Dinesh D'Souza, "The Billionaire Next Door," *Forbes*, October 11, 1999, 55.

15 Katherine Betts, "The New Rich," *Vogue*, April 1999, 346+.

16 Tim W. Ferguson, "Nouveau Riche," *Forbes*, October 8, 2001, 78.

17 Rich Karlgaard, "Digital Rules," *Forbes*, August 10, 1998, 37.

18 "The New Rich."

19 Jim Gorman, "Celebrating the Ultra-Rich Computer Nerd," *New York Times*, June 13, 1999, AR1.

20 "The New Rich."

21 Adam Bryant, "They're Rich (And You're Not)," *Newsweek*, July 5, 1999, 37–43.

22 Beth Brophy, "You've Got Money," *Washingtonian*, October 1999, 59–61+.

23 Melanie Warner, "The Young and the Loaded," *Fortune*, September 27, 1999, 78.

24 Eryn Brown, "Valley of the Dollars," *Fortune*, September 27, 1999, 102.

25 Kerry A. Dolan, "Purple People," *Forbes*, September 1, 2003, 72–76.

26 James Atlas, "Cashing Out Young," *Vanity Fair*, December 1999, 214–233.

27 John Greenwald, "Luxury's Gaudy Times," *Time*, March 25, 1996, 48.

28 Sarah Bernard, "The Helpless Rich," *New York*, July 27, 1998, 13–14.

29 Bruce Nussbaum, "The Summer of Wretched Excess," *Business-Week*, August 3, 1998, 35. Steven Gaines's *Philistines at the Hedgerow: Passion and Property in the Hamptons* is an enjoyable romp through the East End.

30 Joe Queenan, "Don't Worry, Be Happy," *Forbes*, October 12, 1998, 42.

31 "This Year, It's Chic to Shop Cheap," *Business Week*, November 16, 1998, 216–18.

32 Rene Chun, "Spree Well," *New York*, June 14, 1999, 28–31.

33 Douglas Brinkley, "Palace Envy," *Time*, December 7, 1998, 97.

34 Wendy Moonan, "Designing Megahouses: When Money Is No Object," *Architectural Record*, November 1998, 75–78+.

35 Ralph Gardner, Jr., "Class Struggle on Park Avenue," *New York*, June 14, 1999, 22–27.

36 "The Billionaire Next Door."

37 "Class Struggle on Park Avenue."

38 Gary Rivlin, "If You Can Make It in Silicon Valley, You Can Make It . . . in Silicon Valley Again," *New York Times*, June 5, 2005, SM64.

39 James W. Michaels and Victoria Murphy, "The Mass-Market Rich," *Forbes*, October 9, 2000, 58–62.

40 Evan McGlinn, "Barbarians at the Beach," *Forbes*, October 9, 2000, 378, 384.

41 Melanie Warner, "Where Have All the Beemers Gone?" *Fortune*, May 15, 2000, 68–70.

42 Alison Samuels and David Noonan, "Baby's Bounty," *Newsweek*, December 4, 2000, 54–55.

43 Cynthia Hacinli, "Drooling Over Kate Spade," *Washingtonian*, March 2001, 903.

44 M. Edelstein, "Secret Service," *Harper's Bazaar*, August 2000, 200–203.

45 Melissa Ceria, "The New Velvet Rope," *Time*, Fall 2004, 53.

46 Andy Serwer, "The Best Therapy $10 Million Can Buy," *Fortune*, July 12, 2004, 122–28; Gary Rivlin, "Where Everyone Knows Your Portfolio," *New York Times*, October 14, 2007, 26–31.

47 Brendan Vaughn, "How to Have Fun for Under $1 Million," *Esquire*, June 2002, 28.

48 Dan Seligman, "Does Money Buy Happiness?" *Forbes*, April 21, 1997, 394–96.

49 Shana Aborn, "The Envy Epidemic," *Ladies' Home Journal*, February 2001, 158.

50 Robert H. Frank, "Why Living in a Rich Society Makes Us Feel Poor," *New York Times*, October 15, 2000, 62.

51 Paul Johnson, "Riches Breed Innocence But Not Happiness," *Forbes*, April 14, 2003, 43.

52 Lisa Gubernick and Dana Wechler Lindren, "The Perils of Family Money," *Forbes*, June 19, 1995, 130.

53 Peter Carbonera, "Heal the Rich," *Money*, May 2000, 108–114.

54 Leigh Gallagher, "Having It All—But Needing a Grip," *Forbes*, October 8, 2001, 112–113.

55 Michelle Conlin, "When Billionaires Became a Dime a Dozen," *Forbes*, October 13, 1997, 148.

56 "A Century of Wealth," *Forbes*, October 11, 1999, 112.

57 Peter Newcomb, "The Forbes 400," *Forbes*, October 11, 1999, 169.

58 John Horn, "Mise-En-Cents," *The Nation*, April 5–12, 1999, 48–50.

59 Elizabeth Austin, "Why Homer's My Hero," *The Washington Monthly*, October 2000, 32.

60 Marc Peyser and B. J. Sigesmund, "Heir Heads," *Newsweek*, October 20, 2003, 54–55.

61 "The World's Richest People," *Forbes*, July 9, 2001, 110.

62 "The Forbes 400," *Forbes*, October 8, 2001, 127.

63 "The Forbes 400," *Forbes*, September 30, 2002, 99.

64 "The Forbes 400," *Forbes*, October 6, 2003, 136.

65 "The Forbes 400," *Forbes*, October 10, 2005, 89.

66 Freda Germaise, "Gold Diggers of '95," *GQ*, February 1995, 158.

67 Jan Hoffman, "How They Keep It," *New York Times*, November 19, 1995, SM104.

68 Brigid McMenamin, "'Til Divorce Do Us Part," *Forbes*, October 14, 1996, 52–60.

69 N. J. Sales, "Who Wants to Marry a Multimillionaire?" *Harper's Bazaar*, April 2000, 210–13, 239–41.

70 Leigh Gallagher, "Take Back Your Poils," *Forbes*, October 9, 2000, 92–96.

71 J. Van Meter, "The New Dot.Com Society," *Vogue*, April 2000, 380–85.

72 Richard Reeves, "The New Wealth," *Money*, October 1997, 170.

73 Robert Frank, "The Wealth Report," *Wall Street Journal*, June 22, 2007, W2.

74 Marlys Harris, "How to Marry a Billionaire," *Money Magazine*, July 2007, 95–100.

75 "How to Marry a Billionaire."

76 Susan Adams, "For Love or Money," *Forbes*, July 23, 2007, 206.

77 "How to Marry a Billionaire."

78 James K. Glassman, "The Rich Really Aren't Different," *U.S. News & World Report*, April 14, 1997, 68.

79 "Cheap Thrills," *People*, May 5, 1997, 141–142.

80 "$1 Million Worth of Secrets," *U.S. News & World Report*, June 9, 1997, 90–92.

81 Andrew Serwer, "How the Millionaire Next Door Got That Way," *Fortune*, August 17, 1998, 104–107.

82 John Tierney, "Manhattan's Richest Endangered Species: The 'Typical Millionaire,'" *New York Times*, September 7, 1997, SM40.

83 Elizabeth Austin, "Why Homer's My Hero," *The Washington Monthly*, October 2000, 30.

84 Adam Bryant, "A Millionaire Moment," *Newsweek*, March 13, 2000, 48.

85 Andy Serwer, "Can These Books Really Make You a Millionaire?" *Fortune*, July 11, 2005, 51.

86 Hubert Herring, "A Million Here, A Million There. Still Real Money?" *New York Times*, June 25, 2006, 32.

87 Paul B. Brown, "So What if $1 Million Isn't What It Used to Be?" *New York Times*, April 6, 2008, 30.

88 "A Millionaire Moment."

89 Peggy Noonan, "Who Wants To Be a Millionaire, Anyway?" *Good Housekeeping* April 2000, 220.

90 "Can These Books Really Make You a Millionaire?"

91 Andrew E. Kramer, "New Czars of Conspicuous Consumption," *New York Times*, November 1, 2006, C1.

92 Natasha Singer, "Not Down and Out in Moscow," *New York Times*, November 29, 2007, G1.

93 Brooke Astor, "Weighing the Benefits," *Vanity Fair*, October 1995, 156.

94 Robert Lenzner, "The Mouth of the South Puts His Foot In It," *Forbes*, October 14, 1996, 40–41. For more about "the mouth of the south," see Ken Auletta's *Media Man: Ted Turner's Improbable Empire*.

95 "The Fine Art of Giving," *Time*, December 16, 1996, 48–49.

96 Robert X. Cringely, "High-tech Wealth," *Forbes*, July 7, 1997, 308.

97 Katie Hafner, "The Wealth and Avarice of the Cyberrich," *Newsweek*, December 30, 1996– January 6, 1997, 48–51.

98 Michael Lewis, "What Will Gates Give?" *New York Times*, October 13, 1996, SM34.

99 "Bill Gates," *People*, December 31, 1999, 75.

100 Adam Cohen, "Putting His Mouth . . ." *Time*, September 29, 1997, 32.

101 Howard Fineman, "Why Ted Gave It Away," *Newsweek*, September 29, 1997, 29–32.

102 Stephen Glass, "Gift of the Magnate," the *New Republic*, January 26, 1998, 16–19.

103 "A New Breed of Philanthropist," *BusinessWeek*, October 6, 1997, 40–44.

104 James Traub, "Philanthropy 101," the *New Yorker*, October 20–27, 1997, 33–34.

105 Michael Lewis, "Heartless Donors," *New York Times*, December 14, 1997, 231.

106 Jonathan Alter, "The Nicer Nineties," *Newsweek*, December 29, 1997–January 5, 1998, 44–45).

107 Anne Faircloth and Caroline Bollinger, "Fortune's 40 Most Generous Americans," *Fortune*, February 2, 1998, 88.

108 "The Billionaire Next Door."

109 David Whelan, "Who Gives?" *Forbes*, October 11, 2004, 76.

110 Carol J. Loomis, "Warren Buffett Gives Away His Fortune," *Fortune*, June 25, 2006, (online edition).

111 Jane Lampman, "Rich to the Rescue," the *Christian Science Monitor*, November 20, 2006, 13.

112 Dave Denison, "Watching the Rich Give," *New York Times*, March 9, 2008, SM14.

113 Jon Gertner, "For Good Measure," *New York Times*, March 9, 2008, SM66+; Abby Aguirre, "Easy Come, Easy Go for Idealistic Heirs," *New York Times*, March 9, 2008, ST11.

114 Louis Uchitelle, "The Richest of the Rich, Proud of a New Gilded Age," *New York Times*, July 15, 2007, 1.

Conclusion

1 Geraldine Fabrikant, "They're Pinching Hundred-Dollar Bills," *New York Times*, October 4, 2008, 1.

2 Ellen Gamerman, Cheryl Lu-Lien Tan, and Francine Schwadel, "As Times Turn Tough, New York's Wealthy Economize," *WSJ.com*, September 20, 2008.

3 "Russia's Wealthy Hit Hard By Financial Turmoil," *Morning Edition*, October 15, 2008.

4 Christine Haughney, "In Tough Times, Even the Billionaires Worry," *New York Times*, September 10, 2008, 2L.

5 Tim Arango and Julie Creswell, "Goodbye To All That," *New York Times*, October 5, 2008, BU1+.

6 Tom Herman, "There's Rich, and There's the 'Fortunate 400,'" *Wall Street Journal*, March 5, 2008, D1.

BIBLIOGRAPHY

AUTHOR'S NOTE

Rich relies primarily on period magazines and newspapers as its sources of material, because I believe journalists serving on the front lines of the scene represent our most valuable resource for recovering unfiltered stories of the wealthy. From these hundreds of journalists' reports from the field, many of them obscure and largely forgotten but important firsthand accounts of the goings-on within the lives of the day's rich, we really do get the first draft of history.

Other books about the American rich have also been a valuable resource and may be of interest to the reader. Our literary landscape has in fact been littered with attempts to, as recently expressed, decode "the millionaire mind." A virtual flood of books about the robber barons of the Gilded Age was written in the twenties and thirties, almost all harshly and deservingly critical of these men who turned the term "rich" into a four-letter word. "In any considerable library of Americana the bibliography devoted to the defamation of rich men is ample," thought Lucius Beebe in 1962; he was of the opinion that besides approved (or paid for) biographies, "the well-to-do in the United States have had an uncommonly bad press." Cleveland Amory's *The Last Resorts* of 1952 looked nostalgically back on the golden age of Saratoga, Bar Harbor, Tuxedo Park, Southampton, Palm Beach, and Newport at the turn of the century (these resorts catering specifically to "any millionaire looking for the shortest distance between the cash register and the social register," as *Time* put it in its review of the book), and in his 1960 *Who Killed Society?* Amory traced how the nouveau riche evolved into the Old Guard. Other books about the rich in the postwar years, notably Robert Heilbroner's 1956 *The Quest for Wealth* and Lucy Kavaler's *The Private World of High Society* of 1960, focused on the human drive for acquisition and, specifically, Americans' common desire to rise to a higher social class during some particularly money-oriented times. As well, classic sociological works like C. Wright Mills's 1956 *The Power Elite*, William Whyte's *The Organization Man* of the same year, John Kenneth Galbraith's 1958 *The Affluent Society*, and Vance Packard's *The Status Seekers* of the following year each explored different dimensions of the wealthy elite as it blossomed during the postwar years.

In the sixties and seventies, as the cult of celebrity emerged, books about the American rich tended to go for sheer shock value. Revisionist historians in the early 1960s helped to restore in part the reputation of men like Henry Ford and John D. Rockefeller, however, tranforming them into something between the ogres they had been popularly viewed as and actual human beings. Ferdinand Lundberg's 1968 bestseller *The Rich and the Super-Rich* made quite a sensation with its argument that a very small number of households effectively controlled the nation through their economic and social power. Kenneth Lamott's *The Money Makers* of the following year showed readers that some of the world's greatest fortunes were the result of human disasters, both natural and manmade. Three other books from the late sixties—George G. Kirstein's *The Rich: Are They Different?*, Roy Perrott's *The Aristocrats*, and Stephen Birmingham's *The Right People*—also peeked inside the world of the rich, the unusual attention being paid to them no doubt a response to the changing winds of society. Still, despite all these books, the nation's bicentennial American wealth culture remained largely a mystery to the man or woman on the street. "The rich are the least studied—and least understood—class in the U.S.," argued *Newsweek* reporter Kenneth L. Woodward in 1974: "While sociologists probe the poor and measure the middle classes with computerized efficiency, the rich remain largely ignored by social scientists and journalists alike."

Much has changed in the past couple of decades, especially relatively recently when baby boomers' careers and earning power peaked; it became difficult to ignore the escalating presence and influence of the American rich. Some of the sharpest critics of the day have recognized that the rich offer an ideal lens through which to view American society, understanding the extent to which the upper class has both reflected and helped shape our operative values. There was a flurry of books and films about Wall Streeters in the late 1980s and early 1990s, not surprisingly, when the money being made by investment bankers and other paper pushers became the source of both lust and disgust. Two of them—Lewis Lapham's 1988 *Money and Class in America* and Galbraith's *The Culture of Contentment* of 1992—were particularly vitriolic. These A-list authors convincingly argued that the size and greenness of New Money was vile, shameful, and, in short, were turning the country into a worse place.

Over the last ten years or so, however, social critics have been more fascinated with the rich than angry at them, an "if-you-can't-beat-'em, join-'em" attitude taking hold among keen observers of the current scene. David Brooks's 2000 *Bobos in Paradise: The New Upper Class and How They Got There*, for example, showcased the lives of "bourgeois bohemians," the mash-ups of mainstream culture and 1960s-era counterculture who, according to the author, "define our age," represent "the new establishment," and "govern social life." In his 2002 *The Natural History of the Rich: A Field Guide*, Richard Conniff offered an interesting exploration of the richest members of the human species; the author compared the super-rich to the animal kingdom to provide a frame of reference for their particular (and often peculiar) behaviors and actions. Michael Gross's *740 Park* of 2005 was a voyeuristic historical tour of "the world's richest apartment building." In *Richistan: A Journey Through the American Wealth Boom and the Lives of the New Rich* of 2007, *Wall Street Journal* reporter Robert Frank took a trip through that foreign land, exploring the exotic lifestyles of the new American rich. Finally, the explosion of how-to-get-rich books (and seminars) in the late 1990s and early 2000s confirmed that Americans' love affair with money had become more passionate than ever. It was now reasonable to conclude that our culture had become mostly about how to get more money in order to spend more of it on the increasing number of "luxury" goods and services.

Books

Aldrich, Nelson W., Jr. *Old Money: The Mythology of America's Upper Class*. New York: Alfred A. Knopf, 1988.

Allen, W. H. *Modern Philanthropy: A Study in Efficient Appealing and Giving*. New York: Dodd, Mead, 1912.

Amory, Cleveland. *The Last Resorts: A Portrait of American Society*. New York: Harper and Brothers, 1952.

———. *Who Killed Society?: The Warfare of Celebrity with Aristocracy in America from the "First Families" to the Four Hundred to "Publiciety."* New York: Harper & Brothers, 1960.

Bach, David. *The Automatic Millionaire: A Powerful One-Step Plan to Live and Finish Rich*. New York: Broadway, 2003.

Barton, Bruce. *The Man Nobody Knows: A Discovery of the Real Jesus*. New York: The Bobbs-Merrill Co., 1925.

Bernstein, Peter, ed., and Annalyn Swan, ed. *All the Money in the World:*

How the Forbes 400 Make—and Spend—Their Fortunes. New York: Knopf, 2007.

Beroff, Art and T. R. Adams, *How to Be a Teenage Millionaire*. Topeka, Kansas: Tandem Library Books, 2000.

Birmingham, Stephen. *The Right People: The Social Establishment in America*. New York: Little Brown, 1968.

———. *Our Crowd: The Great Jewish Families of New York*. New York: Harper & Row, 1962.

Brooks, David. *Bobos in Paradise: The New Upper Class and How They Got There*. New York: Simon & Schuster, 2000.

Burrough, Bryan and John Helyar. *Barbarians at the Gate*. New York: HarperCollins, 1990.

Conniff, Richard. *The Natural History of the Rich: A Field Guide*. New York: W.W. Norton, 2002.

Davis, William. *It's No Sin to Be Rich: A Defense of Capitalism*. Nashville: Thomas Nelson, 1976.

Dunne, Dominick. *People Like Us*. New York: Crown, 1988.

Ford, Henry, with Samuel Crowther. *My Life and Work*. Garden City, New York: Garden City Publishing Company, 1922.

Foster, Rich and Greg Hicks. *How We Choose To be Happy*. New York: G.P. Putnam & Sons, 1999.

Frank, Robert. *Richistan: A Journey Through the American Wealth Boom and the Lives of the New Rich*. New York: Crown, 2007.

Frank, Stephanie. *The Accidental Millionaire: Leaping from Chance to Mastery in the Game of Life*. Essex, England: Greenlight Publishing, 2005.

Fridson, Martin. *How to Be a Billionaire: Proven Strategies from the Titans of Wealth*. New York: Wiley, 1999.

Galbraith, John Kenneth. *The Affluent Society*. New York: Houghton Mifflin, 1958.

———. *The Culture of Contentment*. New York: Houghton Mifflin, 1992.

Gross, Michael. *740 Park: The Story of the World's Richest Apartment Building*. New York: Broadway, 2005.

Hansen, Mark Victor and Robert G. Allen, *One Minute Millionaire: The Enlightened Way to Wealth*. New York: Harmony, 2002.

Hayashi, Ken. *Millionaire by 26: Secrets to Becoming a Young, Rich Entrepreneur*. Bloomington, Indiana, iUniverse: 2003.

Heilbroner, Robert. *The Quest for Wealth: A Study of Acquisitive Man.* New York: Simon & Schuster, 1956

Jarrett, R. E. *Discovering the Millionaire in Every Child.* Tarentum, Pennsylvania: Word Association Publishers, 2002.

Kavaler, Lucy. *The Private World of High Society: Its Rules & Rituals.* New York: David McKay, 1960.

Kirstein, George G. *The Rich: Are They Different?* Boston: Houghton Mifflin, 1968.

Korda, Michael. *Success.* New York: Random House, 1977.

Koslow, Brian. *365 Ways to Become a Millionaire (Without Being Born One).* New York: Penguin, 1999.

Lamott, Kenneth. *The Money Makers: The Great Big New Rich in America.* Boston: Little, Brown and Company, 1969.

Lapham, Lewis. *Money and Class in America: Notes and Observations on Our Civil Religion.* New York: Grove Press, 1988.

Lewis, Michael. *Liar's Poker: Rising Through the Wreckage of Wall Street.* New York: W.W. Norton, 1989.

Lundberg, Ferdinand. *The Rich and the Super-Rich: A Study in the Power of Money Today.* New York: Lyle Stuart, 1968.

Mills, C. Wright. *The Power Elite.* New York: Oxford University Press, 1956.

Needleman, Jacob. *Money and the Meaning of Life.* New York: Doubleday, 1994.

O'Connell, Brian. *The 401(k) Millionaire.* New York: Villard, 1998.

Orman, Suze. *The Courage to Be Rich: Creating a Life of Material and Spiritual Abundance.* New York: Riverhead, 1999.

Ostrower, Francine. *Why the Wealthy Give: The Culture of Elite Philanthropy.* Princeton: Princeton University Press, 1997.

Packard, Vance. *The Status Seekers.* New York: David McKay, 1959.

Perennez, Didier. *Lunchtime Millionaire: A Step-By-Step Guide To Building Wealth . . . On Your Lunch Hour.* San Francisco: Pacific Heights Publishing, 2004.

Perrott, Roy. *The Aristocrats: A Portrait of Britain's Nobility and Their Way of Life Today.* New York: Macmillan, 1968.

Prince, Russ Alan and Lewis Schiff. *The Middle-Class Millionaire: The Rise of the New Rich and How They Are Changing America.* New York: Doubleday, 2008.

Rees, Goronwy. *Multimillionaires: Six Studies in Wealth*. New York: Macmillan, 1961.

Reich, Robert. *Tales of a New America*. New York: Crown, 1987.

Ringer, Robert J. *Looking Out for #1*. New York: Funk & Wagnalls, 1977.

Rothkoph, David. *Superclass: The Global Power Elite and the World They are Making*. New York: Farrar, Straus and Giroux, 2008.

Savage, Jeff. *Millionaire by 40*. Oregon, Ohio: Buckeye Publishing, 2005.

Stanley, Thomas J. *The Millionaire Mind*. Kansas City, Missouri: Andrews McMeel, 2000.

———. *Millionaire Women Next Door: The Many Journeys of Successful American Businesswomen*. Kansas City, Missouri: Andrews McMeel, 2004.

Stanley, Thomas J. and William D. Danko. *The Millionaire Next Door: The Surprising Secrets of America's Wealthy*. Atlanta: Longstreet Press, 1996.

Steichen, Joanne. *Marrying Up: An American Dream—and Reality*. New York: Rawson Associates, 1983.

Stewart, James B. *Den of Thieves*. New York: Simon & Schuster, 1991.

Taylor, Jim, Doug Harrison and Stephen Kraus. *The New Elite: Inside the Minds of the Truly Wealthy*. New York: AMACOM, 2008.

Vanderbilt, Cornelius, Jr. *Farewell to Fifth Avenue*. New York: Simon & Schuster, 1935.

The Vanguard Foundation. *Robin Hood Was Right: A Guide to Giving Your Money for Social Change*. San Francisco: Bookpeople, 1978.

Veblen, Thorsten. *The Theory of the Leisure Class: An Economic Study of Institutions*. New York: Macmillan, 1899.

The Wall Street Journal. *The New Millionaires and How They Made Their Fortunes*. New York: Macfadden, 1961.

Wharton, Edith. *The Age of Innocence*. New York: D. Appleton & Company, 1920.

———. *The House of Mirth*. New York: Charles Scribner's Sons, 1905.

Who Wants To Be a Millionaire? Oxford, England: Boxtree, 1999.

Whyte, William H., Jr. *The Organization Man*. New York: Simon & Schuster, 1956.

Wixen, Burton N. *Children of the Rich*. New York: Crown, 1973.

Wolfe, Tom. *Bonfire of the Vanities: A Novel*. New York: Farrar, Straus and Giroux, 1987.

INDEX